TRANS...

ILLUSION

THEODORA'S JOURNEY THROUGH TIME

By Thea Ivie

Gurulight

Transcending Illusion,
Theadora's Journey Through Time

ISBN: TBD

Acknowledgments & Credits
Writer/Editor: Betsy Braun
Design: Blue Moon Publishing, Sedona, AZ
Inside Cover Sri Chakra: Paul Heussenstamm
Cover Image: Sergei Iourov
1st edition (2007) - Cities of Light Publishing

2nd edition published by Gurulight, 2021
Email: info@gurulight.com
Web: www.gurulight.com

Sergei Iourov is a Russian artist who illustrated the cover
of this book, and a very dear friend of mine. Sergei is a
visionary artist who started painting at the age of five. I
feel so honored that after he read *Transcending Illusion*, a
vision of this cover came to him in an altered state of
consciousness. I personally feel that Sergei is a Rembrandt
of our age.

- Thea

"Reading Transcending Illusion totally changed my life! I was stuck in negativity, not knowing how to get out. It helped me to take total responsibility for my state, change it and go beyond the negative 3-D world to a place where I could easily let go. I felt so empowered by the book that I knew that anyone can do what Thea did if they just know the tools."

- Gwen Anderson (Retired School Teacher), Nevada

"Thea's book beautifully assisted me to comprehend the many chapters and highlights of my own current lifetime and of my inner life. This book is an energetic, inter-dimensional experience, and reading it blessed me with healing, integration, inspiration, and a resultant resurrection, a new birth. Read the story – from pre-birth to today – of a current Master of Light, Spiritual Healer, and Eternal Lover of God. Feel yourself in the great weaving of the magnificent tapestry of Divine Plan. This is the story of a woman demonstrating Mastery and Enlightenment in the latter part of the 20th century, joining with the One in bridging and bringing in the Eternal Now of the Golden Age. May it bless the world and all her kingdoms and queendoms!"

- Dr. Jewels Maloney, Sedona, Arizona

TABLE OF CONTENTS

FOREWORD

I have known Thea for over six years and we have managed to stay in constant touch ever since we met. She is
my sometimes partner in healing and together we have
made dreams come true through the miracles of God and
His healing angels. As you read Thea's wonderful book,
Transcending Illusion, you will walk hand-in-hand with her
on her quest for enlightenment.

Thea is a great adventurous spirit. At an early age she
went to India to be with enlightened Masters. After praying to Lord Jesus to take her to a man who truly knew God,
she was led to a great, realized soul, Swami Ramdas of
Kanhangad, South India.

After sitting at the Master's feet meditating constantly,
she experienced a state of Oneness where her mind totally
stilled and she went beyond body consciousness knowing
she was all Spirit. Thea says that while in this state she knew
she was not the limited body. This is the state of beingness,
being all beingness. It is a state of total absorption into the
Self where the sun doesn't know it is the sun: it just IS. As
she returned to the realm of duality, she experienced subtle
thoughts and became a witness to the bliss. Thea could not
maintain this state but realized that this was the purpose of
all human life: *to realize the Oneness of God.*

Thea went through many experiences in India; one was

being bitten by a cobra and having a miraculous healing by a healer saint who was with her when it happened. He simply drew out the poison from her leg and saved her life. After this transforming experience, Thea was able to heal people and see beyond this dimension.

As she states in her book, she has had to release countless lifetimes of karma on the path of transcending illusion and she says if she can do it, anyone who sincerely wants freedom can do it according to their own path. As we travel with Thea, we journey into the unknown, the struggles, the ecstasies and the triumphs of conquering ego to rise above limitation. As we retrace her karma we also retrace some of the ancient history of the earth.

Thea is a never-ending force in this world and a bright light for all humanity. She is a wonderful healer, a bright light in my life, and it is an honor to call her my friend.

Love and light,
Glenn Maxwell
Angelic Healer and Author of Glances at Eternity
November 2006

INTRODUCTION AND ACKNOWLEDGMENTS

This book started as an idea when I went to India in 2002 and had my *nadi* leaves read. Ten thousand years ago the great *rishis*, or illumined masters who have achieved cosmic consciousness, gave prophecies that were recorded onto *nadi* (palm) leaves. These Great Beings are able to see past, present and future as one as they live beyond the illusion of time. Through their clairvoyance they tuned into many souls who would be living on the earth at this time and were able to predict their futures. This was done as an intercession from God, to help those souls understand their path.

Augustiar was one of the ancient *rishis* that tuned into me. Augustiar was the teacher of the great Mahavatar Babaji, an Ascended Master still living in the Himalayas. These readings were recorded on palm leaves and preserved with peacock oil. When I connected to my *nadi* leaf readings by Augustiar, it was mentioned that I would write a book of great significance. Two years later when I was in retreat in India, I met Betsy Braun, a wonderful American lady who ended up being my roommate at the President Hotel in Chennai. I told Betsy stories of my life with the masters in India, and did some healing work on her. She said, "If you ever write a book, I would love to be a part of it."

Several months later after I returned to America, I called

Betsy and asked if she would indeed like to help me write my story. She was thrilled, but didn't know how she could get away from her job long enough to work on the project. As fate would have it, she was laid off from her job and she flew to Sedona with her dictating equipment in tow.

Before we began taping, I tuned into my masters and prayed, "This is your book. Let me be the vehicle for your divine love and guidance." I would go into a trance and talk for hours without stopping as Betsy recorded the story I was telling her. She would then transcribe the tapes and edit the material. I had the easy part. Betsy returned home, and spent the next seven months diligently transcribing the material, and editing as she went along. If it were not for Betsy's hard work, this book never would have been written.

Frances Adams was our first editor, bringing the grammar and story together in a more organized fashion. Thank you, Frances, for your great gift.

Many thanks to my dear friend, Virginia Lloyd, for her further help in the editing of this book.

I would also like to thank my good friend, Lane Badger, publisher of the *Four Corners Magazine*, and her staff, for the layout and graphic design of the book.

I have tremendous gratitude for all of my friends mentioned above, as well as for all the others not mentioned here who helped with editing.

And lastly, thank you to my beautiful parents, who gave me the freedom and support to pursue my path, and to my beloved sister, Wendy, who is always there for me, whether or not she has understood what I was doing! And to my dear friend and former husband, Brian, for mirroring my attachments so that I could release them and experience freedom. He has taught me that letting go is a huge leap to God Consciousness.

I give gratitude to all my angels and masters who are always pushing me forward. You are the stars!

I will mention here that this book is not meant to shock, divide or separate, but only to unify. Everything I have written here is true from my perspective and experience, but I encourage all readers to verify their own truth by going within.

To protect the identity of certain individuals, I have given them fictitious names.

This is the story of my spiritual journey to transcend illusion. My life has been unusual compared to most people because I have experienced many dimensions simultaneously. I thought that all people saw and experienced what I did, but later learned that it was not so.

My soul came in for freedom this time around, and my quest superseded need for attachment, desire or material comfort. My soul yearned to go to India at a young age to be with the realized masters, and they helped me to unfold like a lotus flower. The path to enlightenment is not easy, but I realized at a young age that it was the only way to transcend suffering.

As we begin the inner journey of the soul, all our subconscious imperfections from lifetimes surface so we can let go of all pain. We must go through the pain in order to transcend it. Our pain is caused by past traumas, attachments and aversions to people and objects, fame and fortune, and sensual desires. Holding onto desires always leads to disappointment, because even if they are fulfilled, at some point the joy of the fulfillment will dissipate. Our subconscious mind is full of many unpleasant events we haven't yet cleared.

Growth is letting go of what we are not, and growing into who we truly are—spiritual beings of happiness and joy. Come with me on my journey; it is a journey for everybody, for we are all One.

THE EARLY YEARS

This is a story of my path to enlightenment. I was blessed in this life with wise and loving parents and the guidance of great Masters. After many years of meditation and two near-death experiences, I noticed that powers from God such as spontaneous spiritual healing, clairvoyance, and inner sight started to surface. I was able to see blockages, as well as their cause and whether from this or a past life, and was able to release them through deep faith and prayer. As a beautiful flower unfolds its fragrant petals to the light of the sun, my life has opened to deeper levels of understanding of who I am, why I am here, and why we are all here. The journey has been anything but ordinary and involved a good deal of struggle, beginning with my entrance into this life.

You could say I was a miracle baby. It was 1940 in Santa Ana, California, and my mother was six months pregnant with me when she, my father, brother and sister were in a terrible car accident. My father was pinned under the car, and my mother was thrown through the windshield. My brother and sister were thrown out the back window and by the grace of God, they didn't have a scratch on them. My father survived, but was paralyzed from the waist down; he was told he would never walk again. My mother had lacerations on her face. Due to the tremendous shock, doctors said she would most likely lose the baby.

Mom went to several doctors, all of whom told her the same thing: her unborn child would not survive. She was determined to have me because she said my conception was the most beautiful experience she had ever had in her life. It went beyond the sexual aspect into incredible bliss and union with God. She said her baby had to be born because it was a love baby from God and was destined to be very special.

Dr. Browning, my grandfather's best friend, was a family practitioner who knew our family very well. Mom finally went to him and he said, "Of course this baby is going to be born! I know this family and it has to be born and it will be perfect." My mother was overjoyed that she had finally found a doctor who would encourage her, and he did. Over the following months my mother meditated and prayed for her unborn baby and for her convalescing husband at home.

When my mother went into labor there were complications. Dr. Browning immediately informed the nurses to prepare for a Cesarean section. My father wanted to stay in the operating room and due to the special circumstances surrounding the birth, Dr. Browning agreed, but added,

"You can stay on one condition— don't faint on me because there's no one that's going to pick you up!"

"I assure you Doc, I'll be fine!" my father said smiling. The moment Dr. Browning made the incision my father fainted and toppled out of his wheel chair, but contrary to Dr. Browning's warning, they did pick him up. When he opened his eyes he looked upon his perfectly healthy daughter, and the beaming faces of everyone in the room!

The first few years after my birth were bittersweet for my mother because of my father's disability. Dad was an ancient soul, however, and there was nothing he couldn't overcome. He said that this human body and God, the Supreme Being, could do anything. He swam in the ocean for a year only using his arms. With incredible will and perseverance, he mentally sent messages to his legs, "You can do it, you can do it." When I started to crawl, he said he was like a baby too and had to learn how to do it all over again. Between swimming and crawling he brought his legs back all the way, although the doctors had told him he'd never do it.

One of my great friends from early adulthood, Gayatri Devi, who was head of the Ananda Ashram in La Crescenta, California, said my parents had to go through tremendous trials and suffering as a way to purify themselves, and to prepare for the role they had as parents to me.

My early memories were very joyful. I was the youngest and much loved. In my dreams I was always flying to other worlds, seeing angels and beings of light, and feeling the experience of not being in the body. I had the love of my friends and animals. We always had horses, cats, dogs, and many other animals including a goat, a donkey, a bird, hamsters, and at one time even an elephant! Those animals understood me better than humans did. I would spend hours training and talking with them telepathically. My cats took so much from me. I'd dress them up in baby clothes and feed them bottles! I'd spend hours braiding my horse's mane and putting ribbons in it.

I always had hideouts in nature. I'd get my friends to help me build forts out of twigs and branches with secret doors where only special people and animals could go. It was my own little world and sanctuary. I felt the fairies and devas and the connection to the nature spirits. My father was a pantheist[1] and taught us if we were quiet in nature we could feel the trees, plants, wind, birds, and everything around us, all of which were God.

Thea proudly seated on the family pet donkey, Jenny, and holding onto her daddy.

1   Pantheist literally means "God is All," and refers to one who sees God in all of nature and the universe.

Whenever we kids would cry, he would pick us up and take us to a tree and say, "Just become close to the tree." Nature became our great healer.

From the time I was little, my mom would spend hours rocking me, while she talked to me about God. She was an extremely high angel and beautiful being, and almost too sensitive for this world. Her mother had raised her and her sister, Idie, to believe that all religions lead to the One. My maternal grandmother, Florence Nell, was very psychic and intuitive. She would see someone die before they passed, seeing a great light coming down, engulfing them and taking them up. Florence could see beyond this world.

My maternal grandparents were born in Antre, England, and owned an interior design store there. From time to time, gypsies would stop by the store and Florence would give them remnants of material. The gypsies would read her palm in payment. She was fascinated with the gypsies' free lifestyle and mystical outlook. Because of her own free-spirited, mystical nature and waist-length black hair, she always said she had some gypsy in her. Everything they predicted came true, such as how many children she would have, that she would lose one child, and that she would travel across the ocean and live in a sunny place by the sea.

My grandmother taught her children about reincarnation and how she had seen past lives. She also believed that all paths led to the One. She was brought up with a broad, expansive view of what God was. Mom taught the same philosophy to her children. Between a pantheist father who

Mom and Dad.

believed nature was God, and a mother who believed all religions lead to the One, I gained the foundation for who I would become.

I was always able to see the unseen, and my parents encouraged me to do so. I also had a very vivid imagination, so they never knew when I was making things up or if what I was seeing was real. Nevertheless, they always encouraged me. I could see fairies and nature spirits, which appeared as lights. I would run and feel the wind blow against my skin, and knew that it, too, was a live being. I was ecstatic.

My father owned a summer camp for boys, and from a very early age my sister, Wendy, and I were the only girls there. My dad believed in the power of positive thinking and would never tear a kid down for what he or she couldn't do. A child could always do something well, even if it were just eating lunch or taking a nap, and he would build on that.

Growing up with the boys at the camp was a hoot. We were surrounded by boys from different backgrounds and all types of animals. I learned how to ride horses bareback at three years of age by gripping with my knees. Wendy and I loved the boys' world and didn't care that they weren't girls! We were thrilled with the beautiful world that Daddy had created with his camp and the children, animals, and power of positive thinking.

In a very loving and patient way, Dad helped us to confront our fears. I was afraid of the dark, so he'd walk me down the hall at night and keep dimming the lights more and more, until finally he let me walk down the hall by myself. He said, "Whatever fear you face thoroughly will go away. We often deny and push away what we are afraid of and because we never face it, it always remains."

As early as I can remember I was scared to death of rattlesnakes. Daddy had no fear of wild animals, so to help me overcome mine, he caught a few rattlesnakes and put them in an aquarium in the garage. He would hold the snake's neck down with a forked stick, then grab it from behind its neck and pick it up. Every day Daddy would take my hand and walk me into the

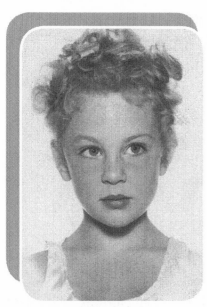

Thea, age 5.

garage and say, "Now send love to the snakes because when you don't send them love they rattle. Fear and hatred are the same to animals." Even behind the glass they still terrorized me and I'd look at them with my little heart pounding, wanting to run the other way. I tried my best to love them but it was hard. My father would tell me to speak honestly to the snakes about how I felt, so from my heart I said, "I don't know why I'm afraid of you. I don't want to be afraid and I really want to love you, so could you please help me love you?"

Eventually I overcame my fear - at least when they were in the aquarium - and they stopped rattling. Dad said, "See? They are total reflectors of what you feel because they interpret fear as hatred and fear you could kill them. All animals are like that." I got very close to those snakes. They were the only ones that laid eggs in captivity because of the love we gave them.

Our parents were incredible examples dedicating their entire lives to raising and loving their children. Mom was always at home for us. I never knew a time when she wasn't there when we'd come home from school. She would have milk and nice snacks for us and we could tell her about the day. We would also share our day at the dinner table and my father would help guide us through any problems.

Dad had amazing ways of confronting situations that disturbed us. For example, if we had a bad experience with a teacher, he would tell us that she was probably upset about something in her own life, and that we should try to love her. He said we could change people with our thoughts. One time we were in a restaurant and noticed the waitress was very sad. Dad said, "We have to send her love. See if you can change her." The three of us closed our eyes, concentrated on her and sent her love and happiness. We saw her change before our eyes. It was an extremely valuable lesson about the power of love sent through concentrated thought.

Our parents' nurturing love provided us with the perfect environment to thrive. Some of my happiest memories were playing with my big brother, Kim, and sister, Wendy. Kim was like a coach, so I ended up being a tomboy. I was always small for my age and even as a tiny little kid he'd have me pole vaulting or doing football wing-T plays. I did everything to try to please him and would work like heck after school. He taught me a lot about perseverance and I have to admit I enjoyed the challenge.

Wendy was a great leader and wise person and I was so proud of her. She always won awards in school and was voted most outstanding student. I stood in the audience yelling with delight as she received her awards. Even when she later became a mother, she received the Arcadia Award for most outstanding teacher of the year. We had a ball growing up together too. We'd take long horseback rides up into the mountains on beautiful trails surrounded by trees. Our horses would gallop up the hills and jump logs while we rode bareback.

A lot of my time was spent training my horse. He was a

hackney pony and trotter, and an incredible friend. I trained him to come like a dog when I whistled and to stretch way down so I could get on, because I was so little. I taught him to buck, which was not helpful later when other kids tried to ride him!

Later, my sister and I discovered that our physical coordination developed sooner than the boys and that even though they were the same age, we were better at swimming and riding horseback. The boys started to resent us because we were outdoing them.

So one summer, Dad sent us to a private camp for girls. Dad had also recognized we were maturing and felt it would benefit our development to be around other girls of our age. It was the first summer we weren't with the boys and we missed them. We enjoyed showing off and being better than they were! It was an upscale girls' camp, but because we had been taught so well at dad's camp we ended up winning all the competitions in swimming and riding. We had learned English saddle from one of the best equestrian teachers in the area, Miss Lesley Proud. She taught me English saddle from the time I was five

Thea (left) with sister, Wendy.

Thea, age 3, with brother Kim.

years old. I would watch her teaching the other kids and then I would imitate posting bareback. She was so impressed that she called me in and taught me with the others. So when we went to the girls' camp, we won so many ribbons! One skill I learned there was how to jump. It was an exhilarating feeling as I went over the jumps because it felt like the horse and I were one being. If the horse was afraid and about to shy, it was important to give him confidence. This was no problem for me because I was telepathic with all my animals. We had a total understanding of each other and were very close.

After two or three years at the girls' camp, Daddy opened his boys' camp to girls. He called the girls' section "Becky Thatcher." My sister and I were proud to be the first Becky Thatcher's along with eight other girls.

Dad had an abundance of patience as we grew up. And he had the same patience with the kids at camp. He truly loved them. The counselors were also trained into the power of positive thinking and how to overcome fear in positive ways. Every year, all the groups thrived.

Each group picked a name for themselves, such as the Cougars, Mighty Kittens or Trojans, and they had T-shirts made and created their own cheers. The groups challenged each other in competition and at the end of the day, each group chose the outstanding boys and girls who had achieved the most that day. Then the entire camp formed a large semi-circle; and the chosen ones from each group stood in front of everyone and were honored for their achievements. That practice promoted teamwork, comraderie and unity con-sciousness.

Dad had tremendous respect for nature, and viewed it as God. He had no fear of animals, even the wild ones. At the end of camp, all the kids sat on logs in a semi-circle and Dad would catch skunks to put in the middle. He would prepare the kids beforehand by telling them if they had any fear of a skunk it might spray them. He explained that skunks were beautiful animals, like kitty cats, and through love they could be tamed. The skunks would be released into the semi-circle with some 300 children and the kids would call out, "Come here little skunky!" The skunks could feel the group's love and affection, and wouldn't try to run away, but in fact would walk right up to them. The kids loved it. Only one year did a child get sprayed and that was because he started screaming!

Children from well-known and wealthy families attended Dad's camp. Usually the children of parents with old money were very mellow. The newly rich children were sometimes spoiled and demanded special treatment but they quickly learned that everyone was equal in our eyes, no matter how much money they had. Many of these children had spent a lot of time with maids and nannies, and didn't get as much love from their parents as they received at camp.

Dad's philosophy was to "get the kids in nature and let them get muddy, we can hose them off at the end of the day." He wrote letters to the parents saying if they didn't want their kids to get dirty, to not send them to the Tom Sawyer and Becky Thatcher Camp. If they hadn't gotten dirty before, they certainly would when they got to camp. The kids would get down into the mud and cake it all over themselves. It felt like total freedom and they loved it. We'd catch frogs in the mud and have frog races. The kids were allowed to be kids and be happy. They loved horse-back riding, hiking, swimming, adventures and games.

We had a small fleet of buses that went to the various cities to pick up and drop off the children. The children waited on the curb at the designated area, called "curb stoners," and if they were there when the bus arrived they received special notice. One boy, little Harry, came from a very wealthy family and he didn't want anyone to see the huge mansion he lived in. His maid accompanied Harry to the bus stop and carried his belongings. It kind of undid what we were trying to do at camp to make the children self-reliant and independent. Harry would ask the driver to drop him off a block away and when the driver asked why, he said, "I don't want the kids to see my house because they would make fun of me." Not all the children were from wealthy families.

Harry was a little spoiled. The kids went on daily hikes to promote endurance and health, but Harry would plop down in the middle of a hike and start to cry, "I can't go any farther!" He was pudgy and it was harder for him, but not so much that he couldn't make it through the hike. Harry was just used to getting his own way with tears. When it started to become a problem for the counselors, Dad stepped in.

Dad was always there when a difficult situation arose and there wasn't any problem he couldn't heal, because he was very wise and loving. He began to accompany the group during their hikes and as usual, Harry sat down and started crying, "I can't do it, I can't do it..." My dad spent a lot of time finding out about each of the children and what they enjoyed, and he knew Harry liked antique cars. So Dad went up to him and said, "Harry! You can do it! You know that Model T Ford you have at home? You know, we crank those up - that's how we get it going. People are not much different than those cars, and we can crank you right up." He told the rest of the group that Harry was the car, that Dad was going to wind him up, and asked the kids to make the cranking sound. Dad continued, "You're just like the Model T. As we crank you up, like the gas being fed to the car, you'll get a lot of energy."

Group participation and encouragement were continually emphasized at camp, whether it was to help a child to learn how to swim or overcome a fear. The whole group started chanting, "YOU CAN DO IT! YOU CAN DO IT!" As Dad started winding up Harry like a Model T, Harry's frown gradually turned into a huge grin. Then quicker than anyone had ever seen him move, he jumped up and started running up the hill, and was the first to reach the top. The whole group cheered. Harry was honored that day as "Most Outstanding Camper."

After that day we never had trouble with Harry again. All the kids knew when one of them conquered something, and they were all really happy and supportive of each other when it happened. It was incredibly heartwarming to watch their beaming faces when they overcame an obstacle.

Daddy always used positive reinforcement mixed with genuine care to bring children out of their shells, and to overcome negative behaviors or blockages they learned at home. He spent a lot of time with the children and with their parents as well. He would come home from camp, then talk on the phone with the parents, particularly single mothers, and would guide them with wisdom. The kids loved Daddy and he loved them, but he also set boundaries and wouldn't let them get away with anything that wasn't good for them. His whole life was spent helping children and parents surmount obstacles. He was a dad to many people and he was always there for us as well.

One of the children from our camp had an assignment at school, to write about the three most important men in the world. He wrote about Jesus Christ, George Washington and my father! That's the effect he had on children.

When I was twelve I came down with scarlet fever. Even though I had a high fever, I remembered it as a beautiful time. My dad read the children's book *Heidi* to me and we got a new German Shepherd puppy, Blitzen von Heidelberg. One of the most amazing things that happened at that time was when I went out of my body and ended up on the ceiling. There I was, looking down at myself in total joy, feeling free and happy. I didn't know it then, but it was a near-death experience. It didn't last very long; moments later I was back in my body. I told my mother about it, and she explained to me about astral travel (although she didn't call it that). She told me that sometimes we go out of our physical bodies into our subtle bodies[2] and that we could go wherever we wanted when we were in our subtle bodies, which was what had happened to me.

After that, I started leaving my body at night, and decided it would be great fun to teach my friends how to fly! I gave them a class during recess, and was convinced that I'd take off. But to my dismay I couldn't get off the ground. My friends didn't laugh at me, because they knew that I was sincere. I didn't understand that it was my astral body flying at night. The experiences were so real that I thought I could do it during the day too.

At home I asked my mom why I couldn't fly, and she said, "At night you are in a more subtle body and it's just as

2   The subtle body is a non-physical energy that all beings possess. Just as the physical body is made up of matter, each non-physical body has its own attributes and exists around the physical body. The physical body is the densest, and each subsequent body is progressively more refined and resonates at a higher frequency.

Our beloved Shepard, Blitzen von Heidelberg, with Kitty.

real as during the day. During the day you forget your subtle body, and you are in your physical body." She helped me to understand the difference between the bodies, and the experiences of each body.

It wasn't unusual for me to communicate with people who were out of their physical bodies. I could see them and they would talk to me. When I was seven, my uncle died of a heart attack on the golf course. That night he appeared to me. I ran into the living room and said, "Uncle Ted's here! Uncle Ted's here! He's talking to me." My mom said, "Oh my God, he died today, and he's out of his body." He had been trying to talk to other people and I just happened to be able to see him. A lot of kids can see the unseen, but because their parents make this ability wrong or don't believe them, the kids suppress it.

From the time I was young, I had a fantasy about going to a monastery to be with the holy people who lived there. That fantasy was rekindled when my parents and I went to Ojai Valley to see Krishnamurti, a mystic and realized soul. He taught the path of Vedanta, that we are one with God now, and that the only thing we have to do is to release the delusion covering that knowledge.

I had inherited enough mystic in me from my grandmother to know that this was what I wanted to do. My grandmother was an original follower of Krishnamurti. She also knew Mary Baker Eddy, founder of the Christian Science Church and author of *Science and Health with Key to the Scriptures*. The book was based on the *Upanishads*, ancient scriptures from India, and my grandmother studied it thoroughly. We were brought up with the Christian Science philosophy without going to church. We had tried going to traditional Christian churches but it was boring. My brother, sister and I would end up drawing pictures and yawning until my mom said we didn't have to go to church anymore. Truth be told, she didn't like it either. My parents taught us at home about the different religions. One particular phrase from *Science and Health* has stayed with me my whole life: "Man is not Material, Man is Spiritual."

My grandmother was a great inspiration to me. I could always identify with her, because she was a very free spirit and way ahead of her time. She believed that all paths lead to the One. She was a great mystic in her own right. My mystical abilities must have been hereditary as I was always open to these things. My brother and sister had the same teachings as I did, but they didn't go as deeply into it.

I was always very sensitive to teachers. If they loved me and were kind people, I'd do anything for them even if I didn't like the subject they taught. Only a few subjects interested me, such as the Hopi Indians, but mostly I just liked being with my friends and building hideouts. Once in third grade, during an arithmetic lesson, I was sitting next to the window, staring at the bushes and wishing I was building a fort. Our teacher started screaming, "Theda! Theda! Where are you?!" I was in somewhat of an altered state and it yanked me back to my body. I was very shy, and felt my face heat up with embarrassment. She demanded I come up to the front of the class. She barked, "What did I just say?" Of course, I didn't know because I wasn't paying attention, and wasn't even completely back in my body. The children started laughing and I went back to my seat in some form of shock. From that point on I couldn't even do simple math. I told my dad about my experience and he hired a tutor. The tutor worked very hard with me and I made some progress, but I still retained a block to math. It wasn't until many years later that I was able to release the trauma and free that part of my mind.

I received good grades in school, but I don't know how. Most of school was very boring to me and I pretty much faked it all the way through. In high school I took a speech class. I was supposed to research and prepare a speech with an introduction, body and conclusion. The assignment was more effort than I was willing to put forth, so with just a basic idea in my head I walked up to the podium and spontaneously gave my speech. To my delight, everyone loved it! Well, almost everyone. At one point our class critiqued each other's speeches and a classmate said about mine, "She gets up there and her personality just takes over and she acts like she has studied, but she hasn't studied at all." I thought, *boy, he really knows! I wasn't fooling him.*

I still went on to college even though school was drudgery to me. I became the school's mascot, "Tammy Tiger," and got to dress up in a tiger outfit to lead the band. I had a ball! No one knew who I was and I got away with just about anything. I'd lead the band waving my arms and kicking my legs and having a great time. Aside from my mascot escapades, it wasn't until my third year when I took liberal arts classes and studied authors such as Emerson, Thoreau and Walt Whitman that I became so inspired. It brought me back to my own upbringing when my dad told us if we had a problem, to go out into nature and the problem would go away, because being quiet in nature was being with God. I had some incredible teachers for those subjects, although I didn't know that one of my teachers was experimenting with LSD. It was during the early 1960's when LSD had started to become popular, and boy, was that class outrageous.

I did a term paper on Kahlil Gibran. In one of his books, *The Prophet*, he wrote about what real love was. He said that love was spiritual and of the soul, not of the body or mind. I was leaning up against a tree working on my report and was suddenly sucked into a high state of spirit consciousness. I stayed in that state for a long time. I didn't know what it was, just that it felt darn good! It was my first experience of meditation when I felt the presence of God within. I shared it with my mom and she suggested I ask Aunt Idie for her book on meditation by Joel Goldsmith. I started reading it and realized there were other men that had achieved "Oneness" like Jesus. That really thrilled me. I used to read the Bible when I was a child, and I would feel Jesus within and receive silent teachings from Him.

Around that time Dad called me at school and said that Mom was losing ground and needed to visit me. She had thrown her whole identity into being a mother, and since her children had all left home, she had lost her identity in some way. When she came to visit me I noticed that she was very far off, forgetful, and sometimes would lose her sense of time. Both dad and I were worried about her. I was the youngest, and since I had left for college, she hadn't been the same.

That summer when I went home and my mom continued to have periods when she would stare off into space. At one point she didn't know who she was. Doctors called it post-menopausal depression. In those days physicians didn't know about the glandular system. Knowing what I know now, I could have turned it right around but I didn't know it then.

Mom ended up having a nervous breakdown and we

reluctantly admitted her into a mental institution. For her therapy, the doctors administered shock treatments. My world was totally blown apart. I didn't understand why this was happening to such a beautiful soul. My mother was so sensitive, in fact too sensitive, which may have been the problem. My aunt and I visited her and many patients who were such kind souls. Before we went into the facility, we'd shift our consciousness, and pray for all the people. The patients would follow us around because they could feel our love. We grew to love them all, and instead of just bringing tea and cookies to Mom, we'd bring enough for the whole ward. They always looked forward to our coming and we'd have a party. These so-called mentally ill people were some of the most beautiful souls I had ever met. They were like children, simple and pure, and were attuned to the love we extended. It was a crime that the patients were highly medicated. However, it was all the doctors knew how to do in those days.

At Christmas we threw them a party. Dad dressed up as Santa Claus, and we had stockings made up for each of them. We brought along our friend Jenny, who to played the piano while we all sang Christmas carols. One of the patients, diagnosed as manic-depressive, always sat in the same corner. Whenever we visited, we would say hello to her but she never responded or came out of her corner. One day Jenny sat down at the piano and started to play. After a couple of songs, the woman suddenly leaped up, pushed Jenny out of her seat, and started playing the piano like you would not believe! The nurse was shocked, and said it was the first time that the patient had a reaction. It wasn't shocking to my dad, Aunt Idie and me, because we knew the power of love.

We did everything we could for Mom. She was in a sad state because she was heavily medicated and wasn't eating well. She had lost a lot of weight and was a little woman to begin with. But no matter how sick, she always knew who we were, was happy to see us, and loved us.

TURNING TO GOD AND INDIA

A s I turned more to God, there was the need to find answers to the questions within me, "What are we here for? Why do we have to suffer? Are we here to just get married, have babies, build houses, and die? Is that all there is?"

Between reading Joel Goldsmith's books and dealing with Mom's illness, I started praying to Jesus from the bottom of my heart, "Take me to someone who totally knows God like you do."

A couple of days after my prayer, my Aunt Idie called and we talked about my search for a spiritual teacher. She told me that India was a country with many realized souls. She said that Joel Goldsmith had talked about a man in India who was the highest realized soul he had ever met. He was named Swami Ramdas, affectionately known as Papa Ramdas. Joel was also a realized soul, so I listened to Aunt Idie with great interest.

Joel had visited Papa Ramdas' ashram and had written

a letter to his students about his experience, which Aunt Idie then forwarded to me. The letter stated that as Joel approached the gates to the ashram, there was a huge archway with "Anandashram" written at the top, which means Abode of Bliss. He entered into beautiful grounds with mango trees and white buildings, and he said that the minute he walked through the gates it was like dying and going into another realm, because the energy was so high. Joel described Papa Ramdas and Mother Krishnabai, Papa's student, who had also gained realization, as being the most loving and joyful beings he had ever met. All realized souls have different aspects of God that they express, and Papa Ramdas' aspect was the total joy of God.

Papa had achieved such a high state of *samadhi*[3] that he renounced his wife and child and became a wandering *sadhu*[4]. He said he couldn't love just one family, because the whole world was his family. He wandered throughout India, going wherever Ram would send him and later founded the Anandashram. (Papa Ramdas wrote about his life in his books *In Quest of God*, *In the Vision of God*, and *God Experience*.)

I also learned about Hinduism, a religion that embraces all religions and Masters. All lead to the One. I thought about Papa Ramdas and his ashram day and night. Aunt Idie said that I should write to Papa Ramdas and tell him about myself and see if I could go to his ashram and be one of his

3   The Sansrkit word Samadhi refers to a completely absorbed state of God consciousness experienced during concentrated meditation.

4   A sadhu is a wandering monk who begs for his food.

students. So I did. I wrote a long letter, pages and pages of everything about my mother in the mental institution, how I didn't like school and was trying to find myself, that the only thing I was interested in was God, and how I wanted to be realized like Joel Goldsmith, Jesus, and him. I asked if he would please take me as his private student because I was reaching a point in my life where there was nothing else that I wanted to do.

I waited for weeks for a return letter and would go to the mailbox every day. Finally Papas' letter arrived, and oh my God, was I ecstatic! It began with "Beloved Mother". I didn't know that every female was "mother" to him. I said to my father, "Dad, he thinks I'm a *mother*." We both had a hearty laugh over that.

Naturally, I had to call Aunt Idie and read the letter to her. It was so beautiful— he said he'd love to have me come. I had written in my letter that I didn't have much money but that I'd be willing to work in the ashram or do anything. He replied that money was not the issue, that anyone could come free of charge. The main purpose was to bring people into their own realization, and give them a safe place to meditate and be with a master.

I was absolutely beside myself with excitement. This was the big adventure I had been waiting for my entire life, even though I was only 21! I quickly sent a reply letter, which said, "I'm coming, I'm coming, I'm coming!" I sold the car my aunt had given me, and used what I had saved from working at my dad's camp for my airfare. My travel agent made arrangements for me to stay at a very fancy hotel in India because I was so young, and he wanted to make sure I was well taken care of. The only place I had ever flown was to Northern California. There I was three months later waving goodbye to my bewildered parents and Aunt Idie as I boarded a plane to another country thousands of miles away. I was filled with anticipation of meeting a realized soul who knew God fully. It was all I could think of.

When I changed planes in Hong Kong, I sat next to two boys about my age from England who were the funniest characters. They bantered back and forth with a droll sense of humor, and I laughed all the way to India. As luck would have it, they were booked at the same hotel as I in Bombay, and they gallantly acted as my protectors, which I thoroughly appreciated and enjoyed.

India was like nothing I had ever seen before. There were cows in the street, women dressed in colorful saris, people, and poverty everywhere, but it was real. The boys asked me why I was crying and all I could say was, "I love it here." I felt totally at home.

The next day I parted ways with my English friends and boarded a plane going to a village near Mangalore. When I arrived, a crowd of people gathered around and followed me as I walked. The children outstretched their little brown hands begging for money, and I gave them pennies, or whatever I had. It was all so strange to me, but I liked it, and I felt very close to them. They had such beautiful, soulful eyes.

In order to get to Papa Ramdas' ashram I had to take a

rickety train to Kanhangad. I sat with a lovely Indian family who noticed I was young and alone, so they took very good care of me. After some time, the train stopped and there was much commotion, with people yelling back and forth in Hindi. I asked the family in my compartment what was happening. There was always someone who understood English. They told me the bridge was damaged, and it would have to be repaired before we could continue on. I looked at my watch and realized if we were much delayed, I'd end up arriving in the middle of the night at a jungle station. I was a little worried. There was nothing I could do though, and decided to surrender to the moment and enjoy my great adventure. The Indian family was so loving and generous, sharing their food with me as if I were part of their group. I felt right at home with them. They said that if there was no one to meet me at the station, that I could go home with them, and they would get me to the ashram the next day.

After five hours, the repairs to the bridge were completed. Around midnight the train pulled into Kanhangad, a little jungle station consisting of only a thatched hut. I was certain no one would be there to meet me at that late hour, but I looked around anyway. To my surprise, a beautiful young Indian man was standing there and asked, "Are you Theodora?" I excitedly replied, "Yes! I'm Theodora!"

The young Indian man was Papa Ramdas' grandson, one of the most beautiful men I had ever seen in my young life. He took me to the ashram, and told me that Swami Ramdas wouldn't see anyone until the morning and I could meet him then. He took me to the dining hall and gave me snacks and *chai* (Indian spiced tea), and told me to sleep. He said, "You'll probably be too tired to see Swami Ramdas in the morning..." but before he could finish his sentence, I exclaimed, "No I won't!" Nothing would prevent me from meeting this great man I had been thinking of for months!

The next morning I was dead tired. It took all my will power to get up and to dress. I was shown into a room packed with people, something I would get used to in India, and was instructed to take my shoes off, which was Indian protocol. In the front of the room stood a beautiful man. I was taken up to him and introduced as Thea. I shook his hand and said, "How do you do! I'm so happy to meet you!" The correct protocol is to bow or pranam to a realized master, but I didn't know that. Everyone was laughing. His first words to me were, "You're so young!" And I said, "What did you expect, an old lady?" He replied that my letters were so mature. Everyone became very quiet. Papa looked at me and said, "Ramdas' mathematics go like this: "One plus one equals one. Understand?" I replied, "Yes, everything is one!" He said, "Very good!" Then he said, "You've got to know you know nothing."

I said, "Papa, I don't know very much. I went to college for three years, and didn't like it one bit. What they taught me, other than about the mystics, didn't mean much. I am here to find myself."

Papa Ramdas told me he hadn't liked school either, and said he spent most of the time in the corner wearing a dunce cap, because he was so mischievous! He said, "The dunce cap was pointed like a pyramid and probably gave Ramdas great intelligence." His remarks meant so much to me, because I had spent time judging myself for not being motivated in school. Most of the Masters and mystics are bored with the facts, and want something that feeds the soul. I was relieved that he didn't like school either. All the judgments that I had of myself, why I didn't like school, and maybe I wasn't smart enough- all dropped away.

Laughing, he said, "You must go to the dining room. Have some *chai* and be fed, and then you can come and be with Ramdas later." He always spoke of himself in the third person. I went to the dining hall, had *chai* and noticed people sitting on the floor eating with their fingers. One of them was a little man named Sam who I later found out was Sufi Sam, the famous leader of the flower children. He became my guru on Indian etiquette. I was given a spoon, but I wanted to learn how to eat with my fingers as the Indians did. I carefully squeezed the rice and vegetables into a ball until it was firm, and leaning forward over the plate, placed the ball into my mouth. I felt like a little kid using my hands.

Sam was like a mother to me, very kind and happy that I was there. He said I had come to the right place, and that Papa was one of the greatest saints in India. There was also a Canadian lady there, Savitri, who helped me shop for a sari, taught me how to put it on, and showed me how to apply the *kum kum* [5] on my forehead.

The Anandashram, or Abode of Bliss, was absolutely out of this world. Devotees were constantly chanting in Sanksrit, repeating the same mantra over and over. The primary chant was the Ram mantra: *Sri Ram, Jai Ram, Jai Jai Ram, Om Sri Rama Jai Ram Jai Jai Ram Om.* It sounded very funny and I felt like giggling. I went for a walk with Vimala, a lovely Indian woman, and asked her why the chanters kept doing that same tune over again? She said, "Oh, that is Papa's mantra. It is such a holy mantra. *Om* is the beginning sound of creation and the most powerful seed sound in the universe. *Sri Ram* is the name of God and is considered to be the impersonal Godhead, or it can be the personal prophet who was the great avatar [6] Rama."

I didn't even know who Rama was, but I continued to listen intently. "When we chant the mantra, we are giving gratitude and praise to God all the time. *Jai* means victory to God. When you are doing the mantra your focus is on God in a concentrated way, and it is a high form of meditation." I wanted more than anything to learn how to meditate.

The women took turns playing the harmonium to different versions of *Ram Nam.* Every day I would sit near Papa whether he was in the bhajan [7] hall or under the banyan tree.

5   Kum kum is a powder made from turmeric and lime juice and in Hinduism is applied to the forehead during pujas, or sacred ceremonies. It represents a pure soul who sees the divine in all beings.
6   Avatar means "the descent of God" in Sanskrit and refers to the incarnation of the Supreme Being who is free from the laws of matter, time and space. Avatars come to this world to spiritually uplift humanity and to remind them of their true eternal and divine self. Famous avatars are Krishna, Rama, Sita Devi, Gautama Buddha and Jesus Christ.
7   Devotional songs to God in Sanskrit.

I wasn't going to miss a thing. People would ask him questions and he would reply with truth and wisdom. Fortunately for me, he spoke excellent English. He was such a beautiful representative of God.

Vimala said I should get initiated and receive the Ram mantra. She told me when initiation happens, a realized soul takes responsibility for a devotee's spiritual development, and imbues his or her power and blessing into the sacred syllables of a mantra. As the mantra is repeated, it is empowered by the grace of the guru. Initiation is also surrendering to a realized soul, a representative of God. I approached Papa and asked to be initiated into the Ram mantra. He told me to come the next morning, to not eat anything beforehand, and to wear white and bring flowers. I went to his room early the next morning and sat next to him. I felt his love for me. It was so much more profound than the love my parents had for me, and they loved me dearly. I had never felt this deep kind of love before. He was pure joy and beauty. I said, "Papa, I don't know what meditation is, but this is wonderful!" He said, "The sun shines equally on all, but the sun can only enter when the heart is open. Ramdas loves all equally, but you allow him into your heart."

He initiated me into the Ram mantra, which he had me repeat three times after him, and then instructed me to do it constantly, day and night. I figured since I was there, I was going to give this the biggest try of my life. After the initiation, the mantra flowed and I could feel the grace of my guru. At 5 a.m. every morning I went to Papa's room;

it was always crowded. There was a large influx of people coming to the ashram, as well as those who lived there permanently. I chanted Ram Nam constantly. I noticed at times that I would find incredible quietude within, then there were times when a lot of garbage would come up and I'd feel horrible. I'd even have dreams of things I had done that I thought were bad. I told Papa about it and he said, "It is the *guru kripa*. When the guru accepts one fully as a disciple, one's karma[8] has to surface and it's helpful if it comes out in dreams. When it gets too intense or if you are afraid, just call on Papa Ramdas and he'll help you through it."

One night I was having a terrible dream. I woke up with a start and yelled out, "Papa! Papa!" The next morning when I went to Papa's room he said, "You yanked on Papa Ramdas so much last night you almost pulled him out of bed!" Oh my God, I thought, he's aware of everything.

He would answer every question I had even if I didn't verbally ask it. One day I asked him if he could read my mind, and he replied, "No, Ramdas doesn't try to do that. Ramdas is just a pure channel from which Ram flows, and if there is a question that needs answering it will come forth. Ramdas is a fiddle and the devotees play the fiddle."

I sat right next to Papa from five in the morning until ten at night chanting the mantra. Wherever he went, I

8   Karma is the Sanskrit word for "action," in the sense that for every action there is a reaction. It's meaning is rooted in the law of cause and effect, or "As ye sow, so shall ye reap."

went. I got very disciplined doing Ram Nam. I decided I was going to do this nonstop and not talk to people, like Papa had told me. After about three weeks I started feeling euphoric. One day Papa gave me the name of Indira, which is an aspect of the Divine Mother[9] Lakshmi, representing beauty and abundance in all things.

Papa Ramdas was the greatest salesman of God that anyone could have. He was total joy, and told captivating stories.

One that I loved was about the frogs and the buttermilk: Two frogs leaped into a can of milk that had not been churned, and they sank to the bottom. They kept paddling to come up for breath and then would sink down again. Over and over they tried. Finally one of the frogs got too tired, gave up and drowned. The other frog, however, kept trying. Going up, taking a breath and going down. Going up, taking a breath and going down. The frog ended up churning the milk and formed a little clump of butter. He then got on the clump of butter and leaped out. Ramdas said, "You have to make a tremendous effort for God. You can't give up. You can leap on the butter island and leap out. Your effort will form an island of grace."

I was so inspired by these wonderful stories that I went for it day and night. I was eating the Indian food with my fingers, and loving everyone there because I was so attuned

9 The Divine Mother is the dynamic and creative force of the Godhead and lives in all things. She is known by many names, such as the Goddesses Devi, Shakti, Durga, Kali, Isis, and Mother Mary.

to myself and to Papa. I felt like Papa was inside me. He used to say, "Papa Ramdas is like a Jack in the Box, when you say the mantra, Papa jumps out." And that's what it felt like. I was getting close to him on an inner level; I felt as though I had a glimpse of what realization might be like.

So there I was, doing the mantra constantly and getting into euphoric states. I wrote my family, friends and sorority sisters and tried to tell them what this was all about, and couldn't. Would they understand? It was a feeling deep within my heart, which I couldn't communicate in words.

One afternoon I was sitting in Papa Ramdas' room listening to his discourse, and thinking about a saying my mother had taught me, "Man is not Material; Man is Spiritual." Papa Ramdas was talking about losing body consciousness and going into the subtle body and more refined states. He said, "When the *kundulini* [10] rises it is like an electrical current coming up the spine. It pierces the *chakras* [11] and you lose physical body consciousness and go into your finer bodies. Sometimes you will feel the physical sensation of your head expanding. Then, the mind completely stops and you go into a Oneness state." I was so impressionable, and listened to every word.

---

10   Kundulini is Sanskrit for "coiled up" or "serpent power" and represents the female cosmic energy existing in every atom of the universe. In humans it originates in the first chakra, or energy center, at the base of the spine and remains in a dormant state until awakened through disciplined yogic practices or by a realized master. The un-manifested kundalini is symbolized by a coiled serpent with its tail in its mouth. When this energy is awakened it travels up the spine to the top of the head where the person experiences a Oneness state with God.
11   In Hinduism, chakras (from the Sanskrit word *cakra* meaning "wheel") are energy centers along the spine that give life force to the body.

The next day I was sitting by Papa in meditation, and again the thought came into my mind, "Man is not Material; Man is Spiritual." Suddenly an electrical current emanated from the base of my spine and rose up like an elevator to my neck. From that point down I couldn't feel a thing. Then I went into a state of Oneness: there was no mind, no thoughts, no body consciousness; just Beingness. I lost the concept of time and space; a state described in ancient Indian texts as *samadhi*. Because there is no time or space, and no thoughts to judge the experience, I had no clue how long I had been in this state. I remembered reading a quote from *The Gospel of Sri Ramakrishna*[12] about the knowledge of Brahman, that said, "In Samadhi one attains the Knowledge of Brahman— one realizes Brahman. In that state reasoning stops altogether, and man becomes mute. He has no power to describe the nature of Brahman.

"Once a salt doll went to measure the depth of the ocean. It wanted to tell others how deep the water was. But this it could never do, for no sooner did it get into the water than it melted. Now who was there to report the ocean's depth?"

When I started to come back to duality, I felt a sense of being a witness to the bliss, which was almost better than *samadhi* itself. Papa Ramdas described this state as being the "sugar." I knew I was the body and was aware of my individuality, but it was the subtle body that was

12   Ramakrishna was a great, realized soul who lived in the mid-nineteenth century. He mastered all the types of religions and proved through the elevated state of meditation or samadhi that every path or religion could reach the final state of Oneness or God.

experiencing and tasting the sweetness of bliss. It was so joyful and high. When I opened my eyes everybody had cleared out of the room. All I wanted to do was find Papa Ramdas and surrender at his feet. I couldn't wait to bow to Papa. Surrender is born of total trust and tremendous

From left, Mother Krishnabai, Papa Ramdas and Thea
at Anandashram, India.

love. You can't really let go to anyone, to a master or to God, unless you have a trust for that being. As that trust comes into the heart, we can let go and let God or higher consciousness take over. When we surrender to a realized soul in India, it is customary to bow at their feet. It's not idol worship, but bowing to ourself as Consciousness in the form of that Being. It isn't anything other than just letting go and totally trusting and feeling completely safe. As we do that, karma just flies off us and we experience a still mind. When I touched Papa Ramdas' feet in total surrender, I felt a tremendous energy of God within me. Papa's toe would go up and tap me on the forehead and I would get such a buzz. He said, "Ramdas is in everything

Anandashram, India, with Papa Ramdas (center), Mother Krishnabai (right of Papa) and group. Thea is seated in the first row, fifth from right.

and everyone. Ramdas is not separate from yourself."

When you surrender, it is not to something outside of yourself but to the God within. The master is the mirror and the way back to the self within. Surrender is a letting go, trusting, and allowing us to just be ourself.

I knew it was Papa's grace that had allowed me to experience this amazing state. He was probably under the banyan tree, but my legs were numb, and I couldn't even walk. Finally managing to get to my feet, I made my way out to him, and totally surrendered at his feet. When I looked up at his face he said, "Very good, very good."

I said, "Thank you Papa, I had no idea."

He replied, "Don't go back, just go forward. Don't try to relive the experience, live in the moment."

I felt it was the best advice he could have given me, otherwise I would have always been trying to get it back. We lose something when we're not in the moment.

Extremely encouraged, and being a bit of a smart aleck kid, I thought, "This path will be a cinch!" Papa had told me that I didn't have much karma left, so I thought that this was it, my karma was done, I'd go into *samadhi*, and maybe go back to the States and teach. Wrong! After that experience, I had to work even harder.

The higher one goes in consciousness and purity, the more it stirs up the unconscious and impurities. As I had experienced such deep states, I seemed to go deeper in the opposite direction, "into the mud." I learned that it was a cleansing process and part of the path, and all that I accomplished was eternal. Finally...I wasn't wasting my time, and knew that seeking God was all I wanted, and why I was here in this life. This was the opportunity I had prayed to Jesus about, and had waited for my whole young life.

RETURNING TO AMERICA AND SECOND TRIP TO INDIA

After six months of being with Papa Ramdas every waking moment, I received a telegram from my father, that my mother had been released from the institution. I had asked Papa to help her, and he did! I wasn't sure whether I should go home so I asked Papa and he told me that it would be good for me to go home because I had to learn that Papa wasn't just a physical body, he was everywhere. He said I could do *Ram Nam* and I would feel his grace. He added that I should serve my mother as God, and I could evolve tremendously that way.

I went back to America to look after my mother. Soon after I arrived, I made a huge shrine in the apartment and put flowers everywhere. My folks didn't mind; they supported me.

Each morning I woke early and chanted. Papa had told me not to try to change their beliefs but to just love God in them. It was the greatest thing I could do. I dearly loved my parents already, and worshiping God in them took my love for them to another level, and they felt it. I would leave flowers on the dining room table and our times together became even more joyful and loving.

It was my opinion that it was Papa Ramdas' grace that allowed my mother to be released from the institution; not because of the doctors' so-called healing techniques. There was a part of Mom's mind that had been damaged from the shock treatments, so she couldn't discern time. Otherwise she was beautiful and fully conscious, although she had to be watched. I took her to Yogananda's Lake Shrine in Pacific Palisades. It was a great honor to serve her and to help daddy out.

My meditations were very deep. Papa Ramdas was right there for me. I didn't need to be with him to feel his presence. Every time I'd chant *Ram Nam*, Papa would jump out like the jack-in-the-box he had promised!

It was a family time for me. My sister had two children, with a third one on the way. I became the grandmother figure called "Aunty-Gram", because even though Mom was still there, I took her place.

About that time, I was really feeling the need for spiritual company. Dad thought there was a Hindu ashram in La Cresenta, California, so I drove up there and after asking for directions, I found it. As I drove through the gates there was a beautiful nunnery, and a nun came out to greet me and confirmed that it was Ananda Ashram.

I was shown the nunnery, and I learned about

Ramakrishna. I had a wonderful time there. During the day, I took care of Mom, and in the evenings and on weekends, I spent my time at the ashram. Papa Ramdas, Ramakrishna and Divine Mother began to merge within me. I loved God and all the Great Beings.

I was in America for a year and a half, looking after Mom, going up to the ashram, working on my spiritual growth, and trying to decide what I should do with my life. Then I received a telegram from India that Papa Ramdas had taken *mahasamadhi*. I was heartbroken and in shock. *Mahasamadhi* is when a realized master leaves the physical body through death and goes into a God-illumined state of Being that is forever beyond karma. Ramdas had told me once, "Ramdas is one with every atom, and when his body drops off, where can he go?"

The head of the Ananda Ashram said if I wanted to go back to India that I should, that the *mahasamadhi* is a very great time. My father reassured me that I had done my duty with Mom, so back to Papa Ramdas' ashram I went.

Mother Krishnabai was Papa Ramdas' most advanced devotee and was a very high soul, but I didn't have the same connection to her as I had had to Papa. She didn't speak English, and didn't have the winning personality that Papa had. He was perfect; there was no ego. Papa was a constant flow of God consciousness. I spent a year at the ashram, but it just wasn't the same— I was so attuned to my beloved Papa and missed Papa's physical presence.

While I was at the ashram, I started to think about

Ananda Moyi Ma[13], a very great master living in India. I first learned about her at Ramakrishna's ashram in La Cresenta when I saw a picture of her hanging in the hall. She was a beautiful woman with long dark hair, like a goddess, and I knew I had a strong connection with her. I asked the nuns who she was, and if she were still alive. They told me about her, and that she was still living. I hoped with all my heart that I would some day meet her.

After that, Ananda Moyi Ma came to me in my dreams whenever I had a conflict. Initially, it had happened when I returned from India the first time. I was confused about the materialism and falseness in America, both of which turned me off. I had changed so much internally that all I wanted was simplicity and honesty, not identification with the body. When I was in college, my sorority sisters and I had worn sophisticated dresses (or so we thought). When I returned I was confronted with a lifestyle that now seemed foreign to me. Ananda Moyi Ma came to me in a dream, admiring herself before the mirror, wearing one of my fancy dresses. She said, "We are all beautiful flowers in the garden. We need to look beautiful." After that dream, I had no more judgment or conflict about outer appearances, and I began to wear my dresses again.

I was starting to get bored at Papa Ramdas' ashram, and didn't know my next step. I had been dreaming of Ananda Moyi Ma quite a bit, and wanted to see her, but since all my

13   Ananda Moyi Ma is mentioned in *Autobiography of a Yogi* by Yogananada, and is called the "Bliss Permeated Mother," one of the greatest aspects of the Divine Mother.

previous attempts at seeing her had been blocked, I knew it wasn't the right time.

Even though I knew Papa was everywhere, I cried a lot, because I just plain missed him. One evening when we were doing *Arati*[14] to Papa Ramdas in the bhajan hall, an amazing thing happened. An older man wearing the *garawa* cloth, an orange robe that symbolizes a renunciate, came into the hall followed by a small crowd of people. I seemed to be the only one who noticed him; everyone else was intent on performing *Arati*, and I couldn't take my eyes off him. At the end of *Arati* everyone bowed at Papa Ramdas' picture, but instead my soul told me to bow at this renunciate's feet.

I walked over to him, *pranamed* and touched his feet. When I looked up, our eyes locked and he shot me such intense energy that I went into a trance. When I came to, he was gone. I looked down and saw tulsi[15] beads around my neck and vaguely recalled his placing them on me after I was knocked out. All I knew was that I had to find him. I spotted Swami Satchitananda (who later became Mother Krishnabai's successor) and asked him about the renunciate. Swami told me that he didn't know who he was, or where he was from, but he would try to find out for me.

The next evening I was up on the mountain with Dr. Hugo Maier, Papa Ramdas' homeopathic physician, watching the sun set into the Arabian Sea. Dr. Hugo Maier was a saintly German man who had spent sixteen years at the

---

14   Arati means holy light in Hindi and is a Hindu ritual where lighted wicks soaked n ghee (clarified butter) and camphor are offered to a deity.
15   Tulsi is an herb (ocimum sanctum, or holy basil) that is highly revered in India for its healing qualities and is used for worship in Hindu religion.

ashram of Ramana Maharshi, a great master and one of Papa Ramdas' teachers. We were walking down the mountain together, and because we were late for dinner, took a shortcut off the path.

As we made our way through the tall grass, a cobra struck me in the ankle. It felt like the puncture weeds I'd stepped on as a kid running around barefoot...and boy, those things hurt. I stood there in shock. Hugo saw what had happened and immediately picked me up. He laid me down in the nearest clearing, sat down next to me and went into a *samadhic* trance. I didn't know him that well, and had no idea he was spiritually advanced. The cobra's venom was so toxic that within a minute I had a fever. Hugo started making sweeping motions with his hand over my leg. I asked him what he was doing, and he replied he was pulling the poison out, and told me to stay quiet. After about ten minutes he came out of the trance and said, "You're going to be all right."

He helped me walk back to my room, and instructed me to lie down while he went to the dispensary to get the antiserum. He told me not to say anything to anyone. He didn't want any negativity to influence me, and certainly there would have been quite a crowd at my door had people known that I'd been bitten by a cobra.

Still in shock, I obediently lay in my bed with my heart pounding. He had told me with such authority I was going to be all right, that I believed him, for the most part. There was a little bit of doubt, and Papa Ramdas had told me that if I ever thought I was going to die, to think of him and he would help me. So I prayed to Papa, "I don't want to give up this body just yet, but if it's your will so be it." I then mentally chanted *Ram Nam,* and suddenly I went into a euphoric state of total peace and surrender.

Hugo came back and gave me the serum. The entire night, he stayed by my bed in a *samadhic* state. He knew everything that was going on in my mind and body— if any fear or negativity came into my thoughts, he'd tell me to stop it! I had to urinate frequently, which was my body's way of releasing the poison, so he held me over the commode near my bed, like a caring mother. By the next morning, I knew I would be just fine.

I was grateful to him for healing me, and for his love and devotion throughout the whole ordeal. I thanked him from the bottom of my heart, and the next morning I found this note from him on my door:

"Don't be grateful to the sign-post, which indicates from afar the way back home. It is not the Guru. But be grateful to Him who has put it there by the very act of going home and remaining there with Him.

"The sign-post is not to be confounded with the Guru himself. The inner pulling, pushing and dragging urge to go home, and the sign-post showing the direction are both His work."

There was a part of me that was falling in love with Hugo, because he was so holy and high. I was amazed that a westerner could go into *samadhi*, heal a cobra bite, and spend sixteen years doing intense *sadhana*[16] at Ramana Maharishi's ashram. He was about 36 and I was in my mid-twenties. It was the first time that I had felt this way about someone, and it was different from the love I had experienced in meditation. Being "in love" with someone prevented me from feeling the love and empowerment within. Suddenly my focus was on an outside object, and even though I felt love, it wasn't the same as feeling the God power within. There was a French woman at the ashram who also had a deep attachment to Hugo, and I became jealous of her. I realized human love and divine love were not the same. Hugo was very aware of what was happening with me. He saw that I was jealous, so he asked, "Do you call this love?" I said, "No, actually I'm quite miserable, but I've never felt this before."

He reassured me that it was okay to have these feelings and to not repress them. He said they were coming up so that I could see the difference between divine love and human love. He added, "Attachment, which people call love, pushes us into control, jealousy and separation." After that I was my old self again, feeling God within. I was able to see human love for what it really was, and chose what I wanted— divine love.

The love stories portrayed in books, movies and television all say the same thing: we are not complete within ourselves until we find our true love, our soul mate, or some other person. When we do, we will live happily

16 Sadhana is a spiritual discipline, such as meditation, prayer and healing, that leads you to God. The purpose of sadhana is to release illusion.

ever after. It's not true. The feeling of "falling in love" typically relates to a past life attachment that has not been completed, and manifests as a strong attraction. When the attachment is worked out, either a very deep connection is established, or a feeling of detachment arises.

Most times when people "fall in love," it is linked to old karmic ties or attachments. When we put God first, and are anchored into our own divinity, we are able to have an ideal relationship, and go to levels of joy which are hundreds of times better than what is experienced in human love. The old way of love is based on attachment, division and approval. Divine love is seeing the higher self of the other, and merging with that one. It is much deeper than attached love, and transforms into the Universal Vision, where we become everyone.

After I released the attachment to Hugo, I was once again able to be close to him, a connection that I had lost when I was jealous and attached. Later he took me into a very high state of spirit where our souls merged into Oneness, which I would not have been able to do before.

I was nearly recovered from the snake bite, and often thought of Hugo's miraculous healing that saved my life. He told me I would become an instrument of God's healing and would surpass him some day, but I didn't believe him. One day I was doing foot reflexology on a man, prayed for his knee to be healed, and the next thing I knew it was healed. The man was so excited that he told everyone he knew, and people started coming to the ashram to see the great healer.

I learned that when I prayed for people they would heal. But being a healer was not what I wanted, or the reason why I was there. In fact, it freaked me out.

About that time, Swami Satchitananda had found out who the renunciate was. His name was Sri Suryanarayan, a great saint who came down from the Himalayas every ten years to a small village called Telecherry. I immediately starting making plans to go there, and Mother Krishnabai arranged for servants to accompany me. When we arrived in Telecherry, we found the disciple house where Sri Suryanarayan was staying. I was welcomed and invited to stay as long as I wished. By then a huge rash had developed on my leg, which was my body's way of cleansing the rest of the poison. My leg itched like mad. When we found Suryanarayan, I prostrated to him and he started laughing! There was a belt hanging on a nail next to him. He took it, wrapped it around his hand and pretended it was a snake. I hadn't told him that a snake had bitten me. The sari I was wearing completely covered my legs. He was letting me know that he knew. Then my leg started itching again, and he started dramatically scratching his leg in the same place where my leg was itching. I started laughing too! He told me to lie down, and that he was going to draw out the rest of the poison. Afterward he said the karma was done. He added that Krishna had sent him to me that day at Papa Ramdas' ashram because I was crying for my beloved Papa.

Suryanarayan was an amazing being with incredible *sid-*

dha[17] powers. The miracles I witnessed, his healing power, and his love of God were extraordinary. I was with him for about two weeks. At night his group did *kirtans*, or devotional songs, to Rama and Krishna, during which Suryanarayan had to be supported because he went into total ecstasy. During the day we'd drive through the jungle in the car that devotees jokingly called "Krishna's Chariot." One day, one of the wheels came off, rolled down into a ravine, but the car stayed upright and continued down the road. I said to the driver that it was impossible, and he replied, "No it's not, things like this happen all the time."

Another time we were in the car (we never knew where we were going) and ended up in front of a house. An old man was standing there, and when he saw Suryanarayan, he started to cry. The old man told us the story that he had been dying, and he had a vision of Suryanarayan healing him. Suryanarayan was there to physically check up on his handiwork.

Sri Suryanarayan

17 A siddha according to Hindu belief refers to perfected masters who have transcended the ego and possess yogic powers over the physical plane.

Suryanarayan stayed with him for a while, and the family fed us. It was such a joyful occasion.

Suryanarayan often tested his devotees by giving them something to retrieve from the jungle. When they were successful, Suryanarayan would pour *chai* (Indian spiced tea) on their head! Only in India could these strange events occur.

After two weeks he said to me, "You never know when you will see Babaji [18], or if he will disguise himself as a beggar. Be kind to all beggars."

I had heard of Babaji. He is an Ascended Master in the Himalayas who is thousands of years old. At that time I didn't know my connection to him. Later I found out that Suryanarayan was one of Babaji's eternal flock, and that he lived with Babaji, who sent him down every ten years.

We were driving back toward Anandashram when Suryanarayan suddenly grabbed his heart as though he was having a heart attack, and started crying "Amma! Amma!"

I didn't know what to do other than fan him, and I shouted to the driver, "What do I do? What is the matter?" He said not to worry, there was nothing I could do, that Suryanarayan was taking on someone else's karma.

When we got back to Papa's ashram, Suryanarayan was still clutching his heart in pain, and I noticed all the devotees seemed very sad. Obviously, something terrible had happened. As we arrived at the bhajan hall, Suryanarayan ran

18   Mahavatar Babaji is an Ascended Master still living in the Himalayas. He is said to be thousands of years old, although no one knows when he was born or where. He is one of the great Masters who watches over humanity and appears to people periodically to impart his message of love and peace. Babaji has yogic, or super human powers, such as great strength and the ability to appear in different forms.

out of the car and up the stairs. By then we were very good at keeping up with him, because we never knew where or how fast he was going to go. We sprinted behind him as he bounded directly into Mother Krishnabai's room. She was lying in her bed, having just suffered a heart attack. Suryanarayan sat next to her and held her hand. He spoke to her in Tamil, so I had no clue what he was saying, but later found out. He told her, "You cannot go now. You are here for the devotees and they need your grace and your physical presence. It is not your time yet. You will be here for many years." He did a healing on her, and she completely recovered, and did live for many years after. Mother Krishnabai was a tremendous boon to all devotees that came to Papa's ashram, and was available for them as only a great saint and master can be.

After Suryanarayan had blessed Mother Krishnabai, he went into Papa's bhajan hall, sat near his chair and became Papa. Papa Ramdas had certain traits that were unique to him, such as his "dancing" fingers and feet that were always in motion from his incredible joy. Suryanarayan started wiggling his fingers and feet just as Papa had done, and I knew that they were merged. Everyone went up to him to receive his blessing. I felt that this might be the last time I would see this great one, so I bowed to him with complete gratitude and said good-bye. Even now I can feel his presence, as I do all the Great Ones. He is only a thought away. As Papa said, "Where can I go? Ramdas is everywhere."

Hugo was still at Anandashram when I returned, and

was thrilled about my experiences with Suryanarayan. Suddenly I had a yearning to know everything about Lord Shiva. Hugo told me that he would like to take me back with him to Arunachala, the mountain behind Ramanashram, which is the sacred mountain of Shiva. Hugo educated me about Arunachala, which is said to be Shiva himself.

The mountain is where the famous Master Bhagavan Sri Ramana Maharishi had his pivotal death experience, and where he experienced total Oneness as a teenager. He stayed in that state the rest of his life. He also did many years of *sadhana* there as a young man. He lived in different temples in Tiruvannamalai and then retired to a cave. Later his devotees founded the ashram at Arunachala. I had known about Ramana Maharishi, because it was he who had given my beloved Papa Ramdas the final Universal Vision. I called Ramana Maharishi my grandpa, because he was Papa's papa!

Papa Ramdas had many experiences as he traveled to the Himalayas, and then to the south visiting many Masters. He had already achieved the state of Oneness, but as he read the *Bhagavad Gita,* he realized there was another state he had yet to achieve, called *sahaj samadhi*, the Universal Vision, where one beholds one's self in every atom. In a cave outside of Mangalore, Papa had an experience where he merged with Jesus, Buddha and Krishna. Papa was open to all the different avatars. He was continually in the Oneness state, but he longed fnor the state of Universal Vision and prayed to God for it. He went to Pondicherry for the *dharsan* (blessing) of Mother Mira and Sri Arobindo, but for some reason they were in solitude, and didn't come out that time.

He met another *sadhu* who told him there was another Great One for him to see, and took him to Ramana Maharishi's ashram at the foot of Arunachala. Papa Ramdas waited to receive blessings from the great Ramana, who would transfer tremendous amounts of energy to anyone he looked at. Everyone was envious of the person who received Ramana's eye *darshan*. Papa went up to Ramana, asked him for the Universal Vision and surrendered totally. Ramana looked at him and poured divine grace into his eyes. Papa said he became a madman, rolling in ecstasy.

After that *darshan* Papa went up to the mountain of Arunachala, found a cave and chanted Ram Nam day and night, eating only a small amount of rice every day. He was in the cave for three weeks, and when he emerged he beheld everything as himself. Papa said he was 'mad with God.' He embraced the rocks, the trees, and felt that everything was the Beloved. Ramana Maharishi had given him the highest of all visions. I don't know

Ramana Maharishi

how many years it took him to stabilize that state, but when I met him, Papa Ramdas was fully established in Universal Vision.

Because Papa Ramdas had told me of his experiences, and having heard so much about Arunachala from Hugo, I was more than ready to experience this great holy mountain for myself.

I arrived at Ramana Maharishi's ashram during the full moon, when devotees do *pradakshina,* or walk around the mountain. Ramana Maharishi said you should go around the mountain like a pregnant woman in her ninth month, very slowly and mindfully. I walked with Hugo and Ramana Maharishi's nephew, Ganesh, and ended up getting so blissed out and attuned to Shiva and the mountain, that I could hardly stand up. I just wanted to sit in the road and meditate, but I had nine miles to go. In my mind I prayed to Lord Shiva, "I want to stay here in Arunachala with you. I have run out of money and don't know what to do." I didn't want to wire my father for money. Going to India was my thing, and I didn't want to take any more of his money. Not only that, but my visa was about to run out.

Lord Shiva granted my wish to stay. After the *pradakshina,* I went back to my room and on my pillow there was an envelope with money, and an anonymous note saying, "You can stay here as long as you want. This is a gift from Lord Shiva." I was dumbfounded and ecstatic!

I had been staying at a beautiful guesthouse of Mother Talyakan, a direct devotee of Ramana Maharishi, and men-

tioned my expiring visa plight. She said, "We'll fix this."
Mother Talyakan had connections with the Indian government, so she made a few calls, and my visa was extended
another year. I ended up staying at Arunachala for nine
months.

Mother Talyakan was quite a character. With fair skin
and blue eyes, she was a Parsi, a Hindu sect that migrated
from Persia. She was tough, and used to beat the *sadhus*
on the head with her cane when they would get out of line.
Ramana Maharishi used to laugh and say, "Give it to them,
Mother!" She had a heart of gold. She raised chickens and
brought me back to health with eggs, as I had gotten very
anemic from my strict vegetarian diet.

At night we had the most amazing *kirtans* at her house.
We sang devotional songs to Lord Shiva and different
hymns written by Ramana Maharishi about Arunachala. My
devotion to Lord Shiva, Rama (I had a strong connection to
him through Papa) and Hanuman, Rama's greatest devotee,
became deeper and deeper.

One night there was a *kirtan* for Rama and a man
started jumping around like a monkey as if Hanumanji
had possessed him. He was dancing from person to person, blessing each one, and we all felt Hanumanji come
through him. After the *kirtan* he went and climbed a tree!

The next day I went to the big temple in Tiruvannamalai
where a holy festival was being held. There was a parade
with elephants, and all the shrines were opened. The poor
were fed, and blessed food called *prasad* was passed around

later to everyone there. The same man who climbed the tree the night before was at the temple. He saw me and looked at me with tremendous love. He brought me *prasad,* and smeared tumeric powder all over my face. Although, at the time I had developed a deep devotion to Hanumanji, I wasn't aware then just how strong a connection I had to him. Because I was fearful that this man might be crazy and was going to dump the *prasad* on my head, I started walking

Thea (center) pictured with devotees at Ramanashram.

away from him. I walked faster and faster to the point where he was chasing me! As an American, I wasn't used to seeing anything like that. Finally he came up to me, and lovingly handed me the *prasad*, and then I realized it was Hanumanji coming through him again, and that it was a great blessing.

As the weeks passed, I felt the presence of Ramana Maharishi overtake me to the extent that I couldn't even do Ram Nam. It was such a profound place for practicing a lot of self-inquiry[19] and asking, "Who am I?" Every day I sat before Ramana Maharishi's photo, and let myself sink deeper and deeper within, until I went into blissful states. One day I looked into Ramana Maharishi's eyes in his photo and wished he were alive, sitting before me, staring at me like Papa. Suddenly I mentally heard, "Go to Hugo's room." I immediately went to Hugo's room and knocked on his door and he told me to come in. Hugo was seated on the floor in a deep meditation. I had seen home movies of Ramana Maharishi where his head would shake with the *Shakti* when he was transferring energy to devotees, and Hugo's head was shaking just like Ramana Maharishi. He asked me to sit down, and he looked into my eyes and became Ramana. I got an incredible transference of energy, and when I went back to the hall, I went into *samadhi*. Because devotees in India recognize these states, they started coming up and bowing before me. I knew that they weren't bowing to me, but to the incredible grace of Ramana.

Arunachala became God to me. Everything was Shiva, Shiva, Shiva. I was doing such deep self-reflection that if one bad thought came into my head, it came back to me instantly. I realized the responsibility I had to really keep my thoughts pure. I would take bucket baths every day with

19   Spiritual Self Inquiry is a method of going directly to the higher self within. Whatever question you pose, the answer comes from within in the form of a realization.

water warmed by the servants. There was a vine coming in through the barred window, and one day I accidentally broke the vine. Suddenly my arm felt like it was broken. I tried to put the vine back, to no avail, and apologized to the poor plant. I knew that Ramana had given me that experience to show that all is One, that we are everything and everybody.

Many of Ramana's original devotees were there, and they told me many stories about him. One was about Ramana's birthday, and how people had come from all over India to celebrate, and to be with him. Ramana had a rule that the ashram animals and *sadhus* should be fed before him or anyone else. At his birthday there was such celebration that they forgot the rules. Everyone was waiting for Ramana to come to his place in the hall and he didn't come. They went to look for him and found him sitting with the *sadhus*. He said, "I am a *sadhu*, and you must feed us first before the guests."

Ramana had a vibrant love for animals, and they for him. A crow would come into the hall every day to see him. A dog would take people around the mountain and Ramana loved this dog. He told people that the dog was a great being and to be very kind to him. There was a cow that had been raised in the ashram that Ramana had named Lakshmi. He said she was an old devotee, who had reincarnated as the cow to be near him. She came every day for years for his *darshan*, putting her head down and he would stroke her. When Lakshmi was dying, he put one hand on her head, one hand on her heart and gave her total liberation.

After nine months it was time to go back to America to

see my family. On the way back, I stopped in Bombay and stayed with my good friends, the Parihks. Sunealbai, a funny man whom Papa Ramdas loved, stopped by the Parihk's and wanted to take me to a very great saint in Ganeshpuri named Muktananda, who was a devotee of Lord Shiva.

I was like a drunkard for God, going from saint to saint, knowing that any opportunity to meet a great saint was a boon. Sunealbai and his mother took me to meet Muktananda, who was strong and virile like an athlete. I totally surrendered at his feet. He told me to sit down and called me Indiraben, or sister. At the time I didn't have a clue what *Shaktipat*[20] was. All I knew was how to sit straight and still in meditation so the *kundulini* could rise up my spine. The next thing I knew Muktananda hit me on the head, and I was in an altered state of consciousness flat on the floor, unable to move! The only other saint who lifted me to that state of consciousness was Suryanarayan when he looked into my eyes.

When I eventually came to, Muktananda was laughing at me. He reached over and hit me again and out I went. I didn't know what had happened to me when I came to again, but it was okay because it was such a beautiful experience. This was before Muktananda became famous. At the time he had a small ashram. He took me to special places in the ashram where I later learned others had not been allowed.

20 *Shaktipat* is an ancient Sanskrit word that refers to the transmission of divine energy by a realized being, or *guru*, to activate the *kundulini* energy that lays dormant in all humans in the first chakra (one of seven energy centers) at the base of the spine. *Shakti* is the creative energy that animates all life, and *pat* means to descend. When a *guru* gives *Shaktipat*, it awakens an individual's own inner divine energy and leads to spiritual awakening.

Muktananda gave me a *dhoti*, a saffron-colored cloth typically worn by men and similar, but not as long as a sari. It was the cloth of renunciation and he told me that I was a *sanyasini*. It was not an initiation, but an acknowledgement of the life I was already living. He was happy that I was wearing that color, which is also the color I wore when I first came to Papa Ramdas' ashram.

After I returned to the Parihk's, I started dreaming about Ananda Moyi Ma again. I still hadn't met her, but by that time I had given up on the idea because I was running out of money and my visa needed updating again! One day we went to visit the Vasudevas, good friends of the Parihk's. Their home was beautiful. As I walked into a large room, I saw pictures of Ananda Moyi Ma all over their wall. I was in shock! I learned that the Vasudevas were great devotees of Ananda Moyi Ma and had been with her for many years. They said to me, "Have you heard of our master, Ananda Moyi Ma?" I started crying, and said that I knew her very well, and told them about the dreams I had had. The Vasudevas said, "We are going to see our great master in three days and we would love for you to go with us. Can you come?" I started crying again and told them I would love to!

I didn't have any money left, yet I couldn't pass up this wonderful opportunity, so I just surrendered the problem to God. When we got back to the Parihk's home, they said to me, "How are you doing with money?"

"Well, I could wire my dad for more money because I really want to see Ananda Moyi Ma," I replied.

Swami Muktananda (seated in chair) and group.
Thea is seated in the first row, second to left.

Mr. Parihk smiled and said, "We thought you might be
low on money, and we would love to help you. It would be
our greatest gift to send you to Ananda Moyi Ma."

So there it was. I went first class to Dehradun with the
Vasudevas, along with their servants who carried many gifts
for Ananda Moyi Ma. The whole way there I was stunned.
I just couldn't believe I was finally going to see her in the
physical body. She was a goddess to me. We arrived at
her ashram in Dehradun, which was in the foothills of the
Himalayas in the north of India. As we entered the grounds,
I could see Ananda Moyi Ma reclined on a couch in a huge
hall filled with crowds of people. When I walked into the

hall, she waved at me as she said "Hah!" I thought she was waving at Mrs. Vasudeva because she didn't even know me. I looked around and Mrs. Vasudeva was way over at the other end of the hall, so I realized it was me she was waving at!

The room was so crowded, I didn't know how I was going to edge my way closer to her. Luckily Mrs. Vasudeva immediately came over to me, and being the large, formidable woman she was, pushed her way through the crowd like a bull with me trailing behind her. I fell to the floor in front of Ananda Moyi Ma and started crying. I had never seen such a radiant being in my entire life. I loved Papa Ramdas, but this was a feminine being, an aspect of the Divine Mother. Mother Krishnabai was a realized soul, but I didn't feel she was an aspect of the Divine Mother. Ananda Moyi Ma was an avatar and someone I had known before at a very deep level. As I prostrated, I totally let go and gave everything up to her, and knew she would carry me through a new phase of my life.

Ananda Moyi Ma

That evening Mrs. Vasudeva asked if I would like to have a private interview with the Mother and I replied, "Are you kidding? Absolutely!" So Mrs. Vasudeva arranged the meeting, and accompanied me as a translator. As we approached Ananda Moyi Ma's room, a group of tough Indian women stood guard to prevent any uninvited guests, and by their expression I could tell they were thinking, "Oh no, another Westerner." Westerners had a bad reputation there because they didn't know the protocols. They didn't take their shoes off, or would be high on LSD (it was the 60's) and generally broke all the Hindu rules. I had been there for over a year and was getting familiar and felt very at home with the protocols, such as wearing a white sari (the color of purity) when around a master. In fact, I felt more like an Indian than a Westerner at that point.

Mrs. Vasudeva and I went into Ananda Moyi Ma's room and sat down on the floor. I looked up at Ananda Moyi Ma and became totally tongue-tied. What in the world was I going to say to this high being? She gazed at me with incredible love and complete knowing. It was as if there was nothing she didn't know about me. She lovingly said, "Tell me about your life."

I told her about the time I had spent in India with the masters, and that she had come to me in many dreams. She said to me, "Those weren't dreams. Mother was coming to you. You are very close to this body[21] and Mother has been watching you since you were three years old."

21 Saints often speak of themselves in the third person because they do not identify with the body.

I was dumbfounded! Who was I to have someone so great looking after me? Continuing our conversation, I said, "In some of these dreams you were teaching me about attachments and aversions." She asked me to tell her about them.

I mentioned my conflict between looking beautiful and glamorous in America versus living the simple life of a renunciate in India. When I had returned to America, I had not wanted to focus on my outer appearance or wear my fancy dresses or lipstick. I told her how she had worn my dress in a dream, and said we were all flowers in the garden and needed to look beautiful.

Another situation occurred along the same lines. I had become somewhat judgmental toward my sorority sisters, thinking they were phony and superficial because they focused on material things, such as going to cocktail parties. In a dream I was at a cocktail party with my sorority sisters and Ananda Moyi Ma, who was wearing high platform heels and a tight cocktail dress. She was smoking a cigarette in one of those long cigarette holders and blowing smoke rings in my face and said, "You must see all women as the Divine Mother." After that, there was no more judgment about my sorority sisters!

Ananda Moyi Ma told me it wasn't an accident that I came to India when I was so young, because I had spent many lives in India going for God. She said my karma was very good, and that I would always have a realized soul in my life, and not just one master, but many masters. She said, "Each will lead you to a certain state. You have come for God realization. You don't need to marry, but you can. You have come here for God and that is what you need to do." She then gave me the vow of a *Brahmachari*[22], which is what I had really wanted, but had not asked her for. She gave me very strict instructions, such as not to look into men's eyes, and to repeat the name of God constantly. She gave me the mantra, Ram Nam, which Papa had given me, and said, "Now Papa and Mother are both in it."

One of the protocols I wasn't familiar with at that time was not to touch a master. I had touched Papa's feet, which is why I thought nothing of putting my head in Ananda Moyi Ma's lap. She lovingly started rubbing my head and transferred so much energy into me I could hardly walk afterward! Papa Ramdas had given me the name Indira, and she said, "In-dir-a, one, two, three, and In-du, one, two!" So now my name was Indu, which was short for Indira. I was very honored and touched.

It was a profound interview and I felt very close to her. She poured her grace on me and gave me more than I could ever have imagined.

Hugo had told me that everyone follows the saints around because they think that is how a spiritual connection will be made; however, the divine nature of a master cannot be found through the body, but only within oneself. I took that advice very seriously when I saw Ananda Moyi Ma.

I was outside in the courtyard meditating on Ram Nam

22 Brahmachari in Sanskrit refers to a spiritual student dedicated solely to God who has renounced the physical pleasures such as sex, alcohol, gambling, eating meat, etc.

and a crowd of people had gathered and was waiting for her to come out. When she came out of her room, she bypassed the expectant crowd and instead, walked directly over to me and touched me on the head to let me know I was doing the right thing. I was so touched and glad I had heeded Hugo's guidance.

I learned Ananda Moyi Ma was going up the street to a Rama temple to imbue life into a statue. I should have been excited to go with her, but I decided to stay in meditation. I continued to silently chant Ram Nam and reached a very blissful state.

About a half hour after she had left I was getting a yearning for the Divine Mother, but this was no ordinary yearning— it was in the depth of my soul and I couldn't stand being without her. Inwardly I hysterically cried out, "MA! MA! MA!" It was as if I was possessed with a feeling that I had to have the Divine Mother or I would die!

Within ten minutes Ananda Moyi Ma was standing before me with no one around. She leaned forward and softly said, "As you yearn for the Divine Mother now, always yearn for Her. She will always be with you."

Gradually the people came back from the ashram and by the expressions on their faces they were a little confused. I overheard that Ananda Moyi Ma had apparently disappeared. One moment Mother[23] was standing next to the statue she had just imbued and the next moment she was gone! No one could find her. I smiled to myself as I real-

23 An affectionate name for the Divine Mother.

ized she had teleported[24] before me. I also knew it had been God crying out through me; there was no way I could have evoked such deep feelings.

Mother would secretly call me to her room where I spent a lot of time. She asked that I not tell anyone, so no one's feelings would be hurt. One time she called me to her room and gave me a beautiful sari with golden threads. She would wear different saris during each celebration, and I believe she had worn this one for a Radha Krishna celebration.

One day I received a telegram from my family wanting me to return home. I asked Ananda Moyi Ma what I should do. She said to go back and be with my family. After my flight arrangements had been made, I went to Mother to say goodbye.

My time with Ananda Moyi Ma was like being with a very old and dear friend and mother. She wanted me to sing for her, so I sang a chant to the Divine Mother. She looked into my eyes the whole time I sang, and lifted me very high; it was such a privilege to sing to the Divine Mother herself. Then she sang back to me: Hari Bol, Hari Bol, Hari Bol, Hari Bol, Hari Hari Hari Bol. I was already late for my train, but there was no way I was going to interrupt her beautiful *darshan* to me. I was in total ecstasy and bliss when I left and not surprisingly, and only in India, the train was still there when I arrived at the station.

---

24 Teleporting is physically arriving at a destination by just the thought of being there.

GOING INTO SOLITUDE

When I returned home I realized my time in India had changed me. I had reached higher levels. I continued to correspond with Ananda Moyi Ma and I received such beautiful messages from her via Mrs. Vasudeva. She would relate to Ananda Moyi Ma how I was doing, and Ma would convey her blessings to me.

I also corresponded with Muktananda. Before I left Ganeshpuri, he had introduced me to Amma, his secretary, and she would always get my letters to him. One letter I wrote said, "Beloved Baba, I just want to be like you. Please give me the grace to be like you." Through Amma he wrote back and said, "I am you."

I was a child of the Masters, a child of bliss, and was in the state of bliss all the time. My parents were totally accepting of me. They just wanted me to be happy because they loved me so dearly. They were accepting of my experiences and didn't resist anything. My mother and father knew my soul and supported me in my goal of attaining God in this lifetime.

Whether I was going to the Ananda Ashram in La Crescenta, visiting my brother, sister, nieces and nephews, or the kids at camp, everything was beautiful. I often looked after my sister's five children, and I'd show them pictures of my Masters and talk about my experiences with them. My sister was raising them as Christians, but I was determined that they were not going to be narrow Christians. I would teach them about Hinduism and how all paths lead to the One.

One day they wanted to learn how to meditate. We went into the living room and found comfortable seats, and I explained that the whole purpose of meditation was to still their minds so they could feel God within their hearts. They made me smile because of their sincerity and determined effort. My nephew's face was all scrunched up and I told him not to try so hard, to relax and just naturally let God come in. They all loosened up a little bit. I noticed tears streaming down my nephew's face, and asked what he was experiencing. He said, "I feel so much love in my heart and I know it's God. The love made me cry." I told him that was meditation when you feel God in your heart. They all had really great experiences.

If a saint came to Los Angeles I would take the children with me for *darshan*. They met Bhakti Vedanta, who was head of the Hari Krishnas. He blessed them, and my niece danced to *Hari Ram, Hari Krishna*. I told my sister how I was determined they would not be narrow minded, and she said they wouldn't be anyway, but with me they surely wouldn't!

During the day I took care of my mother, and at night I resided at the Ananda Ashram, which provided me with spiritual nourishment and opportunities to meet others who loved God. I struck up an immediate friendship with one of the regular devotees there. Yogi Jim was a cute, homespun older man who was full of love for God. He was originally from Kansas and had been an engineer. After attending a lecture of Yogananada, he decided to live only for the Divine Mother and became a wandering *sadhu*. Several close coworkers had attended the lecture with him, and they also renounced the world and became monks at Self Realization Fellowship. Another very pure man who came up to the ashram was Eden Abez, who wrote *The Nature Boy, Where are You Going*, a very famous song in the 1960's.

The hippie movement was taking hold, and people were experimenting with LSD at the ashram. Gayatri Devi, who was the head of the Ananda Ashram, was fairly broadminded about it. LSD allowed people to get into very deep states and made it easy for them to give up the world. She said if it could awaken people to God it was not a bad thing, although she discouraged its misuse in any way. One person who had tried it was Kali Kananda, who had been with Timothy Leary, and had a vision of Mother Kali[25] while on LSD. When he met Gayatri Devi he took the monk's vows of renunciation. I was rather naïve about who was or wasn't using LSD. I really had no desire to try it, because I was hav-

25 The Hindu Goddess Kali is the warrior aspect of the Divine Mother who cuts through illusion with fierce aplomb. According to ancient text she was born from the brow of the goddess Durga, a slayer of demons, during a battle between the good and evil.

ing blissful states through the grace of God and the Masters.

It became our tradition at the full moon to have big bonfires and kirtan in nature. I had read *The Gospel of Sri Ramakrishna*, which described how people would sing and dance in ecstasy with love for God; that's precisely what we did. Eden Abez would steal the show with his songs and drum playing. One song he wrote was, "Buddha John, he went to town, he went to town with no shoes on..." We'd get so tickled and inspired by Eden's songs and powerful mantras, that we felt like we were living during the time of Ramakrishna.

At night I stayed in the cloister with the nuns and a few of them would join me at the *kirtans*, although it was mostly men. Sister Amla lived in the cloister next to me, and she was rather judgmental. I would invite her to go to the *kirtans*, but she always refused. She had a habit of making snide comments and putting people down, yet everyone seemed to tolerate it. Behind her back she was called The Whip— there is always someone at an ashram that is good for "whipping" the ego, but in her case it was based on judgment and self-righteousness and was not done through love. We all had our amusing names for her, and mine was "Sister Omelet." One evening we were all having dinner and she said, "Well, I saw you were out there with the men again. What were you doing?"

I turned to her and replied, "What's it to you, Sister Omelet?" Everyone started giggling. I continued, "We sing God's name, and it would do you a lot of good to go." I put her in her place and she never bothered me after that.

I began to realize that I wanted to go into solitude and do uninterrupted *sadhana*, just going for God with all my heart and soul, so I prayed for a place where I could do this.

Elwood Decker and his wife, Ann, were friends of mine who lived in Hollywood in the mid 1960's and were great devotees of Ananda Moyi Ma. Ann was a healer for the movie stars. She had power in her hands, a kind of "psychic" plastic surgery, which enabled her to rejuvenate cells and sculpt the faces of her clients. She said whoever she worked on would change inside as well, because if they didn't it would be too difficult for her to do her work.

Elwood and Ann invited me for dinner one evening so I could meet a friend of theirs, Lester Levenson. He was a lovely man who owned 160 acres in Sedona, Arizona. When I met him he exuded depth and inner stillness, and I sensed he was a high being.

Lester told me he had been a physicist in New York City. A pragmatic man by nature and a staunch atheist, Lester had spent his life tenaciously seeking material success. However, at the age of 42, he suffered a heart attack and was told by his doctor if he took a step up a flight of stairs, it might be his last. The thought of being an invalid, or of dying, scared him to the core, and forced him to seriously reevaluate his life.

Lester holed up in his penthouse, and began a concentrated effort of deep self-reflection. What did he *really* want out of life? Everything in his life seemed flat to him in the face of death. He realized he wanted love. But when he reflected on his past love relationships, he discovered that being loved brought only temporary pleasure, and often included an ulterior motive of pleasing people to get them to do what he wanted. As he went through the process of letting go of his selfish desires, he began to love people unconditionally. He felt lighter and happier than he had ever felt before.

Next, he discovered that the mind is a creative force and that, unconsciously, he had been holding on to a negative view of his body. This realization enabled him to replace his negative view with positive visualizations of a whole and healthy body, and he not only healed his heart condition, but also many other health problems he had had for years.

These amazing realizations gave him such joy that he vowed he wouldn't stop his quest until he understood the total picture of what life was all about, and why he was here. At the end of two months, he went from being a total atheist, to seeing God in everyone and everything. He had sought love from others, particularly beautiful women, as a way to attain happiness, and now he felt tremendous joy from loving unconditionally. He was grateful to people who opposed him, because that gave him an opportunity to practice unconditional love.

During this process, he experienced such tremendous energy flowing through his body that he walked the streets of Manhattan for days at a time. One day he passed a metaphysical bookstore, and bought a book by Swami Vivekananda.

Before his realizations, he had thought religion and meta-physics was for the weak-minded. He had no language to explain what he had experienced and no knowledge of the ones before him who had attained the state of Oneness. Later, someone gave him a copy of *Autobiography of a Yogi* by Paramahansa Yogananda. He put the book on the floor by his meditation chair and would stare at the picture of Yogananda on its cover, until one day Yogananda stepped out of his picture and talked to Lester. As time went by, other Masters appeared to Lester, such as Krishna and later Jesus. When Lester was a child he was often beaten up by the neighbor-hood kids because he was Jewish, so when Jesus appeared, Lester's subconscious fear said, "Oh no, not you!" Jesus laughed and said, "I too was born a Jew, and look what happened to me! I'm your friend." Lester let him merge into his soul, an experience so profound, he couldn't talk about it for years after.

It was during this time that the Masters told Lester to go to Sedona, Arizona. He had no clue where Sedona was, and had to look it up on a map. Lester was in such a high state of Oneness he didn't hesitate to sell all his material belongings, buy a trailer and head west. Yogananda had been guiding him, so he decided to first visit Yogananda's ashram in Encinitas, California before going to Sedona.

Once he arrived in Sedona, the Masters told him to look for land. He didn't have the money, but was a madman for God in those days, and knew the money would come. A week later he found a beautiful 160-acre parcel with two houses on it. About the same time, a man from New York, who owed Lester a large sum of money contacted him out of the blue. The man said he was now able to pay Lester back. It was enough to buy the land! The seclusion and security of his property enabled him to stay in *samadhi* for long hours every day with no distraction. As in New York, he attained Universal Vision with the geckos and other native creatures, and felt they were all himself.

At Ann and Elwood's, I told Lester about my desire to go back to India and go into solitude, and he said his ranch in Sedona would be perfect for me. He had two houses on his land: one where he resided and the other he made available to serious seekers of God. After his own experience of concentrated, deep reflection and his miraculous recovery, it was his way of sharing with others what he had experienced. He added that only a few could stay, because most people couldn't take solitude. There were several women living there, and he suggested I give it a try and see if I liked it.

At the time I was living with my parents and taking care of my mother. I wanted to lead a life of solitude, yet felt no one could take care of my mother better than I could. Lester told me that I had to put God first, and that the karma between my mother and father was not up to me, but was my father's responsibility. Lester told me, "If you go for God with all your heart, don't you think God will look after your mom?"

Lester's words resonated true in my heart and helped me to break the need to be my mother's caretaker. As always, my father fully understood and supported my decision. He was actually quite happy that I would only be one day's drive away instead of across the world! I headed out to Sedona to continue my *sadhana* in earnest. There I met Frances and Laurel, whom he had met back in New York City. They graciously welcomed me and looked after me as if I were family. I soon discovered that Frances had published a small book of Lester's teachings a few years before called *The Eternal Verities*; it became my guide book at the ranch.

My focus was to be with Babaji, and to prepare my body for a state beyond the need for food and shelter. After a couple of weeks of meditating nonstop, I decided to go on

Thea, Frances and Lester at his ranch in Sedona, AZ.

a water fast, to begin letting go of the need for food. Babaji was an Ascended Master who did not eat, and if I wanted to be with him, I needed to be in a place where I didn't need to eat either.

Five days into the fast, weak yet very focused, Babaji appeared to me in a vision, as a youth surrounded by an effervescent golden aura. I was dumbfounded and ecstatic, and from the depth of my heart I said I wanted to be with him in the Himalayas. I told him that I thought of him day and night, that he was my master and how deeply I loved him. He said, "Your *dharma* is in the West. You are not to be with me in the Himalayas in this lifetime. I am with you at all times, just think of me and I will be with you."

Babaji then showed me a past life where he had been like a parent to me in the Himalayas; that was why I had such a deep yearning to be with him. I told him if my *dharma* was in the west, to please remove the desire to be with him, and Babaji granted my wish. I gave up the idea of going back to the Himalayas to be with Babaji in the physical, but as he said, whenever I became still and thought of him, he was with me.

I spent eight years on the ranch and went through lifetimes of karma. Lester wouldn't let anyone stay there unless they were growing, and that meant pulling up the unconscious ego and letting it go. We had to grow really fast to be qualified to stay on the ranch. He called us the "Go-Go Girls"—we had to either grow or go! It was such a great opportunity to be alone and meditate with no interruption, that we didn't waste any time. The momentum enabled one lifetime after another to come up. The only time we left our rooms was to eat, tend the garden, do chores or go to the outhouse.

Meditating in solitude was not easy. There were times when I wanted to run, but there was no place to go and no diversions, like television or movies. Lester told us when the subconscious tendencies come up, to go through it, otherwise it takes tremendous energy to bring it up again. He taught us discipline, and knew exactly where we were in our spiritual growth, and what we were doing. My concentrated effort to become free automatically brought up past lifetimes. Lester taught us that all the answers can be found within, and all we had to do was ask ourselves, "Why do I feel this way?" So when I would start to feel terrible, because old tendencies were coming up, all I knew was that I needed to get through it.

One of the old tendencies was the attraction to men. I was young, good-looking, and still had an interest in men, although I didn't act on it. It was something to be transmuted as far as I was concerned, because people or objects could not provide me with the kind of happiness found within. If I were to be with a man, it had to be with someone who loved God, and loved me in a pure way. After being with the Masters, most men didn't thrill me at all. Papa Ramdas had told me that I would meet every past tie, attachment and aversion in this life. I would meet all my husbands and enemies from the past. The truth of this was starting to become apparent even in my isolation at the ranch. When we'd go into town for supplies we'd meet people. One day in town I waited in the car while Frances had film developed in the camera shop, and this handsome cowboy came up to the car and said, "Howdy ma'am. My name is Jake and I'm your neighbor." My heart started pounding! Only in town for a short time and already I had my first test.

Jake was totally hooked on me. I could feel his energy enveloping me, and I did my best to block it. One day he came looking for me at the ranch, and was so bold that he went right into my room looking for me. I have to admit that a part of me was a little bit attracted to him. Papa had said I would meet all my past ties. Jake was one of them, but I just wasn't ready to deal with it. Like a scared schoolgirl, I ran out the back door and hid behind a bush when I heard his truck pull up! At one point he walked so close to the bush I thought he'd find me, but he didn't, and he finally left. I called Lester, told him about Jake and asked for his help. He said that when I was ready to let go of the attachment, it would be released. Eventually I let it go and prayed that Jake would find the right wife, which he did.

As I released these tendencies, my mind became so still that I would often see Babaji, Jesus and the Divine Mother. They were my Trinity and were always with me. I had a drawing of Babaji on my wall, and at one point his image turned into Krishna.

RELIVING THE FRENCH REVOLUTION

I had known about past lives from my grandmother, and
in high school I would hypnotize my friends by swing-
ing a necklace to and fro to see if they could remember
their past lives. My friends were very aware and totally
open to my attempts. I had glimpses of my own past lives,
but never in detail. Feelings and somatic memories started
coming up, and I began retracing the story of past lives.

At the ranch the first big past life karma I got into was
the French Revolution. I was a fancy lady wearing a beautiful gown and wig, and Marie Antoinette was a close friend
or cousin. We were having a ball being royalty, dressing
up in pretty dresses, wigs and riding in carriages to parties
and operas. Sometimes we'd travel incognito to avoid being
noticed. Marie and I were actually simple women at heart,
and there was a part of us that wanted to live simple lives.
With Marie's means we were able to indulge our every
whim, so she secured a country hideaway. We would pretend to be farmers' wives, wear plain clothes and care for
the animals. We loved that life, as it was a time when we

could get away from our high profile existence. Apparently neither of us was happy in marriage, but we had many things in common and enjoyed them together.

Marie was a very high soul and devotee of St. Germain, as was Napoleon. St. Germain's goal was to make a United States of Europe. He tried to guide Napoleon to this purpose, but Napoleon took the path of power instead. Louis the XVI was a weak man, and Marie Antoinette was strong and yet innocent. She didn't have a full picture of what was going on around her politically.

Behind the scenes was a group of influential and powerful people, who were plotting to overtake the royalty. This group was led by dark souls called the Illuminati. They are a combination of fallen angels and the reptilian race who have been on earth since the beginning of time. Their primary goal is, and has been, to rule this planet and make a slave race. They are an ancient bloodline of dark souls who want to be the elite, and have nearly succeeded. (More will be discussed about them later.) During the French Revolution, the Illuminati took control again and began to do away with key members of the royalty.

Suddenly, from a life of fun and frivolity, I found myself in a dark dungeon in the most horrible of conditions. I was cold and sick with some type of bronchitis, and had my period with no cloths to wear. The cell was dirty, foul smelling and rat infested, and screams and cries could be heard from the other prisoners. I realized we had been summoned to court, found guilty and were sentenced to death, all at the hands of the Illuminati. It happened so swiftly that we didn't even know what we had been accused of!

I prayed to God and meditated. As my death approached, I had became so ill that I wanted to die. As I relived this experience, somatic pain came up in my neck, and I realized I had been beheaded. I was killed before Marie Antoinette, and remember becoming her spirit guide on the other side to help her out. They wheeled her out in a wooden cart in complete disgrace to be executed. The people loved her, and watched in horror and shock, but they dared not express allegiance for fear of losing their own lives. Marie was in a catatonic state, and I stayed with her in spirit the whole way until her death. The blade was so sharp and fast that death was instantaneous.

I hadn't told Lester about the past life I was reliving, but it shouldn't have surprised me when he came back to the ranch after a trip and said, "For God's sake, get out of the French Revolution! It's all *maya*, it's all illusion!"

"But Lester," I defended, "I'm fascinated with it!" I had been researching that time period in books, only to find inaccuracies compared with what I knew. He was right to tell me to move on, and I finally did.

In solitude I realized I had accumulated many lifetimes that were unfinished. It was a cycle of birth, creation of new circumstances on top of previous lives' events, and then death before they could be completely worked through. Many things that I had not worked out were coming up and manifested as feelings of depression. When these feelings came up I'd ask, "What is this about?" Or if I had an attachment or aversion I'd ask, "Why can't I let go of this?" Then the pictures would be shown to me and I'd learn the story line. I realized that feelings should not be judged or brushed aside. They are there for a reason and have a source or origination point.

Through this process more past lives came up. For some reason whenever the wind blew, it brought up deep feelings of sadness. Lester suggested I go within and ask why, so I did. I saw I was a Protestant with broad beliefs that were unacceptable to the Catholics, and I was hung because I wouldn't conform to religious dogma. At the moment I was killed, the wind was blowing, which became a lock in my unconscious. After I released that life, I no longer became sad when the wind blew.

During the summers I would go home and work at my father's camp. Even there I continued my growth. I would fall in love with a counselor, and recognized it for what it was— an attachment to be worked through. I was taught we don't have to get entangled sexually when we are attracted to someone. Through meditation, prayer, mantra repetition and self-inquiry, I would release the tie. It wasn't always easy though. There were times when I wanted to leap into bed with somebody, but instead would release the desire. Afterward, I became detached from the person as if I didn't even know him.

Lester taught us that meditation and self-inquiry could bring up very intense emotions related to an attachment.

Everyone we fall in love with, or to whom we have an aversion, is an old tie from the past. The attachments and aversions are stored in the subconscious. It is our job to bring them up and release them. This enables us to become free.

My effort at the ranch was to let go of these past attachments and aversions. There were times when I would meet a person who would hate me for no apparent reason. By tracing my connection to that being, I would get the story line, understand what was really happening, and be able to release it.

Visiting a movie set at the Honanki Indian Ruins a mile from Lester's ranch. The crew let me hold a cheetah, who loudly purred!

We rarely had visitors at the ranch, a rule Lester strongly encouraged so we would maintain our concentration. However, he made an exception for a woman I had met one summer. I invited her out and something curious happened when she arrived— I suddenly hated her! I was so distracted by this hatred that I burned our dinner and couldn't function very well. I told Lester I needed to go to my room and pull it up, and he nodded and said I'd be surprised at what I'd find. I learned that she had been my husband in a past lifetime in England. I was having an affair with another man, and my husband (my present time friend) discovered us in bed together and killed us. Once I saw it, I released the feelings and we were friends again.

These deep pockets of unconscious feelings linger until they are brought up and released. I learned there is a reason for each person we meet and don't like or fall in love with, and I was going through these karmas right and left, making spiritual progress very quickly.

MY FATHER PASSES
AND MY LAST DAYS AT THE RANCH

My dad had a stroke. We were all very worried about him because his left side had signs of paralysis, and his speech was affected. After a number of tests were done, the doctors found a blood clot. It was too close to his brain to remove, they said, and suggested we not tell him. They told us another miracle could happen, just as had happened when he regained the use of his legs years before. We followed their advice for a while, but his condition worsened, and I felt a responsibility to tell him. He came to Sedona to visit me, and we found a lovely spot in nature to sit and talk. I told him everything I knew about the blood clot, and that he could go anytime. I said, "Daddy, you can bring yourself back from anything."

It wasn't long after he left, I was in deep meditation, when thoughts of death came to me. I knew someone was going to die, but I didn't think it was my father. Later that afternoon I was still meditating and felt Jesus, Ananda Moyi Ma, Papa Ramdas and my father, and we merged together into a Oneness state. I didn't know what it meant, and was just happy to share this glorious state with my father and my saints. I thought, "Good show, Dad!"

I realized that he had attained an incredible state. We had made a pact some years before that if he attained realization before me, he would pull me up, and if I attained realization before him, I'd pull him up.

Soon after, my brother called, and told me that my father had passed away. I thought, "Why didn't it hit me before?" I said I would come home as soon as I could, and then went back to my room to get plugged in again. I saw a celebration with beings from all realms honoring him. He went higher and higher into heavenly realms, and with each one he passed through, there would be another celebration. I also saw relatives coming in from this life, such as his mother, brothers and sisters, as well as beings from other dimensions. It was an incredible party!

On my way home I lingered in my father's heavenly celebration and felt his support for our entire family. Upon my arrival, I was jolted back to reality. My family was in deep grief. I took over, and began the difficult task of informing all the people who had been close to my father of his passing. My brother and uncle made the funeral arrangements. I wasn't plugged in to where my father was anymore, and was feeling sad that he was gone.

The funeral was beautiful, with about three hundred

people in attendance. It was open casket, and when I walked into the church I saw the spirit of my father, his mother, and Jesus! They lifted me up again, and I was in bliss. The family was behind a curtain and saw each of the guests as they came up to the casket to pay homage to my father. I always worshipped the God in my parents with flowers, which my father always loved, so I brought him a dozen roses, and placed them on his body. I could see him above me, laughing and lifting me up higher and higher. I was basking in ecstasy and didn't know how I was going to get back to my seat. Every eye was watching me and expecting me to be sad, so with great effort I toned it down and walked back to my chair. My mom was being cared for by family, so I didn't stay very long and went back to Sedona.

When I returned to the ranch, I didn't feel my father as much. I knew he was adjusting to the other side. I missed his physical presence. When he was alive I could pick up the phone anytime and call him, but he wasn't there anymore. I felt that my father was with Jesus, and so high that he was beyond my consciousness and ability to reach him. Fragments of a past life surfaced about my father. We had been Essenes during the lifetime of Jesus and both of us were very close to Jesus. Then it hit me that Jesus had taken my father to do a very special mission on a space ship between dimensions. That was as far as I could take my own consciousness to learn where he currently was.

Throughout my time at Lester's ranch my guides were always with me— Jesus, Papa Ramdas, Babaji and the

Divine Mother. When I was in meditation I could also see other people's guides and Masters and who they were close to. During the summers when I would work at my father's camp, I could see where people were stuck. With their consent I would call in their Masters and guides and act as a conduit to release the blockages. I loved the work and began to help quite a few people. Then I would return to the ranch and work deeply on myself.

Another experience I had moving into higher dimensions after death was with my mother's best friend, Margie. Before Margie's death we had conversations on the phone concerning her feelings about death. She said she thought it would be a beautiful experience and that she would end up in a peaceful place. When she passed away, I represented the family by going to her funeral. I arrived early, and stopped by the casket and meditated. The next thing I knew Margie was pulling me up into an incredibly peaceful state saying, "This is even better than what we talked about!" I merged with her and by the time her family arrived, I was in a state of bliss. She talked to me telepathically during the whole funeral, and told me to tell her daughter Julie, and her family that she is happier than she has ever been in her entire life. I did so, and it was a great comfort to all of them.

I loved the girls at the ranch. Due to our constant meditation I became telepathic with them, especially with Nancy, who had moved in five years after I did, and lived in the adjoining room. I knew exactly where she was on her path, and she was able to tap into my high experiences.

If one of us became stuck, that girl could sit in the "hot seat" during our evening meditations when we were all together in the living room. We would pray for that person. One evening I felt stuck, so I sat in the hot seat while all of us prayed. I had been reading a book about Krishna and Radha, so when I was sitting in the hot seat, I was inwardly calling to Radha for help, and of course I had had that experience with her in the temple in India. So I silently prayed, "Radha, Radha, help me, help me, I feel stuck."

Suddenly she came to me as the most beautiful woman I had ever seen. I realized she was an aspect of Lakshmi in her Ascended body. The artistic renderings I had seen of her just didn't do her justice. She lifted me so high, it was the most profound love state I had ever experienced. Radha came toward me and touched my head, and then she went around to each of the other girls and gave them her blessing. The only one who really saw what was happening was Nancy. After the evening meditation we always retreated to our rooms in silence, so I couldn't verify with them what had just happened. I walked back to my room in ecstasy, feeling Radha around me, and stayed in that beautiful state for hours. The next morning as Nancy walked out of her room I couldn't get to her soon enough and excitedly asked, "Did you feel anything last night?"

Nancy laughed incredulously, "Are you kidding? The Divine Mother blessed us all, and I knew something profound was happening to you. I got the aftermath and really sailed with it!"

I asked Laurel and Frances if they had seen anything, and they said they had felt something, but were not able to see any details.

Radha really opened me up. Babaji, Krishna, Radha, Rama and Sita are all the love energy of Vishnu. My third eye opened up so I could see the Masters better, and my intuition grew by leaps and bounds. It was difficult to be around other people, which Lester had warned me about, because I could see through their blockages. Because I could see things other people couldn't see, it made them uncomfortable if they didn't want to grow. Lester said, "You have to learn how to play the game, to act normal in the world. If you react to what's going on behind the scenes, it means that you still have ego, and you have to release that."

I was reacting to things I was seeing behind the scenes because I could read some people like a book. It wasn't something I wanted, but was a result of repeated meditation. My heightened awareness also told me I was almost through with my time at the ranch, but at the time I didn't know why.

In my eighth and final year at the ranch I felt my time to leave was approaching. I questioned some changes I saw in Lester, which is what he had taught us to do if we didn't understand something. I had been very good at taking ego presentation, which is bringing up painful memories hidden in the unconscious. Lester said it was the greatest thing a master could do, and he was very good at it. Always done with love, a spoken word or phrase from him could pull up the hurt and I'd feel like hell. I learned to get through it very fast because it was quick growth, and sometimes even looked forward to him pushing my buttons!

At this particular point, however, I was seeing some reactivity in him, as well as a decline from his high state. He had made a conscious decision to come down into the world to be more like people, and as a result I didn't feel his teachings were as powerful. So when I questioned him about the discrepancies I had observed, I was not prepared for his response. He reacted and told me I wasn't growing anymore and that I had to leave the ranch. I drove back to California in confusion, wondering why Lester thought I wasn't growing. I felt like a spiritual failure, but later realized there is no such thing as failure, just moving on.

MUKTANANDA BRINGS BACK THE SHAKTI

Before I left the ranch, Muktananda had come to me in dreams. I hadn't seen him since India, although I had kept in touch with him through his secretary. I had fond memories of him because he was the one who had given me *Shaktipat*, the powerful transference of energy and grace. In one of my dreams Muktananda was calling me, "Amma! Amma! Come to me!" (Amma is another name for the Divine Mother.) Then it changed, and I was a child sitting on his lap. I was so ecstatic when I awoke, I knew I wanted to see him again, and wondered where he was.

When I returned home, I worked at my father's camp and had some free time to go to the Bodhi Tree, a famous metaphysical bookstore in Los Angeles. On the wall was a poster: "Swami Muktananda Coming to America!" I was beside myself! I called the contact number and learned that a large mansion in Pasadena had been rented for the program. My offer to help prepare for his arrival was gladly accepted, and I did so with complete enthusiasm and antici-pation of seeing him again.

Just before his arrival we formed two lines to greet Muktananda. The moment he saw me he exclaimed, "Indiraben!" I was overjoyed, because I didn't think he'd even remember me! I went to every meditation or program that was offered at the house. It was absolute bliss— I was getting into the *Shakti* again. It was so revitalizing after leaving Lester's ranch. On some level I felt I had failed. Lester had told me that I wasn't growing anymore, although I thought I was.

Muktananda showered me with love and couldn't wait to give me *Shaktipat*. I was so ready. *Shaktipat*, the divine transference of energy, was a delightful contrast to ego-presentation, sitting in meditation for hours, and releasing karma. I experienced beautiful states at the ranch; howev-er, it wasn't the same as being at the feet of Muktananda, and receiving such incredible *Shakti* and grace.

Due to my dear friend Amma, I was able to have a personal interview with Muktananda. I explained to him how I had been at Lester's ranch for eight years, going for God, and how, at the end, Lester had said I wasn't grow-ing anymore. Muktananda exclaimed, "What?! You *were* growing. What happened is that another door was opening and you needed to move on. Lester did attain a high state of consciousness, but he didn't undo all of his karma, so he slipped back into what was left. You are not a failure!" Then he added, "When I saw you, the glow you had in India was gone," which I confirmed was due to my reaction to Lester's words. Muktananda took me up from that point on. He transferred so much *Shakti* to me that I was flat on the floor most of the time. I loved it!

I had rented a cute apartment. One morning at about 3 a.m., I awoke and felt Muktananda merge with me. I thought if I looked down at my arms they'd be brown! We merged together and went into a magnificent state of bliss and total Oneness.

This great master worked on me day and night from a distance, and I was so ready for him. He quickly brought me back to the high states of spiritual bliss I had experienced in India. The *bhakti,* or devotion to God, was returning, so different from the arduous hours of self-inquiry at the ranch. Because of God's grace, the karma was lifted painlessly and effortlessly.

I spent as much time as I could with Muktananda, and went to his retreats. At one retreat in Big Bear, I noticed how people would squirm and make weird body movements and sounds from the *Shakti.* I was going into bliss, but thought I was missing something because I wasn't wiggling around. During one of the breaks I took a walk through the woods, and who should I bump into but Muktananda and his secretary, Amma! Without thinking I blurted it out, "I think something must be wrong with me, Baba, because I'm not moving around or making noises like the others. I want to do that if that's what I'm supposed to do!"

He said, "You don't need to do it, Indira. You have been

meditating for so many years that your nervous system is very refined. The shaking is when blockages in the *nadis*[26] need to be shaken loose. You'll go into a more subtle manifestation of the *Shakti*, such as bliss and dancing mudras, where your hands or body will dance, but not the harsh manifestations that clear the *nadis*."

I was relieved, but then another issue came up. While sitting in the traditional meditative posture with my back straight, my upper body wanted to bend forward to the floor. I tried fighting it, because it was like a sleepy state, and I thought it was *tamasic*[27]. Each time I'd fall forward, I'd force myself to sit back up again and remain erect. It became increasingly difficult, because every time Muktananda went around the room, he'd hit me on the head with more *Shakti*! Finally he said, "Don't fight it [falling forward]. This is a lower *samadhic* state where you'll go to *lokas*[28]."

What a relief it was to not fight it. The next thing I knew I was down, down, down. I'm double-jointed, so it didn't hurt my body when my head was on the floor. I would be there for hours in blissful states and realms. The first place I went to was Shiva's *loka*. I saw people with three lines of ash on their foreheads. It was like a movie, and I did get a little attached to it because it was exciting, but it was the

26 *Nadis* are subtle energy channels in the body that are connected to the physical nerves, with the main *nadi* running up the spine from the base to the crown *chakras*. Depending on the source, there is said to be anywhere from 1,000 to 72,000 *nadis*.

27 Tamasic is a Sanskrit word that describes one of man's three attributes, or gunas, which are: tamasic (darkness, inertia); rajasic (activity, passion, the process of change); and satvic (purity in mind, body and soul). Tamasic represents laziness, clouded power of reasoning, dark emotions, anger and greed.

28 Heavenly realms.

bliss state that enthralled me the most.

One evening at the retreat, we chanted all night long the *Hari Ram Hari Krishna* mantra that Muktananda loved. The women and men, seated separately in groups on either side of the hall, would take turns singing, *Hari Ram, Hari Ram, Rama Ram, Hari Hari, Hari Krishna, Hari Krishna, Krishna Krishna, Hari Hari.* Earlier that day when I saw Muktananda in the woods, he pinched the skin on my third eye and pulled me along as he walked, and it hurt! Amma gave me a look that told me not to resist. Nothing happened after he let go, but Amma whispered in my ear that something big was going to happen. Something happened all right. I had the worst diarrhea anyone could imagine! By the time I arrived at the evening chanting, my body was pretty well cleaned out and I tingled all over. I was able to surrender and dance to the chanting.

The next morning Baba Muktananda came into the hall, and somehow I ended up right next to him. The next thing I knew I was in some kind of love trance. I fell backward to the floor as an incredible love vibration went through my entire body. I felt every cell of me was love. It was different than the peace or bliss I had experienced because it was centered in my heart, and every atom of my being was love. I reveled in that state and the transference of energy, which I realized was the result of Muktananda pulling on my third eye.

I became addicted to *Shaktipat,* and started asking for the Shiva *Shakti* energy to come directly to me. Sometimes I would go into these crying fits, but I was taught that it doesn't matter whether you cry or are in bliss, the *Shakti* brings up everything. All the sadness about leaving the ranch was gone, and in fact, I was elated to be away from there. I had worked hard shoveling the karma for years and years, and with Muktananda I felt tremendous grace and everything was effortless.

Receiving the *Shaktipat* sent me into another whole state of surrender and bhakti. The emphasis at the ranch was the path of wisdom, but I was missing bhakti. I had chanted the mantras and brought in my own bhakti, but it was nothing like *Shaktipat*, which is the path of grace. The path of grace is opening up to the energy of the Divine Mother and Shiva. *Shakti* in Hinduism, or *Holy Spirit* in Christianity, is the transferring of Divine Energy of the Heavenly Father and Mother God.

Muktananda asked me to travel with him to other cities, and said if I could spend more time with him, I would become realized very quickly. He took me to high states, but there was an element of magnetic sexual energy about him I didn't trust. I had been with the Great Ones and felt they were above that. Muktananda gave outrageous *Shaktipat* and I certainly didn't think he was less because of the sexual energy. I just didn't feel I could totally surrender to him. It was an amazing opportunity, but my soul told me not to go.

LIFE AFTER THE RANCH

My brother, sister and I had to sell my father's camp because of a bad investment Dad had made. He had taken a huge amount of money out of the camp to invest, and every cent was lost. This incident put him into shock. I feel this is what caused the stroke. We tried to save the camp but it just wasn't possible. As a result of this, I had to find a new career.

I wasn't sure what my next step was. Babaji had told me it wasn't my *dharma* to be with him in this life. Papa Ramdas had passed away, as had Ananda Moyi Ma. There was no one to pull me back to India at that point. I needed a career to bring in money. I hadn't finished college or pursued classes in healing yet.

I was having lung problems around that time. Lester had taught us that every organ in our body was connected to a mental/emotional aspect, so I knew it had to do with rejection. It was also hereditary. My grandfather suffered from consumption in England, which was why my grandparents migrated to the dry air of California. My Aunt Idie was worried about me, and convinced me to go to the doctor. Dr. Browning, our family doctor and friend, was on vacation, so I saw Dr. Richards, his assistant, in his absence. I took one look at him and fell in love! I said to myself, "Oh no, another past tie."

Dr. Richards examined me and diagnosed that my left lung had collapsed. It was fairly serious, but it seemed to me that he was worried beyond measure. He became very flustered and emotional, a reaction I had never seen in a doctor before. I didn't want to go to the hospital, and he agreed it would be acceptable to have a nurse care for me at home.

As I convalesced at home, Dr. Richards was constantly on my mind. I knew he cared for me also; the magnetism he exuded when I spoke to him on the phone or in person was very palpable. I was "madly in love" in the human sense, and found that I could hardly function. It was a sort of Oneness experience, but it was all related to the ego.

It took nearly six months to recover from the collapsed lung. I spent many hours in meditation and self-inquiry, asking for the root of the attachment to Dr. Richards to be revealed, as well as the cause of my lung problem. It came to me that in my last life I had lived in a beautiful colonial house on a large cotton plantation in North Carolina. My father raised me, and he was none other than Dr. Browning! In that past life, when I was three, my mother had died of consumption, so I had a mammy who raised me as one of her own. She adored me, and I loved her and her children.

We considered them to be our family. When the Civil War struck, I recalled living in terror for the lives of our servants. Then I saw the connection to Dr. Richards in that life. He had been a handsome young southern man whom I loved very much, and to whom I was engaged. Before we were married I contracted tuberculosis, and my health declined very quickly. In that lifetime also, Dr. Browning was a doctor, and Dr. Richards was training to be a doctor, but neither of them could save me, and I died.

It was clear why Dr. Richards had reacted so emotionally to an apparent stranger when I went to his office. The trauma of losing me was fresh from our previous life together. I admit I did consider marrying him in this lifetime. I loved him and could have had great material wealth. He was into acupuncture, and receptive to holistic techniques, so I could have continued as a healer and had a good life. The other aspect of marriage that posed a conflict was sex.

On the ranch Lester had helped me transmute sexual desire, and I was not good for any worldly man. I didn't want that anyway. If I was going to be with a man, it had to be with someone pure, who loved me as a soul and wanted realization. I asked myself if Dr. Richards could give me the freedom I needed for my path and my inner voice said, "No." On one level I understood the attachment and knew we could never marry; however I still felt a deep affection and friendship for him.

Dr. Richards recognized how well I got along with people, and suggested I work for him. I had been praying for a new career, and this seemed like my next step. He said, "You have a tremendous love for people, which would be very advantageous for a patient's recovery." Helping people appealed to me greatly, and it felt right, so I agreed.

Dr. Richards taught me a number of practical tasks that LPNs and RNs perform, and then sent me on private duty cases. I loved it!

For three years we cared for Delita, a wealthy woman who lived in a beautiful home in Laguna Beach, California. I had been her husband's nurse for a short time until he passed away, and then was kept on to take care of her when she had a stroke. As a result of the stroke, Delita's left leg was paralyzed and fitted with a special brace. In order for her to walk, we had to hold her up, and manually push her leg forward from behind. The other nurses and I took shifts serving her, and we called her "Delightful Delita," because it was like going to our mother's house. She was slipping mentally, but we enjoyed being with her. We'd perform our duties and take her on rides and out to lunch.

I worked with three other nurses, and taught them how to meditate and pray for the patients. We set up a meditation room in Delita's house and worked as a prayer team.

I was living in Laguna Beach when I heard about another incredible master named Shri Dhyanyogi Madhusudandasji who was touring in Los Angeles. He gave a program at the East-West Cultural Center, which is where I first met him. He had spent 40 years on Mount Abu, a famous mountain in India, and was supposedly over 100-years-old. Dhyanyogi was a great

Shaktipat master and he loved Ram, as I did.

A group of us were chanting the *Ram* mantra with him, and sitting in front of me was a nineteen-year-old Indian girl in a white sari. Her name was Asha Devi. She was touring with him. Suddenly Asha Devi went into a *samadhic* state, and fell back into my lap! When one goes into *samadhi,* the body becomes very stiff. The energy was so amazing that, like a domino, I too fell helplessly backwards and went into a state of bliss. I thought Dhyanyogi was great, but I was even more enthralled with this girl who was totally one-pointed for realization! Dhyanyogi brought forth the Ram energy, but Asha Devi brought the Divine Mother energy in, and I felt a deep connection to her. She was the Kali aspect of the Divine Mother who destroys ignorance, and when she went into a trance, her tongue would protrude from her mouth, a phenomenon I had seen in India.

When I wasn't taking care of Delita, I would spend as much time as I could with Dhyanyogi, and serving Asha Devi. Dhyanyogi taught me how to bring Asha Devi out of *samadhi*, which she'd go into at the drop of a hat. Her body would get stiff with her tongue sticking out, and fall back onto the floor. I liked her in *samadhi* and didn't really want to bring her out! But of course I did use the technique Dhyanyogi taught me by whispering OM into her ear, and gently bringing the energy down her spine. Just touching her would make me high also. I made her clothes, and lovingly took care of her as if she were my own little sister. I felt very privileged to have met these holy people.

A personally signed picture of Shri Dhyanyogi Madhusudandasji.

My spiritual life blended well with my professional life. The nurses and I regularly prayed for the saints to come in and heal Delita's leg. I knew it was possible. One day I had a brilliant idea. I called Dr. Richards and asked if we could take her off her medications. Due to depression and bouts of anger, she had been put on antidepressants after her stroke. I had seen the effect that allopathic medicine had on people. It was okay for a while but the side effects were not good. I felt the medications were suppressing her muscles and emotions. I suggested we take her off the antidepressants, and instead give her natural vitamins, as well as wholesome foods and juices. Since we spent so much time with Delita,

Dr. Richards trusted our judgment and agreed to the new plan. I cautioned that emotions could surface again once she stopped taking the medications.

I told the nurses repressed emotions of anger might come up, and to be prepared. Sure enough, Delita was a maniac! We took a lot of abuse for a while but we got her through it. One day I was walking her down the hall and her paralyzed leg moved forward on its own! I almost fainted. The drugs had been affecting her muscles, so once her body was cleansed of the toxic medications, everything started working again.

I called Dr. Richards and told him I was bringing her in, and he asked, "Is she all right?"

"You'll see," I replied. I took her to his office in her wheel chair and Dr. Richards came out. His expression was one of trepidation, not quite knowing what to expect. I helped Delita up out of her wheel chair. To Dr. Richards' astonishment, she walked on her own. All of us were overjoyed beyond words!

I loved my job, and my experiences were helping to expand my knowledge and ability as a healer. I was grateful for the opportunities Dr. Richards had given me, but part of me was still in conflict with my strong feelings for him. Was working with him really good for me?

If we didn't work together, would I still have the attachment anyway? I knew I needed to talk to someone because it was interfering with my meditation. I enjoyed working for him, but I also felt that the attachment between us was interfering with my spiritual growth. Anything or anyone that comes before God interferes with the path to realization. I thought of Dhyanyogi and decided to seek his counsel. He patiently listened as I began, "I'm kind of embarrassed about this, but here goes… I'm in love with this man and cannot stop obsessing over him. I can't meditate or do anything without his being on my mind. I can't put God first when I'm doing this. I hesitate to tell you, but I just didn't know who else to turn to."

Dhyanyogi was kind and understanding, and told me it was a very deep tie. He gave me this long prayer in Sanskrit to Lord Rama, which essentially said I would put Lord Rama first and only think of Him. It took me a while to memorize the lengthy prayer, but after I did, within three days that whole attachment to Dr. Richards was gone. It was amazing. I was in my own power again.

Later I learned about ectoplasmic cords between people, how they are formed when there is an emotional attachment or aversion, and how to sever them. (This is described further in the chapter on healing.)

During this phase of my life my mother had moved in with my Aunt Idie, who lived in Laguna. One day my Aunt Idie, Mom and I were in a restaurant, when my mom felt faint and collapsed. We took her straight home and called Dr. Browning, who immediately came to the house (in those days, doctors still made house visits!) He told us she had had a stroke, and that we needed to take her to the hospital. She went into a coma, and Dr. Browning didn't think she would come out of it. Two weeks went by with no change, and I asked within why she wasn't letting go. Then I saw that my brother was subconsciously holding onto her. It wasn't good for any of us to have her hang on, so I prayed to Jesus to release the attachment between my mom and brother. She died the next day. We were at the hospital when she left her body, but I didn't get to experience my mother's death as I had with my father, because I wasn't in concentrated meditation at the time. Still, I knew that her passing was a wonderful experience for her and that she was now free.

THIRD TRIP TO INDIA

The thought of going back to India started to play on my mind again, because being *there* meant a certain state of consciousness, growth and getting closer to God. The long delay in returning to India had been a conscious choice. I didn't go back while my parents were still alive, because I didn't want to worry them. They had eventually found out about the cobra bite, and knowing that they almost lost me was overwhelming for them. Between concern for my parents, and Babaji telling me my *dharma* was in the west, I had not thought about returning to India until my mother's death.

Eventually, I made travel plans for my third trip back. My first stop was Papa's ashram. Shortly after my arrival, I contracted jaundice. I turned yellow, had no appetite and lost weight. There was a beautiful swami from the Himalayas who wore his hair rolled up on the top of his head and when he let it down, it would drop to his ankles. He was a *Ram Swami,* and it is their tradition to never cut

Yellow Swami, at Papa Ramda's ashram, sang to me when I had jaundice and introduced me to Brian.

their hair. To help me recover, he would come and sing to me. His name was Yellow Swami, because he wore yellow robes, not because he helped people with jaundice! Every day I would anxiously await Yellow Swami's arrival to hear his songs.

One day he told me about an American man living in his dormitory, who had been a Buddhist monk in India. Yellow Swami was genuinely enthused for me to meet a fellow American who was also dedicated to realization. The American man had jaundice too, so both of us were confined to our rooms. We kept hearing about each other, and finally when we recovered we met. This tall, handsome man walked up to me and said, "Hello, I'm Brian." I looked into his big blue eyes and instantly felt we had a soul connection that was beyond time and space. I wasn't in love with him, but felt a deep spiritual connection. This was completely different from feelings I previously had for Dr. Richards. It was a deep soul bond, as if he were my twin flame.

Brian and I became fast friends and were elated that we both shared a love for Babaji. I couldn't really express my devotion to Babaji at Papa's ashram, because the focus was one-pointed to Rama. Ashrams recognize all the deities, but they are typically dedicated to one particular aspect of God. Not that I would have been ostracized for talking about Babaji, but the energy there was permeated with Ram, and it didn't seem appropriate for me to talk about any other master.

I was so eclectic — I loved Papa, Babaji, the Divine Mother, Jesus and many others — and so was Brian. When I told Brian how much I loved Babaji he smiled and said, "I love Babaji too! My first teacher was a personal devotee of Yogananda and she taught me about Babaji, and since then I have adored him."

Brian had been a Buddhist monk for many years, and previously attended the University of Delhi to obtain his Masters degree in Indian Philosophy. He didn't like the professors, said they were dry, and dropped out of the program. He really came to India to see the Masters, so with only a backpack to his name, he left New Delhi to live the monastic life.

On his way through Sri Lanka to update his visa, he ended up at a Tibetan Buddhist monastery. He said the monks had all been waiting for him! It was an amazing experience. It triggered a deep memory in him, and he realized he had a deep tie to the Tibetan Buddhist path. He easily went into deep states of meditation, and knew he had been a Tibetan monk in many past lives. It was easy for him to shave his head, put on the robes and become one of them. Becoming a monk was the most natural thing he had ever done. He achieved very high states in the monastery, and stayed for about three years. He said he was never so happy in his entire life. He loved the simplicity of a monk's life in meditation, and felt so close to God.

His father, a prominent attorney and graduate of Harvard, and his mother, a Radcliff College graduate, came to Sri Lanka to visit him. They were appalled to find their son so emaciated, and felt it their duty as good parents to save him. They took him to all the local hotel restaurants to fatten him up. His father convinced Brian he really didn't need to live such an austere life. Brian also realized that his path in this life was to experience all religions, not just Buddhism, so he left the monastery, and went to Papa Ramdas' ashram where I met him.

Soon after our meeting, Brian had to go back to America, because his visa had expired. I was sad because I had become so close to him, and suddenly he was being taken away. I stayed a year and a half longer in India doing *sadhana* and going to different places with a wandering *sadhu*,

A very thin Brian at Papa Ramda's ashram where we first met.

Swami Prem, whom I had met at Papa's ashram. He had spent a lot of time in the Himalayas and loved the Divine Mother. As a child he had become very sick and was healed by a Durga *puja*, so his parents dedicated him to Durga. He started going into Mother Durga trances and *samadhic* states as a child, and his family treated him as a saint. He would later turn out to be bad news for me, but I didn't know that at the time.

When I first saw Swami Prem, his face was shining. He had just returned from a recent trip to the Himalayas. Deep feelings of connectedness to Rama and Krishna were opening in me, and he offered to take me to the holy places of these Great Beings. It was impossible for a westerner, especially a woman, to make a trip like that alone. Westerners had no clue where these holy sites were, and the Hindus wouldn't tell us unless they knew we were really devoted.

We traveled to Vrindavan and then to Iodia, a place sacred to Rama. There was a large Hanuman temple there, and we took *ladus*, or offerings to him. There were monkeys all over the place and people were singing the praises of Rama, Sita and Hanumanji and reliving the story of the epic *Ramayana*. Some men were dressed as women. I thought they were gay, but later found out that the men were trying to balance their feminine side by taking the part of Radha. It would have been a weird thing in America, but not in India.

Then we went to places connected to Lord Krishna and I learned the history of each location. My body was getting weak and I was hypoglycemic, but I wasn't about to miss out on anything. We went to where the baby Krishna, Gopala, was born and to the place where all the *gopis* danced with Krishna. One could feel the ecstasy there. Something big was awakening within me, and every time I heard the name of Krishna and Rama I felt incredible joy and just wanted to dance.

Swami Prem told me I'd like Barsana better than Vrindavan, because it wasn't known by many people and I'd feel the *gopis* more. When we arrived, Swami Prem took me to see a great saint to receive his blessing. The saint had been a professor at a university at Banaras, but when Krishna appeared to him, he renounced everything, except for one blanket, and became a *sadhu*. The people in town knew he was holy and lovingly looked after him. He eventually founded an ashram.

Swami Prem and I went to another holy site, the Radharani temple in Barsana. When I sat down I cried for two solid hours. I asked Swami Prem what was wrong with me and he said, "You were close to Radha and Krishna. You were a handmaiden of Radha and your memories are being awakened. You want to go back to that time."

It was then that I knew my connection to them. Everything became Radha for me; I would call out her name, "Radha, Radha, Radha!" Memories of her and Krishna started flooding my mind and I recalled what a beautiful time it had been. It was a reign of peace. After Krishna had killed all the demons, we entered a golden age where people lived in total love and abundance, both inwardly and outwardly. My heart was crying to get back to that time, to dance with Krishna and to be in ecstasy again.

After the Rama and Krishna pilgrimage, I felt it was time to return to America, and I took Swami Prem with me. I spent a lot of money getting him to America, because I thought he was representing the Divine Mother, but he turned out to be a real brat. His virtue declined as he started sleeping with women, and he became arrogant over his status as a spiritual teacher. His teachings were dull because they were not coming from purity within the heart, and I could no longer represent him. I called Brian at the Ananda Retreat, Kriyananda's ashram, and said, "I need help with a swami I brought over. He's like a teenage boy and I have to get him back to India."

Brian came to the rescue and helped me with Swami Prem. One of Swami's promises to me before we even came to America was to impart a Durga mantra that could put one into *samadhic* trances. He played all sorts of mind games with me, and avoided giving it to me. But Brian, acting as my protector, demanded he do so. Brian was formidable- he was a tall, well-built man with a square jaw, and could be very forceful. Brian was as fed up with him as I was. He glared down at Swami Prem and said, "This woman has done everything for you, and *you owe it to her!*" Swami Prem knew it was futile to argue with Brian and sheepishly relinquished the mantra.

I knew receiving the mantra, as well as working out some karma with him, was why I had to meet Swami Prem. I traced our connection back to another life, where Swami Prem was a king, and I was one of his many wives. In that time period, when a king died it was customary that all of his wives die also by committing *sati*, or jumping into a pit of fire. This is what happened to me. I also learned there were many degrees of realization - Swami Prem could zap people with *Shaktipat*, but he was not in the highest state of realization. It was a lesson of discernment for me.

The experience with Swami Prem also enabled Brian and me to see each other again when he came to my rescue. Brian told me he felt we were supposed to be together; I was delighted because I had also felt that way. So we decided to go into meditation and ask for divine guidance. I had a friend we stayed with in Mount Shasta, and that was where we did our vision quest. We fasted and meditated day and night, asking for our next step. The fifth day of our quest, spirit told us we were definitely supposed to be together. Brian tenderly said to me, "I love you dearly, and in a way that is not connected to the senses. We can have a celibate marriage, and I'll be your friend and protector." I felt the same way. He was my unconditional friend and buddy. We fondly called each other "Buddy."

We asked God where we were supposed to go, and both of us received the inner guidance to go to Sedona, Arizona. So we did. Soon after we arrived, Brian and I were married inside a beautiful circle of trees, with two of our close friends looking on as witnesses. We wore white silk, said our vows and exchanged rings. It was a spiritual marriage, to get closer to God, and to one another. In our vows we said we would be protectors of each other, but if ever we held each other back in any way, we would release each other with love.

Our relationship was pure. We would hold each other

in bed, and go into high states of ecstasy. Brian and I were both in our own power, and did not look to each other for our joy. We came together in purity, and there was no desire for anything other than God. It was the real *tantra* between man and woman— the *kundalini* energy would rise to our crown chakras, and we would lose body consciousness.

There was no thought of sex, and in fact we would have had to come down from our high state to enjoy sex. Who wanted to have sex after experiencing such ecstasy? We would go out of our bodies, leave the planet and sometimes be on spiritual journeys for half the day. He was my dearest friend and soulmate. We were together for 17 years.

One important dynamic of our marriage was our ability to mirror, or trigger, each other's karma. Through deep meditation I learned that he was my soul mate from the ancient civilization of Lemuria. We had shared many lives together in Lemuria, Atlantis, Egypt, the time of Jesus and countless others. In these lifetimes our mission was to hold the light against the dark forces.

These dark beings hit us psychically with negative energy and usually go to the third chakra to disempower and deplete our energy. They use dark spirits or demons to attack and drain us. They attach psychic cords to one's fear or negative quality stored on the unconscious from a past life or implant.

After our marriage we battled the dark forces. Some of the same beings we had battled in past lives came into our lives this time around, and the psychic battle continued. It was like a time warp. I will talk much more about this later.

Brian and I were so accepting of all spiritual disciplines, that we didn't belong to any particular one. I had tried to be a nun at the Self Realization Fellowship because I loved Babaji. Not only did I not fit in there, but I couldn't even talk to them about Babaji! One of the nuns recognized this as well, and told me that I was too free to be there. She said, "You have so much freedom on your path now, that you would feel like you were living in a box here." She was right.

Shortly after Brian and I were married, his father gave us a huge chunk of money to go back to school. We began by taking healing classes in Sedona, and realized we were very good at it. We took classes in kinesiology (muscle testing), which applied to all bodies: mental, emotional, physical and spiritual. We also learned herbology, entity release work, Jin Shin Jyutsu, and acupressure. As we took these courses, something interesting happened. While in meditation we remembered healing techniques we had used in previous lifetimes. As we applied the newly learned healing methods from our class, the techniques from past lifetimes would naturally blend in.

VISITING OTHER REALMS AND SPACE SHIPS

W hen I received the *Narvana* mantra from Swami Prem, he said, "This is the most powerful of all the Mother mantras. It is a Durga mantra, and will put you into trance-like states, and take you into other worlds."

The state of bliss resonates at the same frequency of certain heavenly realms and is why they can be experienced. When Muktananda gave *Shaktipat* I went into a lower *samadhic* state. It was kind of like a drug— it was absolutely delightful going to these beautiful realms. I would go to the Shiva *loka* where I saw many beings with the three lines of ash across their foreheads.

Using Divine Mother's mantra I received from Swami Prem, I would go to her *loka* where she sat on a throne in a magnificent hall. She was laden with jewels and more beautiful than any painting I've seen of her. Incredibly high beings were there worshipping her with pujas. It became a practice for me to go there and do puja to her; later I did my own inner puja where I gave her a bath and asked what color sari she wanted to wear. I put jewelry and a crown on her, then led her into a beautiful hall where she would sit on her throne. I would place a garland of flowers around her neck and wash her feet.

As Swami Prem said, the *Narvana* mantra put me into trances, and I started going into realms other than *lokas*, such as on inter-dimensional "Christed" space ships. They are operated by very high beings established in Christ consciousness, and can go anywhere in the galaxy. The Christed space ships are under the command of elevated beings, such as Jesus and Archangel Michael, as part of a huge mission to protect and monitor the earth. They know what is happening at all times. If it hadn't been for these Masters, the earth would have been blown up long ago. In a trance state I was able to see incredible details of these ships, such as healing rooms saturated with light, color, and sound that can heal anyone instantly. The Masters can put people into their Ascended form when they are ready. The ships were very familiar to me because I had spent much time on them in between lives. I started to get addicted to going there, and wanted to be there all the time, but it only happened once in a while.

One year while at Lester's ranch, I flew home for Christmas and while on the plane, I suddenly shifted dimensions and was in a huge mother ship. The ship was occupied with very evolved, transparent angelic Beings who lifted me up to where they were. I felt I was home. I was in a deep state of ecstasy and it felt very natural. I pleaded with them, "Please, do not make me go back! It's awful back there!"

Actually, it wasn't awful being at Lester's ranch. It was one of the happiest times of my life, but after experiencing the contrast of the ranch to where I was now, suddenly it seemed undesirable. They told me I could not stay with them because I was on a mission. They didn't tell me something like, "If you just think of us we'll be with you," as Babaji had said. Instead, I was instantly back on the plane!

I think they may have been Sirians. The see-through type of angels and Masters are usually in their Ascended bodies. The higher they get in the light, the higher they are in their causal bodies. I felt they were my family, and I had the consolation that maybe I could be with them some day.

I had another experience on a space ship, when I went to the Grand Canyon with two friends. Both were very spiritually elevated beings and just plain fun to be with! That day we all felt kind of weird, as if we were going through some type of clearing or cleansing, and unbeknownst to one another, we were each praying to God for help to get through it. We were driving along the rim of the Grand Canyon and I was sitting in the back seat when suddenly the *Shakti* hit me; it was all I could do to keep my eyes open. My friend who was driving looked back and said, "Oh, they're getting you, huh?" I said, "Ya! The *Shakti* is really knocking me out!" My companions were affected too, so I suggested we pull off the road to a grove of trees ahead, put our blankets down and just go with it. As soon as we lay down we all got knocked out and ended up on a space ship! We were in a healing room where space beings showed us some of their healing technology. They led us to tables where we reclined, and instantly our chakras were cleared through light, color and sound frequencies. The lights were so bright and the sound so subtle, it was beyond anything we have here on earth. When we came out of our meditation, we all compared notes and each had had the same experience. When we went back to Sedona we were in a totally different state than before we left!

One evening while I still was at Lester's ranch, I was driving back after seeing the Hopi dances in New Mexico. The dances were to invoke the rain spirits, and not only was the energy very powerful from the ceremonies, but when they were finished, all of us watched as the clouds rolled in and the rain came down. It was an incredible experience. I got home very late, around midnight, and was driving along our twelve-mile dirt road to get back to Lester's, when I saw a blinking red light. I looked over and there was a huge, huge space ship! I was so excited and wanted witnesses, so I pressed the pedal to the metal and raced ahead to the ranch.

I ran into the house and woke up the girls screaming, "SPACE SHIP! SPACE SHIP!" They rushed out half asleep, and there before us, big as life, was a UFO hovering over Loy Butte (a large butte behind our cottage). We scurried into the front yard waving our arms and yelling,

"WAIT! TAKE US WITH YOU! WE WANT A RIDE!" Lester had always taught us that the only way to meet these beings was with a quiet mind, but in the heat of the moment, practical thinking flew out the window. After a few moments, the ship simply disintegrated into thin air. I knew they had changed frequencies, which gave the appearance of disappearing. When we told Lester about it, he said, "No wonder they disappeared. You were too loud! You have to be quiet and meet them in a meditative state."

I learned about "bad" space ships from a popular book on extraterrestrial beings. Lester said we would never meet low-frequency beings if we had no fear, because our frequency was high enough.

The Greys are a species of low-frequency space beings. They take people to their ships at night when they are sleeping, remove their eggs and sperm and then genetically engineer clones in order to create a new race. This is interference of free will.

I discovered that some of my clients had been abducted, implanted or experimented on by the Greys. The implants block the meridians in the brain and third eye, and make one confused. The implants are physical matter, not like the psychological ones the Reptilians used, and are planted into the brain or different parts of the body of the people they abduct, so they can monitor them. At that time I was learning about healing with prayer to the angels, and so I prayed to them to remove these implants. The angels got right in and disintegrated them at once.

Because I am from the angelic kingdom, I had a hotline with the angels. They would do whatever I asked, but only if there were no doer-ship or ego involved on my part. If there were, they'd say, "You do it!" So I learned to be a channel between heaven and earth, anchoring in their energy from the higher realms so they could do their work. They needed my intention, prayer and physical body to funnel in their energy. The angels can take the implants out very easily, and if the dark forces ever do the *"mark of the beast"* here, the angels will just take them out en masse. I have worked on many people throughout the years who had the Grey and Reptilian implants from the past, and have become an expert at removing them.

I realized I wasn't afraid of the dark ships, which were ships used by the Greys and Reptilians, after I learned how to work with the angels, especially with Archangel Michael. It was easy for him to surround any disqualified energies or dark spirits in light, and take them to a sphere of light where they could evolve! Once I realized God was so much more powerful than any of these dark forces, I wasn't afraid of them anymore. I could ask legions of angels and Archangel Michael to come in, and do whatever was needed to be done with the dark ones. My fear of the Greys, dark forces and Reptilians was gone, because I also realized they were here to play a role of duality. Our role as light workers this time is to go beyond the dark forces instead of fighting them, as we have in so many incarnations. This time we are fighting them with light, love and connectedness to the Divine. When we go beyond the delusion, they can't get to us anymore.

I've recalled past lives where I resided on space ships. It was a time before we came to earth, when galactic wars between the light and dark took place. In one case I was the commander of a ship, and was ordered to blow up a planet, but I wouldn't do it. My superior had me killed because I wouldn't follow orders. The fight has been going on for a long time, even before this planet.

There are thousands of Christed ships that are monitoring this planet, and many other places. Archangel Michael, Sananda (Jesus' oversoul[29]), Ashtar, and other Ascended beings command fleets of ships. They are protectors. When my dad died, and I experienced his state of going into realization, I saw that he went so high I couldn't reach him anymore. He went beyond me. I knew he was with Jesus, on one of the Christed space ships.

I feel there is a part of me that is simultaneously living on one of those ships. The vibrational rate is so high and so blissful that my soul longs to be there, and I am just a little envious Daddy got to go back! When we pass, we have duties according to the state of achievement we reached on this physical realm. We go to the realms where we can be of the highest service and evolve the fastest. The heavenly realms have places of frequency and when we leave the body, we go to the place of frequency that matches the one we achieved in our physical body. On this planet we can

29   Jesus' life on earth was just one aspect of his being. Sananda is the culmination of his whole being. When you gain Mastership, you receive a name from God that signifies the vibrational frequency that the master has accomplished through all lifetimes and experiences.

go all the way into the state of Oneness, and beyond all the worlds. This planet is a tremendous launching pad. (As Shankaracharya, the great aspect of Shiva, said, the three greatest gifts are the human body, the ability to get free through the intense desire for liberation, and association with the sages.) At this time, there are many souls who are on a waiting list to embody on earth, because it is an opportune time to grow. Everything has been speeded up on this planet.

The space ships are heavenly realms and after experiencing one, we don't really want to be here anymore. My understanding is we have to Ascend into our light or subtle bodies this time in order to stay on one. We cannot leave the physical body behind through death or astral travel, but must bring the body with us. It must be transformed by releasing all karmic memory through the cells, RNA and DNA and all bodies. The trick is to integrate all of the bodies (physical, mental, emotional and spiritual), which has been a challenge for me. Although I'm in a physical body, there was a time when I didn't identify with the physical. I had to take care to pick my feet up and not stub my toe, because most of the time I was in another realm. I was *in* the body, but felt that it was getting lighter and lighter, and freer and freer.

There are beings that are in a high state of consciousness, and are transforming the body all the way through the DNA and RNA to come into their Ascended form. They are called the "first wavers", because they are showing the way for everyone else. Releasing karmic memory from the cells can be very intense at times. I was living in New Mexico with Brian when I relived an Egyptian life where I was tortured and implanted. The cells in my physical body hadn't yet released the experience, and I literally became crippled! I knew I needed extra help getting through it. I had the Divine Mother Meera's phone number in Germany, and knew she could be called at a certain time when she'd be in a room with her assistant.

We could ask her assistant the question, and she would relay the question on to Mother Meera. I told her that I was suddenly crippled while reliving a past life, and that I needed Mother's help to get out of this pickle. Mother told me to go into my puja room (I don't know how she knew I had one; I guess because she's omniscient) and to stay there and do non-stop japa (mantra repetition). I did exactly as she said. I constantly repeated the mantra and did not leave that room. I even slept there and Brian brought me my food. Within a weeks' time I was totally healed, and I knew it was through Mother Meera's grace.

I understand that we are going through tremendous cellular changes now, that are necessary so that we can get into our light bodies. There are also natural resources that can crack the cellular membrane where all the RNA and DNA are holding these memories, such as a very pure and unprocessed form of Aloe Vera, antioxidants, berries and "programmed" water.

From what I have been getting from my Masters, we are being asked at this time to transform the physical body into a higher frequency, or light body. This is called Ascension. In order to transform the physcial body, the cellular memory must be totally purified. The cells hold onto past traumas and they are held in the body. As we release all the traumas and karmas from the body, it will become less dense, and will transform into the light body. When this happens, the law of gravity will no longer apply. It will be possible to transport to any location with just a thought. Those who do not Ascend in this lifetime will go to those heavenly realms that match their level of consciousness.

OUR NEXT STEP AS HEALERS

During the full moon of May, the Wesak Festival is celebrated. This is the time of Buddha's enlightenment. Brian and I climbed up Cathedral Rock, one of the holiest rocks in Sedona, to meditate during this auspicious time. For hours we stayed in deep states of meditation. When we came out of meditation it was getting dark. We quickly started down the mountain, but the shadows from the moon made it difficult to see, and I slipped on some loose stones and fell. My hand landed right on the thorns of a cactus plant. Luckily my fall wasn't serious, but we both agreed it was better to stay up there until dawn, because we didn't want to kill ourselves going down! We went back to our spot and meditated the entire night on top of Cathedral Rock. I kept going in and out of altered states, and at one point, I merged with a beautiful Native American goddess with long black hair blowing in the wind. She was dressed in white buckskin and high boots. We became one being running through the woods in total ecstasy and unity consciousness.

I later discovered there was a being called White Buffalo Calf Woman who had come from the stars. She was an extraterrestrial, who came down to unite all the Indian tribes using the peace pipe. There are stories that she was the most gorgeous woman one could imagine. Indian lore talks about a man who looked upon her with lust, and as she gazed at him, he disintegrated into ashes because of his lack of purity.

White Buffalo Calf Woman then told me, "Your next step is Santa Fe, New Mexico; it is the healing capitol of the world." She told us we would receive tremendous knowledge about the healing arts there. Brian and I had attended several healing classes in Sedona, loved the healing arts, and knew it was what we wanted to do.

We followed my vision and went to Santa Fe. As White Buffalo Calf Woman had predicted, all the doors opened up to us. We met Dr. J. Victor Scherer, a top healer and naturopath. My dad had always taught me that if you want to get to know someone, to ask them over for dinner. So I did. I called Dr. Scherer and told him I would love to meet him and invited him for dinner. It became a monthly tradition for us to have dinner together at our place, and he became our mentor and close friend.

Dr. Sherer was in his 60's and had never married. I was impressed by the fact that he had been raised as a vegan by his naturopath mother, and had maintained a strict diet throughout his life. He was totally dedicated to working with natural medicines. He was an incredibly pure and spontaneous being who lived for St. Germain and the "I AM " teachings.

Brian and I became quite successful. We took private classes with the best teachers. We studied Jin Shin Jyutsu with Mary Burmeister, and acupressure under Richard Kroft. We appeared on television to demonstrate acupressure. Richard happened to watch the show and was so proud of us! We were private students under another incredible being, Lois Bimford, who was very skilled at psychic release and clearing negative entities. Not only were we healing people physically, but we were also clearing them of dark spirits.

I initially learned about dark entities when I was caring for my sick mother and noticed a weird energy in her room. I had met Pir Viliyat Khan, the head of the Sufi Order, at the Ananda Ashram, and we became good friends.

One day he came to my house for lunch and I told him about the energy in my mother's room. He explained that my mother was attracting dark spirits because of the medication she was taking; it weakened her aura and created "holes" where dark entities could enter. He taught me how to clear the dark spirits by firmly stating, "In the name of Jesus Christ I command all dark spirits to go NOW!" It worked like a charm. The energy in the room completely cleared. Throughout the years, I have encountered dark spirits and experienced psychic attacks. Although I knew the basic rules that governed them, I was by no means an expert. Lois, however, gave us advanced knowledge on releasing dark entities, and protecting ourselves against psychic attack, and Brian and I became very good at it.

As budding new healers, we wanted to practice on each other all the time. We already knew how to get into past lives and release them, so we were having a ball healing each other. As in Sedona, through deep states of medita-

Our very good friend and teacher, Dr. Scherer (left), Brian and Thea in Santa Fe, NM.

tion, we remembered healing techniques from past lives in Egypt and Greece. I was also a Native American shaman, and an Essene during the life of Jesus. I remembered how to work with the chakras and to see and release karma. We used these techniques in our practice natural-

ly as if we had performed them for years. When I prayed for people I could see the angels and Masters come in, and as the karma was lifting, I could also see its cause.

In one case I worked with a woman who had cancer. The angels gave me x-ray vision to see it. As I prayed I saw the dark mass go away. I didn't tell her what happened, because I feared she would think I was responsible for her healing, and I had nothing to do with it. God healed her. Later that week, the woman called me and said, "You know that cancer is gone, you know the tumor went away."

I said, "I saw the tumor disappear, but God is the one who healed you." I was afraid that what had happened in India would happen now, the word would get around that I was a miraculous healer. I wanted to be an instrument of healing, but did not want to be thought of as The Healer.

Because Brian and I had been together from the beginning of time and were parts of the same soul, our karma would mirror each other. Sometimes we had to cancel appointments at our clinic because we became so distraught going through our own karma and needed to work on each other. Once we got through it, we resumed our sessions again. We were a great team and helped each other grow tremendously.

We developed our own healing system, and became very popular in Santa Fe with months-long waiting lists. Our healing center was located in a beautiful adobe house and the entire upstairs was devoted to healing. As one walked up the stairs, the view of the Sangre de Cristo Mountains loomed through large windows that encircled the room. We taught our healing classes and meditation at our center, and at Dr. Scherer's healing colleges in Santa Fe.

Dr. Scherer always said there is a superimposed light world in the etheric realm above Santa Fe, and it is the holistic healing capitol of the world. At the right time, the light city will merge with the physical plane.

Santa Fe certainly was a place that reawakened our healing arts. I learned quickly there couldn't be any doer-ship in anything I did. The minute I felt doer-ship, the angels and Masters would retreat, saying, "You do it." Then I'd cry out, "Help! I'm sorry! I can't do it, please come back!"

When I first began healing work, I didn't know the difference between compassion and sympathy. I started taking people's problems on, and Brian would call me The Compassionate Sponge. It wasn't compassion, however; it was sympathy. Compassion is staying in your high state and bringing people up to where you are, sympathy is going right down to where they are, which helps no one. Detachment is the key. Although I care about everyone's well being and want them to be healed, I have to release any feeling of responsibility for the healing. I am neither the healer nor the doer. I am a co-creator with God. Healing is not my responsibility— it is God's alone.

Brian and I became very well known for the healing technique we developed called "tape release." We realized huge amounts of karma could be released by focusing on one tendency, such as rejection, and praying for all of the incidents of rejection to come forward and be released. If the original occurrence of rejection was brought up, the entire tendency could be wiped out. Incident after incident came up, and we compiled a whole page of tape releases or tendencies. We then muscle tested for which tendency a person had, and prayed to the Masters to release it. We also incorporated other mental and emotional techniques of healing, but the tape release was huge.

During a healing, I could see karma being lifted by beings of tremendous light. Very quickly, one occurrence after another would come up, and the person would feel awful until it was completely released. Brian could measure megahertz[30], and as the karma lifted the person's megahertz would rise. Our work became popular in Santa Fe. People were rushing to us to get tape releases to increase their megahertz, then they'd compare megahertz levels with each other!

Dr. Scherer, Brian and I were like family. We decided to start a holistic foundation, to bring all the healers in Santa Fe together to share our abilities. We also created a healing guide, listing each healer and their specialty. Regular meetings began with prayer and meditation. As more healers joined the foundation, the pool of healing resources increased. We traded information and shared special cases with each other. If we couldn't assist somebody, we'd ask the healer with more expertise in that area for assistance. Dr. Scherer had an aversion to allopathic medicine, and made sure all of the healing techniques brought in were natural and holistic. It worked well for a while until the foundation grew too large, and ego and competitiveness came in. The pure and innocent sharing of talents was gone, so Dr. Scherer, Brian and I withdrew from the group.

30 Electromagnetic radiation is often described by its frequency - the number of oscillations of the perpendicular electric and magnetic fields per second - expressed in hertz. Radio frequency radiation is usually measured in kilohertz, megahertz, or gigahertz. (http://en.wikipedia.org/wiki/Megahertz, 4/5/07)

NATIVE AMERICAN PAST LIVES

When Brian and I moved to New Mexico, it
brought up many memories of being Native
American. One day we went on a long hike in
the Pecos Mountains with our roommate Karim. The guys
could hike a lot faster. I was always behind, but liked to go
with the boys because they would look after me. On our
way back I was exhausted, but I also felt horrible and like I
wanted to cry. I couldn't wait to get back home so I could go
into meditation to find out what was going on. I knew something big was surfacing, having to do with losing someone
whom I'd loved very deeply in a past life. I got home and
went into meditation, and started asking for it to come up.

I saw myself in the Pecos Mountains with a beautiful
tribe of Indians. I had been trained to be a medicine woman
from childhood, a great honor in the Indian tradition. It was
a position in the tribe, which came before everything, even
one's own family. I rode a pinto pony to tend to those who
needed me, worked with herbs and delivered babies. In that
lifetime I met Brian, who was a mountain man. We had fall-

en in love with each other again. We became man and wife and lived with my tribe, although my people didn't totally accept him because he was white, so it was somewhat painful for him. I loved him dearly, but had to keep up with my duties and as was the custom, put them ahead of him. Brian became bored and needed to go out and trap food.

Somehow my soul knew he wasn't going to stay with me. It broke my heart because I loved him so much. In the middle of the night, during a snow storm, I left to deliver a baby, and when I returned I saw footprints in the snow and knew he had left. I was afraid he wouldn't make it out safely, because of the storm or enemy tribes. Tearfully, I followed his footprints. This was what came up after our hike together, losing Brian once again. It was a wrenching pain. He was the love of my life. There was no one else I wanted to be with.

I recalled another lifetime that happened around Santa Fe. Again, I was an Indian woman living in a very happy and peaceful tribe. My friend Robert, in this life, was my four year old son. It was a beautiful village and I had a great love for everyone. Many of the people I was meeting in Santa Fe in this lifetime had been part of that tribe. It was a close-knit, loving group. I was married to Brian in that life as well, and he had gone on a scouting trip. Spanish men on horses invaded our village, brutally killing every person they approached. I saw my son decapitated. In an instant I went from heaven to hell. The Spaniards raped me before killing me. In the meantime, Brian was on a scouting trip, and had a dream vision that his whole tribe was being killed and burned, so he rushed back as fast as he could to save us. He rode up to the cliff overlooking the village to see everything in smoke and all of us dead. He became extremely bitter in that life, and swore revenge to those who had killed his people.

Karim, Brian and I were renting a large, beautiful adobe house in a Hispanic neighborhood. I felt the racial prejudice in Santa Fe between the Native Americans, Hispanics and Whites. It's ancient, has been so for many centuries, and the tension still exists in the region.

The seers and medicine people had dream visions in which the Great Spirit told the Native Americans about the white man coming, years before they arrived. The Great Spirit told them that in order to survive they must not drink the white man's firewater or fight amongst each other. The warriors, however, did not listen. I saw warriors from all over the continent turning against the holy people, not listening to their wisdom or visions. This is how the division of the tribes originated and led to their demise.

I recently had a lifetime open up in which I was a man, and the spiritual leader of my tribe. I was married to a beautiful woman and had a daughter, who, in this life are my friends Jeannie and Sue. The recollection came up when I bought a used car from Sue's boyfriend. There were all sorts of problems with the car, and I kept trying to tell her boyfriend that he had misrepresented it. I had wanted to get the car checked out before I bought it, but he had assured me that was a waste of money because the car was in great shape.

As Lester had taught me so well, I went into meditation and asked the notorious *why?* The story surfaced that Sue's boyfriend had been a warrior in that Native American life. He had not listened to any of the wise leaders who said revenge and fighting was not the way. To make things more complicated, he wanted to marry my daughter (Sue). There was no way I was going to let my daughter marry him, because I saw his anger and lust for killing. He was furious about it. I tried to tell him his ways were violent, and he had to embrace the ways of the Great Spirit, but he didn't listen. In a vision I saw him doing a war dance dressed as a buffalo to curse me.

After the dance he was in a state of such hatred that he went out, and commissioned one of the other tribes to come in and massacre us, including my daughter, the one he loved.

I saw all this karma, and I was seething— I wanted to kill him! But, as always, we have to let it go and forgive otherwise we're stuck, so I released it. I called Sue and told her a little bit about what I had seen, but she became very defensive. I saw that her karma was to work through whatever she needed to with him. It wasn't about me. I wasn't a parent anymore and wasn't here to protect her, or tell her what to do. I had to detach from the situation.

The Native Americans misused the law the Great Spirit had laid down for them by fighting and drinking firewater. I have met many Native Americans in this lifetime. Two medicine men I met were into misuse of power, sleeping with many women and living amoral lives. When I visited the different Native American nations, I saw that they are living in some awful conditions, including poor diet and abuse of alcohol. It came to me, during one visit, that these depraved souls were actually the reincarnation of the Calvary men who had shot the Indians a hundred plus years ago.

In the early times there were great wisdom tribes. Author Ken Carey wrote *Return of the Bird Tribes* about the early tribes in this country living in total harmony. They reached deep states of communication with the earth, God and Spirit. The Indians revered Sedona as a very holy place, and they came there for their initiations. It's peaceful and I don't feel that any battles took place there. Another tribe in the eastern part of America, the Iroquois, were a circle of wise and holy elders who governed and lived in a real democracy.

There are some real shamans left. When Brian and I were living in Sedona, we went to a sacred Hopi dance where white people are usually not allowed. We had a friend who was very close to the Hopi. They let us watch a snake dance, which was one of the most sacred ceremonies I've ever seen. They each put a rattler in their mouths, and came out and danced in twos. If one man gets out of rhythm, it ruins the whole power of the dance. The twelve-year-old boys danced for the first time for their initiation into manhood into the Snake Clan. They were given the little ones that are the most deadly. Before they even dance with the snakes, they love and tame them (just as my dad taught me when I was young). A boy carrying a snake came up to us, and tried to tease and scare us, but I knew not to be afraid. It was an amazing dance and a great privilege to witness. They were real shamans and knew the art of concentration, love and dancing in harmony. I felt a unity consciousness there.

There was an old prophecy by the Hopi, that when the Red Hat came to the Hopi Nation, certain things would occur. The leader of the Tibetan Buddhist lineage, called the *Karmapa,* wears a red hat during ceremonies. The Hopi have been the earth keepers for a long time. When the *Karmapa* arrived, accompanied by Tibetan Monks, and performed a ceremony in his red hat, the Hopis greeted them with open arms as the one they had seen in visions. I feel there is a strong connection between Native Americans and the Tibetans. I had just come back from India when I went to the Hopi dances, and got lost in the chanting, which was similar to the Sanskrit chants.

The government found uranium within the lands of the Hopi Nation and tried to take back the land, the supposed "wasteland" they had given them a century ago! It is atrocious what the government has done with these beautiful people. I guess it's all karma somehow.

The great Native American tribes were, at one time, so close to the Great Spirit, that they could make corn sprout instantly. I knew a lady who was brought up with the Hopis, and as a girl she saw the ceremonial dance and watched the corn sprout right in front of her eyes; it was total concen-tration, faith and prayer. All the elementals, nature spirits and devas gave to them because they were in harmony with Mother Earth, as many still are.

The Divine Mother is very prevalent in Native American history. In the old teachings Native Americans look to Spider Grandmother as the Divine Mother image, and it dawned on me one day that Spider Grandmother is Durga! She has ten arms and looks like a spider, which is why they call her Spider Grandmother. Another aspect of the Divine Mother is Gaia. There is an opening in the Grand Canyon that goes to the very center of the earth and to a crystalline city where Gaia lives. I've heard that Gaia is one of the greatest aspects of the Divine Mother, and has taken over this whole planet as the overseer of Earth. She lives in the crystalline city and is in charge of all the devas, fairies, angels and nature spirits that are working for this planet. The Native American shamans call her Crystal Woman, and in my meditation groups, I used to ask her if we could go down to the crystalline city in our subtle bodies to heal us. She has departments of gnomes, fairies and elves who worked on us! Everyone would come back feeling incredible.

White Buffalo Calf Woman also is an aspect of the Divine Mother, and I've had two experiences with her. The first one, which I spoke of earlier, was when I was on top of Cathedral Rock during Wesak Festival, about 25 years ago, with Brian. We had gone up there to meditate because Cathedral Rock is one of the most powerful vortexes in Sedona. It is a feminine vortex, and it is said there is a crystalline city underneath. When Sri Karunamayi, an aspect of the Divine Mother whom I talk about later on, was visiting some years ago she went into *samadhi* looking at that rock. When she came out, she said, "*Rishis* inside the rock, above the rock, below the rock." She tuned into some very great beings around that rock.

The other experience I had with White Buffalo Calf Woman was when a friend asked me to come to his house and help him get through some very difficult times. He had a substance from South America called San Pedro— it was a cactus shamans use to make tea for ceremony and healing. He wanted to take the substance and have me monitor him through the experience. I agreed, but said we must dose test to make sure it wasn't toxic to his body. I wouldn't do it unless I knew he was going to be all right. I muscle-tested the dose, and saw that it was a fairly mild substance and would not be toxic, although I didn't know what its effects would be.

He took the tea and said, "Take just a teeny bit to be attuned to me, otherwise you might get into judgment. Take only a little so that you won't get off on it, but enough so you'll at least be attuned to the substance."

I felt it would be safe so I took a small amount, an eye-dropper full, then prayed for him, and set out our intentions that he would go through whatever he needed to, and I could help him with that karma.

The next thing I knew he was screaming! He was experiencing a life from Atlantis where he was tortured, so I started helping him through it with concentrated prayer. As I

*Thea pictured in front of Cathedral Rock,
one of her favorite places in Sedona.*

prayed, I happened to look out the window at the beautiful
sunflowers in his garden. It was a perfect day outside and
the next thing I knew, I was merging with the sunflowers.
That little bit I drank had an effect on me. I went into total
Oneness and started doing this dance of Ascension with the

grand helix. I was in ecstasy and beyond duality while my friend was screaming! Actually, I felt there was nothing to heal, because I saw only perfection. I was trying to help him while I was experiencing inter-dimensional levels of consciousness.

I had a memory of a Mayan lifetime, and suddenly I was in Machu Picchu, Peru, coming in on a spaceship. I was a star woman, and then I turned into White Buffalo Calf Woman. It was the port of entry where she came in. I thought, "My God! Maybe I'm an aspect of her!" I saw that Machu Picchu was my origination point to the earth from the stars. I've never been to Machu Picchu, but I'd love to go. My friend, whom I was monitoring, goes to Lake Titicaca every year to study with shamans. They put him through a lot of tests, one of which was going into the water with alligators to conquer fear.

I managed to get my friend through the San Pedro experience, and afterward said to him, "Holy cow! It's unbelievable how something so little can do so much! It brought me into a unity experience with all the rocks and plants and trees; I totally merged with everything." I felt very fortunate for that experience.

White Buffalo Calf Woman has become a part of me. I want an artist to draw her because I haven't seen anyone so beautiful! She's like Lakshmi; the picture I have doesn't do her justice. White Buffalo Calf Woman has a face like Mataji (Babaji's sister) with high cheekbones, and she is one of the most beautiful of the goddesses. Goddesses have a celestial quality that exceeds any earthly beauty because they're so high in frequency and love.

From times as a Native American medicine woman, I've seen that we used peyote, a form of cactus, for rituals and healing. We used it every nine years under very strict circumstances, including fasting, sweat lodge and prayer, and had miraculous results. We were told if we didn't use it for healing we would lose all our powers. I saw that natural plants could be used in a very high shamanic way for healing and speeding up karma, but I still don't recommend it to people, because I see how it can be misused. People want the high, but what they really need is to be disciplined and meditate, and leave the poor plants alone. Power plants should only be used infrequently for sacred occasions and with trained shamans or qualified facilitators.

One other time I tried a mushroom that only shamans could use. A neighbor was a follower of Terrence McKenna, and he asked our group if we wanted to try it. I had an aversion to drugs because my Masters always told me they were unnecessary for me as a meditator, so my first reaction was no, no, no, absolutely not! Then he said, "I want you to be open-minded, and go within, and ask if this would be a tool of evolution." So I did, and much to my surprise I didn't receive the definite "no" I expected. I was told it would be a good experience for me, but it would have to be done under strict ritual. So with the permission of the Divine Mother, I decided to try it.

I was able to determine the right dosage through muscle

testing. I went off by myself, totally surrendered to God, and asked for the substance to be blessed before I took it. After I swallowed it, I got horribly sick to my stomach, threw up, and then suddenly was hit with ecstasy. I knew I needed to lie down, and as soon as I got to my bed, I was knocked out into total bliss. I merged with a large eagle and we flew together into the future. I saw the light center on Maui, and understood it was a designated light center, because of the crystalline energy under the earth that was being activated by space beings. The eagle showed me there would be light centers all over the world with beautiful soul groups coming together, praying and meditating, and sending tremendous light to heal Mother Earth. These souls would go into an inter-dimensional realm where we could see beyond the beyond, and go to any galaxy because we were omniscient. I was very grateful for this experience. I've always dreamed of light centers all over the world, where people could grow together in safety and love, and become enlightened.

WALK-INS

O ne of the most beautiful books written about "walk-ins" is called *Strangers Among Us* by Ruth Montgomery. It explains how highly evolved beings from other planets come in by taking over the bodies of people who are karmically exhausted, and want to leave the physical plane without dying. The Masters facilitate the whole process. Once the soul agrees to leave the body — and there is total agreement between these souls — then another soul from a higher dimension enters into that body. It is another way of leaving the body, and a way for an evolved soul to come in, and do high work without having to be born into an infant body. The walk-in does not assume the other soul's karma, other than what they experience in the body at the cellular level. The soul who leaves the body benefits, by getting a rest from karma and going to another realm for a "vacation" until they are ready to be reborn.

When Brian and I were living in the La Cueva Valley in

New Mexico, we were often called to clear energies. Heavy curses were put on that valley by Hispanics who were being harassed by the government.

It involved some old Spanish land grants and the government's refusal to honor them. In New Mexico the Spanish curse each other by going to brujos, or black magicians, who perform all sorts of dark rituals to hurt one another. The Native Americans also have rituals used to curse the Hispanics and white people. It's an intense place for curses! That valley was also loaded with discarnate beings from a huge battle that had taken place in Glorieta during the Civil War. Brian and I cleared the whole valley.

We were known in the area for our work, and one day a woman from Santa Fe approached me and said that a very strange thing had happened to her. She thought I could possibly help. She said, "My husband went to a spiritual retreat in the Pecos Benediction Monastery, and came back a different person. I know it is not my husband. It is his body, but it's a different soul and I'm freaked out. I can't sleep with him or even have him in the same house. I paid for an apartment for him because I don't know what to do with him!" She had prior knowledge of walk-ins and wondered if he might be one. She was a compassionate woman and knew he probably needed help in adjusting, so she asked for my help. I readily agreed, and we made arrangements for him to begin treatment.

I had met and dealt with walk-ins before. Many claim to be walk-ins, but they are not. Such people enjoy the drama of imagining they are some high being from another planet, so they can dodge their karma, or pretend to be somebody different. Authentic walk-ins don't want others to know who they are. They will reveal it only if we are at their level or if we can treat them therapeutically, but they will ask us not to tell anyone.

The woman's husband, whom we will call Joe, came to me for therapy. He was a beautiful soul and a great healer. Her "true" husband had gone through tremendous dark karma, and his soul was very tired and weary. When he was at the monastery, he wanted out, and made an agreement, that when his soul left the body, a very great being would come in. A walk-in takes over the karma of the previous occupant at the cellular level of the physical body, but not the karmas in the non-physical bodies (i.e., astral, subtle, causal). Many people who leave the body are desperate, and have gone through so much karma they just can't take it anymore. Because they have gone through so much karma and emotion, typically their bodies are not in great shape.

I learned that Joe was from a highly evolved planetary system. There were many souls in the Santa Fe area who were replaced with walk-ins that past Christmas. I continued to work with Joe by lifting the cellular memory of his new, albeit used, body. The karma retained in the cells of that body was very painful for him. so we sped up the process by asking the angels to come in, transmute it with the violet flame and release the old programming.

Joe's wife drove him to my place for treatments. Even

though the relationship was still estranged, I noticed she was wearing makeup, and looking more glamorous than I had ever seen her! After some weeks passed she told me one day, "I'm falling in love with this new being. He is so high, selfless and beautiful, and is everything I've ever wanted." To make a long story short, they fell in love and remarried. Their children thought he was the same dad, and only a few people knew he was a walk-in. Joe took over the former soul's occupation, and became a tremendous healer, because he brought in all this knowledge from the higher realms.

Joe was able to go into very deep meditation with me, and one day we sensed we were being psychically attacked. We soon learned it wasn't only us. Based on the number of calls I received, many people in the Sante Fe area were feeling intense negative energies. As usual, my investigative nature took over, and I began to track the source.

Joe and I discovered the energy was coming from alien space ships operated by the Greys. Our government was upset with the Greys over the misuse of energy, and broke a contract they had with them, so the Greys were retaliating with a psychic attack on the area. This was an intrusion on free will, which was breaking karmic law. I don't like to be psychically attacked by anybody. I knew everyone around us was under this energy, so I went directly to the Prime Creator with a petition, "Is it possible for Archangel Michael to bind all these guys in the ships, and get them out and take them home?! They are causing trouble on this planet. The Greys have done horrible things to people, with experimentation and implants, and have really broken their agreement. Maybe we are being kind to let them be here and experiment, but it's time to get them out of here!"

Joe and I worked together holding the energy as we meditated, and soon both of us felt the psychic attack being totally lifted. God had answered our prayers. Not long after, I had an interesting call from my friend. She said she was driving home from work one evening, and saw many lights going into the sky, as if a large group of ETs were going home, or being taken off the planet. She added she felt a huge energy shift as she witnessed it. I said, "Oh yes, that was just the bad guys being sent home by God!"

My primary work with walk-ins is to get them adjusted to the planet. It's a shock when they arrive in spite of the preparation they have done. They study the Akashic Records of the soul's body they are entering, and hang around them in the astral plane for a long time. So in addition to helping walk-ins adjust to the planet, I help them release the cellular memory of the vehicles they embody, which are often ill. It takes a lot of work to free it of the cellular karma and programming, but once the body is cleared, they are able to fully incarnate. That sometimes takes years to accomplish.

Years ago Brian and I went to North Carolina for a seminar, and I couldn't take my eyes off of a certain beautiful woman. It wasn't her physical beauty that caught my attention, but her beautiful energy. I noticed that she was feeling isolated, so I went over and introduced myself to her. After a few weeks of knowing each other, I could tell she wanted to share what turned out to be an incredible story. By then Brian and I had read the Himalayan scriptures[31] and we knew certain information about the Illuminati reptilian plan to take over planet earth at this time. Their intent, planned long ago, was to make us a slave race. We knew about the prominent Illuminati families, who have been written about by David Icke. They have been reincarnating ever since Lemuria as part of the fallen angels/reptilian plan.

The woman, whom I'll call Sue, said she had escaped from one of the prominent Illuminati families in Europe. Her mother had been artificially inseminated with the sperm of Hitler, and Sue, along with five other children were born as part of an experiment. She said from the time she could remember there were "white coats" coming around to observe them, always writing on their clipboards. The children were never shown love, Sue didn't know who her mother was. When she was three years old, she started participating in Illuminati ceremonies and black rituals. She was forced to perform oral sex on men, and witnessed them killing babies and drinking the blood.

Sue said she had a compulsion to have sex with younger men. She would spot a young man and want to hop into bed with him. She was brought up with extreme wealth and was constantly watched. Her guardians picked her friends and whom she would marry. Everything was planned. On the

31   The Himalayan scriptures is a manuscript of the Akashic Records that were dictated by a master telling of the future of Planet Earth. They warn humankind that if we do not change we will be taken over by the dark forces.

Brian and Thea at a seminar in North Carolina.

outside, she appeared to have everything she wanted, but it was a lonely and stilted life. Sue told me she had wanted to die. When she was 15 years old, she was hit by a car. While unconscious, her soul was met by very elevated beings. They gave her a choice of returning to her life or going to a peaceful place of reprieve, so that a walk-in from a highly evolved planet could come into her body. Her soul was very happy to leave the body, so the walk-in came in and took over. The "new" Sue recovered from the accident, and played the game of being the daughter in that family. Of course she had to take on the cellular memory of the body and the many aberrations of programming from infancy. Because she was so beautiful, she was often used for sexual ceremonies.

It must have been the plan for her to leave, because someone within the secret circle took mercy on her, and helped her escape. Both of them knew that if she was found trying to escape, she would be killed. They also knew a formidable effort would be made to find her. Sue changed her name and traveled to different countries, never staying in the same place for long. Her evolved soul sought the company of spiritually elevated people, and by the time I met her she was unfolding like a flower. I was amazed by her story, because I had just learned about the prominent Illuminati families; and suddenly, here was Sue, a woman with first-hand experience.

I've had many encounters with people who claim to be walk-ins, but I want to emphasize it is a very danger-ous game. They are usually people with psychological problems and are trying to escape who they are. The real walk-ins are on assignment, and are humble, and do not want people to know who they really are. Walk-ins are an amazing phenomenon of this planet, and they are all over. Typically they are at the end of their karma and want to evolve.

I met another woman who had been abused, molested, and suffered greatly. This woman had endured hell, and wanted out, and a walk-in came into her body. I've never seen such a change in my life. She went from being a mess, to a great healer with great wisdom. I mention this now because I want people to know that many great beings have come in. If there have been sudden personality changes within a person, or suddenly they are great healers, it is very possible they are walk-ins.

MOVE TO HAWAII AND
ATLANTEAN KARMA

One winter Brian and I were invited to teach our healing arts on the Island of Maui. Brian always wanted to go to Hawaii, and the opportunity to escape the cold temperatures in Sante Fe for a tropical paradise made it an easy decision. Solomon, an old friend of ours, sponsored the course, and since he knew just about everyone on the island, he was able to pull in a large audience. It was an instant success. As we ate mangoes and papayas, and basked in the beauty of this Hawaian Island, Brian pondered, "What are we doing in Santa Fe? It's freezing there! We have an instant clientele here, and are being very well received. I think we should move here. I know we could make it."

I whole-heartedly agreed. We had made fast friends, and knew of many others who wanted healing, so when we returned to Santa Fe, we made arrangements to move.

When we told Dr. Scherer of our plans, he became deeply saddened. We loved each other, and cried over the end of a beautiful chapter in our lives together.

We felt we were being called back to Maui. The island of Maui had an unmistakable love vibration, and we had clients on that island as well. About that time one of our students from Massachusetts, Robert Wesley, a Dartmouth graduate and music major, had asked if he could join us. We were happy about the prospect, and told him we'd find a big house where all of us could live together.

Robert flew out to Hana with his girlfriend, who happened to know of a man, Jim Caldwell, who lived in Kipahulu, on the other side of the island. When they went to visit him, Robert told Jim about a healing course he had just completed with Brian and me. When he mentioned our names to Jim, he exclaimed, "Oh my God! I know Indira![32] I know Brian!" I had met Jim years before at Papa Ramdas' ashram in India. He was a direct disciple of Yogananda, who had made Jim a *yogacharya*, a lay minister, and he had a large group in Southern California. After he remarried a fourth time, he moved to Kipahulu. Jim was ecstatic when he learned we had moved to Maui, and he insisted we be neighbors and work together.

Brian and I had fallen in love with Kipahulu. As our eyes feasted on the most beautiful place we had ever seen, Brian said, "The lucky dogs who are getting away with living here!" Little did we know we'd be two of them!

---

32   Indira was my first spiritual name given to me by Papa Ramdas.

To our delight, we found a big house for rent near Jim, and Brian, Robert and I moved in. We spent hours meditating together, and not long after, we began the Clear Light Retreats to teach meditation, and our healing system. My preference was to focus on meditation and the *Shakti,* because it was a powerful way to reach large groups of people, and the Divine Mother always honored our groups with her grace.

We developed a retreat program to honor all religions. The retreat began with mantras to Lord Shiva, the destroyer of ignorance, and a lot of karma was always released on that first day! The following days were each dedicated to a different religion or deity, including the Divine Mother, Jesus, Mother Mary, and Tibetan Buddhism. The program was designed to release karma quickly, and was balanced with chanting, meditation and healing work.

We all had our talents, and they complemented each other. Jim and I offered the prayers and transferred the energy, or *Shaktipat*. Brian helped with the healing, and Robert was an absolute genius with music. I taught him the mantras, and he could write songs at the drop of a hat and channel energy with perfect tone. He could sing and play any instrument, and do both with incredible devotion. The music was such a science. It unified the group in joy, raised energy levels and lifted the group into meditation.

Jim, Robert, Brian and I did so much meditation and healing work together, that Jim suggested we move to one of the four houses on his neighboring 12-acre lot. Every day we took long walks together and chanted God's name and we would get so high we could hardly leave each other anyway. It was a natural transition for us to move into one of the houses.

We continued our retreats on Jim's land. The location was abundantly beautiful, and had a very high-energy vibration. In meditation, the Divine Mother kept coming to me and saying, "This is your land and it is to be used as a light center." For seventeen years, I had seen a vision of land overlooking the ocean, and it became clear this was the land. The land was for sale; we just didn't know how we were going to buy it. Robert was living off a family trust, Brian and I were living off our healing work, and Jim was living off his savings.

One day Ron Morris, a successful real estate millionaire, came out to look at the land and wanted to buy it with cash. Jim pulled Ron aside and said, "Ron, I know you are in love with this land, but we have been trying to energetically hold it for a light center. We've been told through divine guidance this is our land, but we don't have the money for it yet. Could you please give us a chance to buy it?"

Ron had practiced Transcendental Meditation for years and understood our plight. He said he would love to give us a chance, and if we were successful in buying the land, he'd even buy the parcel next to it, and attend our retreats! Ron and Jim ended up becoming very good friends. We later learned there was an established karmic tie between us. Ron had been my brother in a life in Atlantis, and Jim had been our father.

After Ron left we thought, okay, now what? We had enough money to put the land into escrow, but had no idea how to make the payments. I suggested we go on a week-long fast and pray to God for the answer, which we did. On the fifth day of the fast I realized I had become attached to the land, and had doership in trying to obtain it. I asked God for the doership to be released, and to surrender to the highest purpose for the land and us. I felt the attachment dissipate, and I went into a very high state of bliss. I knew it was not my problem- it was Divine Mother's problem!

After the fast, Jim, Robert and I got together and compared notes. We had all had similar experiences. We learned it was our land, but we had to let it go and give it up to God. Three days after that experience, Robert's father called and told him he was now of age to receive a substantial family trust. It was enough money to buy the land, and Robert bought it. It was a blooming miracle.

Jim Caldwell

Shortly there-after we began the retreats, and the money we made was put back into the land for improvements. We added a bunkhouse, dining hall and built two beautiful octagonal-shaped buildings with pagodas at the top, which intensified the energy like a pyramid. We made it into a beautiful sanctuary.

Between retreats we'd work on ourselves. I fell into the leadership position, and my job was to keep everyone moving.

Brian and Thea toast to their marital union!

An amazing phenomenon began to occur. Each group that came in to attend our retreats had the same karmic time line. The story began to unfold of how we had been reincarnated time and time again not only individually, but also as a group. Each person within the group would add parts to the story. It started with groups who had lived during the Atlantean civilization. I retraced that life and remembered I was a high priestess, Brian was my husband, Jim was my high priest father, and Robert was my son. Jesus was Amelius, the overseeing spiritual head of The Temple Beautiful, and Brian and I were his coordinators.

Brian and Thea formally married in Maui. From left, Robert Wesley, Brian, Thea and Jim Caldwell.

Ron Morris was my brother, and went the way of the dark. Many of the light workers were from soul groups brought down from higher realms beginning in Lemuria, an ancient civilization before Atlantis. We were all together again as a group, and the same dichotomy was happening in Maui.

Near the decline of the Atlantean civilization, the dark forces came to this earth to control it, and make us a slave race. The dark forces were a combination of fallen angels, the reptilian race, and other souls who had misused energy. They chose the planet earth, because it was one of the most beautiful of all planets. The reptilians were a group of souls from another planetary system who were very scientific, into control and manipulation, and not into their hearts. All the groups became a team with the common goal of controlling the world, and preventing souls from being united with God. To advance their ambition, the reptilians created engram command phrases that were implanted into the subconscious while in a state of trauma. The phrases, such as "the more you try, the more you will fail" or "you will never be happy in love," were implanted into a person's subconscious to form a repetitive "loop" that would trap him or her into an endless cycle of failure. For the engram phrase to be successful, a trauma had to be associated with it, so the dark forces would rape or torture a person or loved one until they were in a state of apathy or unconsciousness.

The dark forces convinced many of the light workers that this new technology was positive; of course, they did not reveal the phrases they'd be using, or how they would be implanted!

When I was living during the time of Atlantis, I had serious reservations about it, because I saw it was interfering with free will. One memory came to me where I was projected on a large screen, similar to a movie screen, and I was trying to tell the Atlanteans what was really happening. The dark forces were way ahead of me, however, and had programmed the screens with a subliminal message that said, "She is a fanatical and crazy high priestess that cannot be trusted." They had also programmed me with the engram phrase command, "When you feel the mistrust of the people, you will become powerless." They created the perfect loop to ensure my failure. The subliminal messages worked on the audience, and I could feel their doubt, which triggered the command phrase in me.

They caught Brian and surgically turned him into an automated programmed robot, by performing a sort of lobotomy. I escaped from the temple with my son (Robert) to the mountains, where Amelius had another temple. I'm not sure what happened to Amelius. I believe he escaped after he told all of us to get out. The dark forces could read minds, and although I screened my own thoughts, they used Brian to get to me. The dark forces cleverly sent to the mountain retreat twelve men that I knew, loved and trusted, and whom they had programmed. They overtook me by stunning me with laser guns. They raped and implanted me with, "Everyone you love will always betray you." I died shortly afterward, and they took my son, and raised him to serve the dark forces.

My father (Jim) tried to save his son (Ron), who had been indoctrinated into serving the dark forces, but Ron was too far gone to save. Jim was a powerful high priest, so the dark forces gave him the implant of "If you make a stand, everything you believe in will crumble." It completely derailed his power to stand up against his son. The dark forces were experts in administering this technology, and had everyone exactly where they wanted them.

In the end, the light workers saw through what was really happening and attempted to fight the dark forces, but it was too late. The gross misuse of energy came crashing down onto the Atlantean civilization, to its ultimate demise from a catastrophic earthquake. Whenever there is a gross misuse of energy, the divine law of cause and effect will create circumstances, such as an earthquake, to destroy the offenders. All the light workers were given a chance to evacuate into Christed space ships before the catastrophe.

The same beings that attacked us in Atlantis found us in Maui. The Divine Mother would warn us that they were sending more dark forces in. At first it was kind of exciting, but then it wasn't fun anymore, because we were under constant psychic attack. The Divine Mother told us, "You are retracing the same experiences that happened to you in Atlantis. Just go through it, release it and go above it. These beings that are sent in are getting the chance to choose the light or the dark. They will either go deeper into the dark, or have a change of heart, and go into the light."

As we relived these karmas, we went through hell. When the implants came up they manifested as huge blockages, but at least we knew what was happening, and were able to identify the command phrases through meditation. We ended up with pages and pages of them. Divine Spirit taught me how to release the implants, and move people, including the retreat staff, through these horrendous karmas. Over the course of events, many souls who had been programmed, or had performed the programming came to Maui. Some of them knew who they were and wanted to change, and others were just switchboards to the dark. Everyone who attended the retreats was told how the reptilians and fallen angels had joined forces, and had used advanced technology to prevent the light workers from reaching the step of Ascension.

Our team worked beautifully together until one man, whom I'll call Joe, was accepted into the group. Joe was one of Jim's disciples from many years before and came to Maui to be with Jim. Joe stayed some years until he met and married a bipolar[33] woman, who became an incredible dark switchboard for our group. I knew she was very dark, and felt her psychically attacking me. I couldn't say anything to discourage their wedding, because I felt it would have interfered with free will.

Psychic attack is a phenomenon which uses a person as a switchboard to negative energy. The dark forces can only use a person who exhibits the lower emotions born of duality, such as greed, power, envy or jealousy; otherwise they cannot use them as a means to transmit negative energy. Jealousy is rooted in a feeling of not being whole, and

33 In my experience, I have found that people that are bi-polar have misued energy in the past and are trying to learn in this life the difference between power and surrender.

———

173

wanting what another person has. In divine love, there is enough love for everyone. Psychic attack can also be from unresolved past life karma.

The marriage with the bipolar woman eventually fell apart, and Joe joined our group. It seemed like a good decision at first, because we worked well together. There had to be complete trust between us to get through the karma, due to the vulnerability of pulling up such deep pain and raw emotion. But then the synergy between us began to falter, and suddenly I was the only woman in a man's world. I knew I was very important to the success of our team, and was bewildered when they not only began to turn against me, but also attempted to discredit me. It was very painful to go through because I loved them all so much. We had done incredible work for eight years, but I couldn't fight what was happening and knew it was time for the group to separate. I also saw it was the destiny of the two younger men to get out into the world and marry. The retreat facility was just too isolated for them.

I didn't know it at the time, but we were going into another karmic time slot from Egypt, when a wicked patriarch had taken over. All of us were from the same soul group and had remained unified in Lemuria and Atlantis, but became divided during the Egyptian lifetime.

When it was time to give up our light center on Maui, I prayed that the right people would buy it (and they did). In addition to its magnificent beauty, we had seen in the etheric realm that two Lemurian temples had also been on the land.

BACK TO THE MAINLAND AND
EGYPTIAN KARMA

About the time our group was falling apart, a close friend of Jim's called and asked him to head up a Yogananda community in Michigan. His friend had previously run the 800-acre facility, and had done a wonderful job building it up. Jim, Robert and I decided to move to Michigan and continue our Clear Light Retreats, and Brian decided to go to India for a time. My job was to bring in the Divine Mother and *Shakti,* and lead the retreats, and I was also instrumental in adding to staff.

It went really well for about a year until something happened at one of my women's retreats. There were about 60 women in attendance, three of whom were wives of an established, all male board of directors. During the retreat the *Shakti* zapped one woman and she began to channel Mother Kali. She went around the group fiercely calling out people's egos. With only a touch, she tapped into one's deepest secrets, which one was hiding or denying. In India the Divine Mother comes through many people and it is a natural phenomenon to allow that to happen. I knew it was Divine Mother's grace coming through, and thought it was fantastic, so I allowed her to continue.

The three board-of-directors wives were extremely upset about the strange manifestation they had neither experienced before, nor understood. They were accustomed to formal meditation retreats where everyone sat for hours with straight backs, which we did also, but my retreats were much more than that. I could feel their negativity blocking the energy of the rest of the group, so I prayed to Divine Mother for them to leave. As if in answer to my prayer, the three women left in a huff. The retreat really took off then. We chanted the *Narvana* mantra[34] and went into high states of bliss. If in a group, the energy of one or more people is resistant, the whole group is thwarted. There must be harmony for a group to go into the unity experience.

I knew there might be repercussions from the incident, but little did I know how deep they would go. The women went back to their husbands, told them about the bizarre happening, and how upset they were that the meditation retreat leader could let a "crazy woman" get so out of control.

The following Sunday I was chosen to speak at the temple, and saw the three women in the audience glaring at me. I prayed to Divine Mother, "Please help me to not

34   The *Narvana* mantra is one of the highest of all the Divine Mother's mantras.

be influenced by these women. Keep me above it, keep me in love, keep the vibration we had going from the retreat." When I walked up to the podium the Divine Mother took over and entered me. To this day I don't know exactly what I said, something about love and Oneness, because I was reveling in an incredible unity experience. I was everyone and everyone was me, and when I looked upon the three women I saw them as the Divine Mother. After my speech, or rather Divine Mother's speech, the three women came up to me crying and apologizing. It was a beautiful healing between us. Unfortunately, the healing did not carry over to the board. Even though their wives had experienced an epiphany, the men continued to view the occurrence as an unacceptable format for the retreat center.

In a sort of witch-hunt fashion, I was summoned before them. I had a feeling they would confront me, so before the retreat was over, I asked each of the participants to write a testimonial, all of which were glowingly positive. It made no difference. The men were very patriarchal and regimented about how the Clear Light Retreats *that I had created* should be conducted, and spontaneously letting in the *Shakti* was not part of the plan. I really didn't like these men! Jim was getting more into ego and had started sleeping around with women, so I didn't get any support from him. It seemed like a good time to leave.

After the chastisement I received from the board-of-directors, I decided to fly to Germany for Mother Meera's *darshan*. Mother Meera encompasses all aspects of the

Divine Mother in one.

When I arrived for her darshan, she touched me on the temple and the top of the head, and brought in the powerful light of *Paramatman,* the Supreme Being, the All. Mother Meera is the first one in the history of earth to bring this light to humanity. Being in her presence was like a healing balm on my heart, and put me into wonderful bliss. As I sat in meditation, I asked whether I should continue to work in Michigan, and I felt the answer "No" come to me. It was a fairly big decision, so I decided to seek Mother Meera's counsel.

The protocol for phone consultations with Mother Meera is to contact her assistant. The assistant asks Mother Meera the question and relays the response back. Mother confirmed it was time to move on, and that the Divine Mother's energy would be thwarted at the Michigan retreat center no matter what I did.

Reenergized and spiritually lighter after my time with Mother Meera, I decided to go to Denmark to meet Alf Hibberton, a man that Jim and Brian knew. He was in possession of Himalayan scriptures that foretold the future of our time. Alf owned a shipping company, but loved the Divine, had lived in India, and studied under an Indian master. He then traveled to the Himalayas where he prayed in earnest to be an instrument of God. Not long after, an adept knocked on Alf's door and said, "God has heard your prayer, and I am here to answer it." Under the adept's arm were a number of scrolls, which he explained were

Himalayan scriptures based on the Akashic Records[35]. The adept spent many weeks with Alf, reading the scrolls and helping him understand their content. In short, the scrolls described how the reptilians and fallen angels would come into key positions in government, and try to take over the world, and make a slave race. The adept told Alf it was imperative that the people were made aware of this plan, so they could prevent it from happening.

Alf graciously agreed to let me stay with him while he showed me the scriptures. While I was there I met a couple who lived downstairs, who asked me to do some healing work on them. We all became close, and I suggested we go on a cleansing fast, to help facilitate clarity and a deeper understanding of the scriptures. A few days into the fast, Alf started exhibiting strange signs of paranoia, claiming that the KGB was after us. He told me if I tried to leave the apartment he'd have to knock me out for my own protection! The couple downstairs was also aware of his temporary insanity, but none of us wanted to call the police and get him in trouble. Alf was a large man so I knew I had to be clever about my escape. The opportunity finally arose. The moment he became distracted, I dashed to the door with my heart pounding, and ran down the stairs like I had never run before! I rushed to the couple's apartment and they excitedly ushered me in. We were all extremely relieved. It was Thanksgiving Day and we rejoiced together and enjoyed a

35   The Akashic Records refers to a subtle substance called akasha where every thought, action and word of every human being in existence is recorded and kept for all time.

wonderful dinner. I also made flight arrangements back to Michigan. The next morning I went up to get my things, and Alf had calmed down by then.

When I returned, I went into a period of meditation to figure out what had just happened. It seemed no matter where I went— Maui, Michigan, Denmark— the same dynamic was coming up of being controlled by men. The story line of a past life surfaced, during which I had been a priestess in Egypt. Alf had been my brother in that life, and had been swayed over to the wicked brotherhood, just as all the others had. The brotherhood was into power, not love, and those who made a stand, like me, were a threat, and had to be silenced.

When I stayed with Alf in Denmark I told him I had seen Mother Meera, and he emphatically stated that the Divine Mother was evil. We were living the same scenario that we had lived in Egypt, with all the same characters. In Egypt the dark brotherhood had killed me, and Alf was nearly successful in Denmark!

By this time, Brian had come back from India and set up a naturopathic practice in Boulder, Colorado. During the time we were apart we never lost contact. We wrote often, and when he returned to the states we spoke on the phone. Both of us understood the need to give each other space, and not to hold each other back from our spiritual growth. I rejoined him there, and the Egyptian life continued to unfold. Interestingly, Brian had rented an apartment in the mountains from a man who belonged to an Egyptian society! I was under psychic attack from Alf, who was remotely working with Brian on the Himalayan scriptures, and was trying to "save" Brian from me. What we realized was that we were reliving the end of the Egyptian civilization, when the reptilians had come in with the same goal, to take over and make a slave race. Brian and I had weathered many, difficult karmas previously, and it was a great comfort to be with him to work this one out also.

CALLED TO NEW YORK TO TESTIFY

I was still in Boulder when I was summoned to New York to be a main witness in a trial. One of our dear friends, Christian, had been accused of assaulting and sexually molesting a woman.

The last time I had seen Christian was the previous summer, when I had conducted a Clear Light Retreat in New York. Ammachi, a Hindu spiritual teacher and aspect of the Divine Mother, was also in New York. A group of us went to see her, including Christian, and Debra, a young woman he had just met. We were all high as kites after seeing the Divine Mother, and joyfully headed to an Indian restaurant for dinner. Debra and I started talking, and I was delighted to learn she had attended my dad's camp years before, and I had been her counselor! I was so happy to see her, but sensed she was putting on airs and trying to be more sophisticated than she was. I was glad she was with Christian, and hoped he would be a positive influence on her.

We were enjoying a marvelous meal when I happened to

look up and notice Debra putting something in Christian's mango drink. A weird feeling came over me that something was amiss, and whatever she was putting in there was not good. I didn't say anything because of my past connection with Debra and the fondness I had for her. I just couldn't believe there was foul play. But just to be safe, after dinner I went up to Christian, who was getting a cab to take Debra home, and said, "If you take her home, do not go up into her apartment. Go straight home!" He was getting sleepy, and he agreed to follow my instructions. Well, he didn't. He was so drugged by the time he reached Debra's apartment, that he willingly followed her when she suggested he sleep over at her place. Christian at least had enough sense to sleep on the couch and not in her bed.

The next morning Debra rushed into my hotel room bleeding from a wound on her arm. I shouted, "Debra! What happened?!" She told me that she and Christian had argued and that he threw down a vase, which broke and ricocheted upward cutting her arm. I couldn't understand how a piece of pottery could bounce on the floor like that, so I immediately called Christian to get his side of the story. I noticed that Debra was acting a little strange and wouldn't make eye contact with me. She blurted out that she was going to the hospital, and then rushed out of the room. I turned my attention back to Christian on the phone, and he agreed that they had had an argument that morning, but it was because she accused him of molesting her. He was so angry at the outright lie that he threw a vase, but it in no way touched her.

We left New York, and a few months later Christian called and told me that he was being taken to court, because Debra claimed he molested her. He needed me to come out to be a witness.

Debra turned out to be a call girl for the mafia and she had been paid to frame Christian. He had innocently put a personal ad in the paper that read, "Rich man wants beautiful young wife," which naturally set him up as a target for foul play. Debra drugged him so that she could get him into bed, and claim that he had molested her, which she told the hospital staff when she arrived with her cut arm.

On a mission of justice, I flew to New York to save Christian. The minute I walked into the courtroom I felt I was under brutal psychic attack. Debra and her slick attorney glared at me. Christian's attorney was a kind, honest and salt of the earth type man, but not very dynamic. I couldn't believe my ears when Debra's attorney claimed I was a cult leader. I just looked at him and repeated what he said in a question, "Cult leader?" The witness wasn't supposed to talk, but I couldn't help it; I was stunned. I had a connection to the woman judge and I could tell that she knew that I was a good person and was having a hard time being called a cult leader. The jury saw it also.

During the recess the gravity of the situation took full hold. It also struck me that I had been followed earlier that day. When I left my hotel I had a vague feeling someone was watching me, but I didn't think much more about it.

When the judge called me to the stand, I explained the

whole story from my perspective. Debra looked at me with daggers in her eyes. She didn't want me there and knew darn well I saw through her charade. In spite of her unabashed resentment toward me, I felt sad and sorry for her. I wanted to pull her aside and ask her why she had gotten involved in this mess, but I couldn't talk with her during the trial.

The trial extended over a number of days, and during the weekend I visited a friend from Hyannis Port. He lived next to the Kennedy compound. I had a strong spiritual connection to John F. Kennedy. I loved JFK and knew why he had been murdered.

While I was at Hyannis Port my friend invited me to a huge celebration with friends and families of the Forbes. We took a ferry to Forbes Island and were all having a grand time, when suddenly the *Shakti* hit me. I couldn't function and knew I needed to go meditate in the woods by myself to understand what was happening.

I whispered to my friend where I was going, and as soon as I sat down, I immediately went into a deep state of meditation. Suddenly John F. Kennedy came to me. He downloaded me with so much information that it took me days to sift through it. He began by saying that his whole family was part of the Great White Brotherhood, which is an assembly of Ascended Masters to help evolve humanity, and to break up the dark forces.

Some of his family had sold out due to fear and had been roped into working for the dark side. John added, "You know why I was killed. I want you to come back here, and hold the energy for the United States, because there is an Illuminati headquarters in Barnstable and on Martha's Vineyard." He then showed me a ley line, or energy line, that connected Hyannis Port to Barnstable to Martha's Vineyard, and told me these were key places for me to hold energy.

When I came out of meditation and returned to my friend's home, it all seemed surreal. Here we were, right outside of the Kennedy compound, waving to the Kennedy's as they drove by, and little did they know I had just been in contact with John.

I returned to New York, and to the trial, refreshed and bright, and ready to have justice win out. Dealing with the mafia was serious business indeed, and it was time to call in the power team from God. I passionately prayed to Archangel Michael, Divine Mother, the Justice of Liberty and the Truth Ray angels to come in and help!

Interestingly, the jury requested I restate my testimony so the judge called me back. Before I went into the court-room I prayed to the Masters to bind any negative or dark entities. I could tell the jury was also under psychic attack because they seemed very confused, so I cleared them too. I was called to the stand and presented my testimony again, and as I looked at the jury, I could feel they were totally with me. I felt such love for these innocent beings who were trying to figure out what was happening. All of a sudden I knew we had won. Sure enough, shortly after I went back to my room, I received the call we had indeed won.

I went back to the courtroom to congratulate Christian

and his team, and all of us were ecstatic and tremendously relieved. Before leaving I went over to Debra and said, "I am so sorry you had to get involved with this. You were my five year old in my group at camp, and I loved you so much. I want you to become that five year old again, and the good person you are. Get out of this! Get out of this!" She just glared at me, and I never saw her again.

I returned to Boulder and told Brian about my visitation from John F. Kennedy, and how he had asked me to return to Hyannis Port to hold the energy. Brian and I always followed our own paths, and I assumed he would remain in Boulder to work on the book about the Himalayan scriptures. He surprised me when he said, "No. You need a protector, and I can work on the book in Hyannis Port." Brian also wanted to separate himself from Alf, who had changed the content of the original scriptures and added his own opinions based on research he had done. The original manuscript had been burned and Brian feared the purity of the document would be compromised.

When we got to Hyannis Port, we temporarily stayed with my friend until we found a cute cottage to rent nearby. Brian continued to work on his book, and I focused on my assignment. JFK had told me some of the darkest energy in America was here, and that I had to help disperse it. By then I had learned how to bring in legions of angels and light beings into dark areas. In meditation I asked what the next step was, and the information came forth that a huge shipment of illegal drugs was coming into Barnstable Harbor, and that our government was involved. It was being shipped to different places from this key port. Brian and I sent legions of angels and Masters into this area and to the ley lines, and no sooner would we send the energies when black helicopters would fly over our house. At first I thought it was a coincidence, and then it started to feel like *Star Wars*. The dark forces can monitor where light is coming from, and when there is a shift in energy. The legions of light beings we were sending in created a huge shift of energy.

Wherever we went we always had a meditation group, and we had started one in Hyannis Port. We had been introduced to a number of people who followed the "Course Of Miracles." One person in particular, Lynn, introduced us to Michael, who was also on assignment from God to bring light to that troubled area. We all became a team, and met others who had been sent to Hyannis Port by God, and didn't know why they were there. They all began attending our Friday night meditations, and eventually we decided to join forces and hold the energy together.

Michael owned a newspaper and regularly printed articles about the Illuminati. His father had been the editor of *Time Magazine.* He had taught Michael how to read the Illuminati secret codes transmitted through newspapers and other publications. Michael was an outrageous character and was ready to fight them! The government had tried to kill him many times. They tried to drug him, and seduce him with beautiful women, but he knew their tactics and was always one step ahead of them.

Our new group started working together, and bringing in the light. In our meditations, we included prayers to God to ask where He wanted us to send light next, and then we focused all our thoughts to send light to that place. We learned to ask the Masters to don us with the cloak of invisibility, so the dark forces couldn't track us. It worked because no black helicopters flew over after that.

Many times when we would send energy into very deep and dark areas, large ape-like demons would come at me. They didn't scare me, and in fact I would reprimand them by saying, "You're in the wrong camp! You have to change over to the light — you know the light always wins. It's just a matter of time." Often they would try to deceive me by pretending to surrender to the light, but I always knew. One ape-demon did surrender in earnest. He got down on his hands and knees and started crying. I told him God was a softy and had already forgiven him, and that God would take over. That demon won my heart. I loved him! Brian said, "Did you know that Milarepa[36] tamed the demons and had them come over as *dharma* protectors? Maha Kala was one. When demons get it from the heart and come over to the light they are our best allies."

In between the time we spent bringing in light, we offered healing workshops and sessions on the island of Nantucket. I found it interesting that one out of every three

36 Milarepa was a great Tibetan master whose guru was Marpa. When Milarepa was a young man he used black magic against his family who unjustly stole his fortune. He repented and his guru Marpa was working out Milarepa's misuse of energy by having him build houses and then dissemble them. Milarepa spent years meditating in a cave where demons would come at him, and he learned to tame the demons and bring them to the light.

—

189

people who came to me was an incest victim. I had no previous experience with working with incest victims and asked spirit to help me. I learned when a child is sexually abused, they leave their body as a defense mechanism, and therefore do not have memory of the event. But the body's cells retain memories from all lives, past and present, and is where the memory has to be pulled from. When the victim began to remember, I would ask for release of the promise made to the perpetrator that they wouldn't tell anyone. I would call in their guides and angels to release the promise, and tell him/her it was safe to do so. Then I would ask the whole being to go back through the trauma as quickly and painlessly as possible so that it could be released from their time track.

After a year and a half we wanted to get out of Hyannis Port. Although we had done a tremendous amount of good, fighting dark energies that the Illuminati brought in through black rituals was an intense assignment. We eventually received permission to leave, and headed back to Santa Fe, New Mexico, a place that always had been good to us, and felt like home. It was where our healing practice had started, so upon our return we rented a small apartment, opened an office for our healing work, and our practice quickly took off.

LEMURIAN LIFETIME

It wasn't long after we had returned to Santa Fe that very deep grief began to surface. I had learned long ago that by going into solitude and asking any question, I would learn the answer from within. I asked where this grief was coming from, and the Lemurian story began to unfold.

Lemuria could be considered the Garden of Eden 80,000 years ago, when androgynous beings totally one with spirit came down from the angelic realms. We came in as soul groups in a very high state of consciousness, and volunteered to embody on earth to help free the planet from the dark forces. I realized that many people I was close to, including Brian, Robert, Jim, and others I had met, were part of my soul group who had reincarnated many times together, to hold the energy for the planet. We spent many lifetimes in this magnificently beautiful realm, where everyone and everything was completely integrated into love, unity and God. Our bodies were so refined, and our thoughts so pure, that any thought would immediately manifest. Lemuria was our entry point to the planet earth. Of course, when we volunteered to come to earth from those higher realms, it looked like a cinch because we saw everything as illusion. Well, it wasn't a cinch.

I don't know how or why we started to come into duality from this unified state, but I knew my grief was from this original separation. The grief I was experiencing was so deep, it was beyond description. I'm very brave at going through my karmas, but this one was so raw, painful and vivid, I had to call a friend to hold my hand while I went through it. I felt like I had done something terribly wrong, and wondered why I couldn't get back to God, into spirit, and into that wonderful feeling of peace and beingness. The grief didn't last long, but it was hell while I was in it. This must have been the original feeling of guilt from the fall from grace, by choosing the sense pleasures over spirit.

More of the story unfolded, and dealt with the dark forces, the same fallen angels and reptilians that we knew in Atlantis. Obviously we all agreed to partake in this experience, otherwise it would not have happened. It is my opinion that we agreed to come into duality, because we needed to experience everything human beings experience. As we fell into duality from the high realms of unity and Oneness, we became more human and were able to understand what duality is. We must have been arrogant, thinking we could never fall out of the Oneness state. I do know we needed to go through lifetimes of the human experience to come to the point where we are now, in order to return to our total

Oneness. We had to experience everything we ever had judged, and we have taken many parts in this grand play.

The end of the Lemurian civilization and beginning of Atlantis is the time slot when the reptilians and fallen angels joined forces and came to the earth. They used their advanced technology of genetic engineering and implantation to create duality, by separating the androgynous nature of Lemurians into men and women. As angelic beings identifying with Oneness and spirit, we couldn't conceive of masculine and feminine, because we were totally balanced in both.

The engram phrases the reptilians and fallen angels created were negative, such as "the more you try, the more you fail," which they placed below the unconscious mind in times of duress or unconsciousness. In the Lemurian temples, we had learned neuro-linguistic programming, which used positive, *conscious* affirmations to evolve people. The dark forces always take the light and twist it. There is great intelligence in the dark because they come from the light, but they use their knowledge to gain control and power.

There were twelve temples in Lemuria, as there were in Atlantis. Each of these twelve temples represented a specific ray, such as the love ray, the wisdom ray, the Ascension ray, truth ray, healing ray, and transmuting ray. (More about the rays will be discussed in a later chapter). We were all connected to one of the rays and its corresponding temple, and I was a high priestess to the transmuting ray. When all the temples came together they made one mandala, or complete circle, to form the absolute truth. Everyone in the temples honored one another, and was sincere in their efforts to bring forth that aspect of God.

Only when a civilization is floundering in its Oneness with God can the dark forces come in and implement their strategic plan of manipulation and power; otherwise, they are powerless. Lemuria was descending in frequency and vibration. Those of us that were in the pristine purity of Oneness and love began to feel a decline into duality and ego. The light workers in the temples began to compete with each other, became judgmental, and went into a matriarchal mode by de-emphasizing the masculine aspect of God.

A "great experiment" was going on as well. Because Lemurians were androgynous, the dark forces posed the proposition of separating the masculine and feminine portions of a being into male and female. They wanted to see if those souls could remain in Oneness, all in the name of positive growth. In order to do this, however, the Lemurians would need to undergo genetic engineering through advanced technology. The dark forces were very persuasive in convincing the Lemurians their experiment was for their highest good. As a result, many light workers were coerced into supporting them without truly understanding what they were doing. Genetic engineering tampered with the cellular makeup of humans, and the implantation of engram phrases interfered with free will. Both were meant to slow the process of a soul's spiritual evolution.

The results from splitting us into men and women

seemed to be a success in the beginning. For the first time, we experienced sexual desire, something we hadn't known before, because Lemurians didn't procreate in the animal way. When souls were brought into the physical realm, it was done mentally, through spirit, and the beings involved were in total agreement. The sexual drive was very strong, and created a need to complete oneself with another person. Because we had retained a certain degree of bliss, it was an incredible union both spiritually and physically. But something unexpected happened. No longer were we in the state of bliss and Oneness, complete within ourselves. We needed another to feel complete, and if our partner became interested in another being, the pain of separation was beyond anything we had ever known. Trust issues surfaced, and procreating in the animalistic way pulled us farther down into the senses.

In my particular case, Brian was a soul mate. He was coerced to join the dark side, and was manipulated to work for the dark against his will, although he knew it wasn't right. As his partner, I didn't know what to do. I had lost the ability to rise above it, so my only available option was to fight back. When we fight the dark we use the same techniques as the dark, because we are buying into the duality. When we are anti-something, we are in a negative state. And being in the negative state brings us down to the same frequency as whatever we are against.

Many of the greatest light workers were seduced into the dark, because they didn't fully understand what was happening. They were naïve and trusting, and the dark forces were very clever. It was also a valuable lesson for the soul to understand power and manipulation, versus surrender and love.

I had come into the senses for the first time, and was not able to get back into Oneness of spirit. I experienced a deep sense of loss of self through my separation from Brian, then endured the ultimate betrayal by him when he

Brian and Thea.

was coerced over to the dark. I had a very painful death in that incarnation. I was carrying Brian's child when the dark forces programmed and implanted me, and I was killed after childbirth, so they could use my baby for experimentation. I left that life in a very sad state.

In between worlds we always go back to our Masters,

and remember what it is like to be in the beautiful state of Oneness with God. There I remembered earth's duality is a plan for our evolution, and that Babaji is one of the original planners of this earth plane. There was an agreement among all of us that the light workers would reincarnate as soul groups during various dark periods of time, such as the end of Lemuria, end of Atlantis, and the end of Egypt, to counteract the negativity and hold God-light energies. The light workers would be sent to earth when the dark became more prevalent. Avatars are the world teachers who come to earth during history's darkest times to bring in light so we can be brought back into balance. Rama, Krishna, Buddha, and Jesus Christ were just a few of the great avatars of this world. The original soul groups incarnated at the same time with these great Masters, to work as a team and support each other to bring in the light.

As I relived my time track, I saw how I became more traumatized, and dropped more and more into duality. With each life I tried to hold the light and would end up getting cursed, implanted, raped or killed. I was on the front lines, so to speak, in the temples, seeing through the dark, holding the light, standing up to them, becoming a threat and then being killed. There were times when I was coerced into the dark under the guise of "good." In one life in Egypt, I fought the dark forces with all my heart and ended up becoming dark because of it, and of course, was killed again when I tried to stand up to them. My *sadhana* in this lifetime is to release all the accumulated traumas I haven't yet faced.

During Lemuria, Atlantis and Egypt, many of the light workers became very traumatized with genetic engineering and implants. Those of us who knew our mission was to leap out of this delusion, and go beyond our desires and attachments, kept trying through meditation, and prayer, and tremendous perseverance. All the attachments and aversions we hadn't released from other lifetimes, including forgiving our enemies, were given to us in subsequent lives in order to finally release. They are just mirrors to our own darkness.

The plan has been to return to our original beingness, with the wisdom of non-judgment, by going through every human experience there is. Judgment was our original mistake. Judgment is whatever we deem right or wrong. "The dark is bad." "The light is good." The list goes on and on.

The dark forces have been an incredible mirror to our fear, so that we can go beyond duality and not fight them anymore. Duality is based on judgment and separation, not Oneness. The aim is to go beyond illusion, duality, judgment and pain, by playing out every experience through many lifetimes, both good and bad. After the lessons of all these experiences are learned, the goal is to go into total perfection, bliss, love, peace and the divine qualities of omniscience, omnipresence, and omnipotence.

Every incarnation is an opportunity to teach us more. Those of us who were part of the original soul groups from the angelic realms always knew we needed to get back, but when we tried, we became immersed in delusion again, looking outside of ourselves. Society had duped us into believing we would live happily ever after if we had lots of money, the perfect career, a big house, or if we were beautiful, we'd find a perfect partner and lasting love. Sometimes we do get what we want, but it is always temporary. Every fulfilled desire is impermanent. When we either lose what we've manifested, or become dissatisfied, we are miserable once again. Then what? At some point we all realize permanent happiness cannot be found from anything in this world, and we begin to ask ourselves, "Who am I?" "Why am I here?" "How can I find real happiness?" We experience an emptiness within that needs to be filled, but with what? When our souls cry out for the truth, our Masters, guides and angels come into our lives and guide us back to Oneness again. We have never known such an accelerated time, when many Christed beings are ready to leap back into their perfection. Many avatars of God are here, both in body, and on the other side, to help us take our final step back to perfection.

Lemuria was about the original fall from spirit identity into sense identity. The subsequent lifetimes of fighting the dark forces, and holding energies during strategic times were very important for all of us. As I have unfolded my karmas in this lifetime, I have met dear ones that I knew in the temples in Lemuria, Atlantis and Egypt, many of whom endured the same fate as I, being genetically engineered and implanted. In this lifetime all the implants are surfacing, to be released. It is difficult, because when the implants arise from the unconscious, we feel like we're stuck. It takes tremendous perseverance and discipline to get through and beyond them. The most effective way to achieve release is to petition God for a specialty team to assist us. Invoking the violet flame helps to transmute the karma that has already emerged. We are also doing this for all of humanity.

OUR BELOVED PETS

Animals that have come in as our pets are helping us to evolve tremendously. My pets have given me some of the greatest joy I have ever known, because they are pure, simple and uncomplicated. Ever since childhood, animals have been my unconditional friends. I realized at a young age we could telepathically understand each other. Because there were no barriers between us, my animals became very intimate with me. I've had some very special animals in this lifetime that I have helped evolve and they have helped me as well. They give us a chance to love unconditionally, and give back twice as much, because they are so pure.

Like us, they also have karmic traumas they have to go through, and receiving love from us helps our pets to break through them. We can call in the angels and ask them to release karma from animals just as we can with human beings, although animals are much better patients!

My healing practice also included working on animals.

There were two women who brought in King, their pet German Shepherd, for treatment. He was a huge, beautiful animal, frightened of men. We laid him on the living room rug and asked the Great Ones to come in and help King return to his time track where the trauma was being held, and release it. We watched King go through duress and release it. Then he sighed and relaxed.

When he was a puppy a robber broke into the house. King hid under the bed while his puppy sister bravely stood her ground and barked at the robber. She was too young to understand how vulnerable she was, and the thief kicked her to death. From that point on, King was terrified of men. However, after three repetitions of the healing technique, we knew the trauma had been completely released when he got up and licked Brian on the face!

I also saw that King had been an experiment in Atlantis where he was caged and genetically engineered to mate him with a human, a trauma that we also released from King's time track. These, and other horrific experiences were done at the hands of the dark forces, who were unconcerned with feelings or emotions, and interested only in bold science and experimentation.

Snakes, representing the *kundalini,* were once considered beautiful beings on this planet, but the dark forces manipulated the truth to make them evil. I've seen Masters come in as a white Cobra, a very high spirit snake, and I'm not afraid of them. Every being is a part of the self, a part of God. Poisonous creatures are a result of man's fear and hatred of them.

Another time, my friend called me to say she didn't know where her sheepdog was. We had done a lot of healing work together, so we both went into meditation and saw that he was tied up in her gardener's yard. She didn't know where the gardener lived, and didn't have any real proof he had taken the dog, so she couldn't confront him. We sensed the dog was terribly unhappy, so we sent him telepathic messages to escape and come home, which he did. The pads on his feet were torn and bloody from his long journey, and some of the rope that had restrained him was still hanging off his collar. His escape was a beautiful example of love and loyalty, and how connected we are to our pets.

I have had deep attachments with all of my animals, but for some reason I have bonded more deeply on a soul level with cats, more than any other species. Colonel Mud was an extremely high cat and quite a character. When he was a kitten he loved to jump up on the dining room table, although I always told him "no!" One day as he was about to jump onto the table again, I said, "If you jump up on this table your name is mud!" Without hesitation he jumped onto it anyway, and I stuck with my promise, and named him "Mud"! It wasn't dignified enough, so I added "Colonel" to it. My dad and I were always laughing at him. He was full of joy, fun and mischief, and constantly entertained us.

Colonel Mud and I would go very deep into meditation, and he always knew where my soul was. He never missed a meditation! He'd either get on my lap, or as close as he could, and start purring. We had him for about eight years.

Before he passed away, I kept seeing a man's form around him, and knew he was going to be reborn as a human. After he died, my dad and I gave him a beautiful memorial service, and buried him on the lot where he used to spend hours hunting. We sang songs of honor to him, and strongly felt his presence and love.

Later in my life, one of my former animal companions from a past life came in as a cat. Brian and I were living in a guesthouse in Santa Fe. One day we went out in the patio and spotted a beautiful golden kitten chasing a butterfly. It was love at first sight. He belonged to our landlady who had two dogs, but never a cat, so I don't think she understood them. He would come over to our house almost every day, and we'd play with him. We tried not to feed him because we didn't want to totally adopt him, but he adopted us and never wanted to go home.

We tried to think of a name that would suit our playful golden boy. We decided on Bodhisattva, which means "enlightened one," who comes back again and again, to give joy and to uplift people. I loved that he was so spunky. Brian would try to discipline him with the spray bottle, but Bodhi was not intimidated by a human being and stood up to Brian. Bodhi's behavior infuriated Brian, because he couldn't control him! Laughing, I said, "Brian - you have met your match!" Bodhi had never been a wimp, and eventually won Brian over because of his strong character.

When Bodhi was about a year old he got hit by a car.

It was a cold winter day. I was at the office and Brian was home. Brian called and told me to get home as fast as I could. Bodhi had been badly hurt, and had crawled all the way home after he was hit. His back legs had been crushed, and he pulled himself along with his front legs, and cried until Brian found him. When I got home and saw poor Bodhi I was horrified. We rushed him to the emergency; he was in such horrible pain that he screamed all the way there. The vet gave him morphine and said we should put him to sleep. We asked Bodhi's soul if he wanted to go or stay, and he wanted to stay. Brian was in the waiting room in meditation and complete concentration, doing *powah*, just in case Bodhi didn't make it. This Tibetan practice helps a soul exit through the top of the head in a very high state. We asked if there was anything that could be done, and the vet suggested hip replacement surgery, so we opted to pursue it. I could read Bodhi and I knew he didn't like it there. The staff were very scientific and matter-of-fact, so we took him home.

My dear friend Linda came over and we searched for a veterinary clinic that was more loving. We finally found a very kind doctor and I literally moved, with Bodhi, into the vet's office. My friend Martha helped me with homeopathic remedies for Bodhi's shock, trauma and pain, that I administered to him every fifteen minutes. We also had to build him up with iron before they could operate. I prayed constantly for Bodhi, and he relaxed and surrendered, because I was there with him.

The doctor said he was young enough to make it through the operation, which we spent a fortune on! But he was worth every penny. After surgery, we brought him home and had to keep him in a cage. I continued to pray constantly, gave him homeopathic medicines, and played the mantras. I noticed he relaxed any time we would play the healing mantra to Lord Shiva, and he didn't like any other mantras! Obviously, he was Lord Shiva's devotee.

We got him through that horrible ordeal, and not only could he walk again, but he could run, and climb trees just as if nothing had ever happened to him! The landlady wouldn't pay for the operations, so he became our cat. After that I took it upon myself to really train him.

I'd always felt close to my cats, but my relationship with him was beyond any I had ever had. There was a wild side to him. He was like a lion or tiger, and he would tackle people if they stopped petting him too soon. He would hiss and spit at people if he didn't like their vibration.

I decided to track our deep connection and went back into a lifetime in which he had been my lion in Egypt as well as my very faithful friend. We both came to a traumatic death in that lifetime. The dark forces killed us both at the same time, but now I was able to lift that former trauma from his time track, and mine as well.

Throughout the years Bodhi has gone deeper and deeper into meditation with me, and there are certain mantras he has preferred from the beginning! Recently I asked a friend of mine, who is also a seer, what she saw in him.

She closed her eyes and went into meditation and said, "Oh my gosh! I see him as a white-point tiger in the Himalayas. I see Babaji, you and me sitting there with the tiger as our pet." As I went into it myself, I saw that as a child I found the cub tiger, whose mother had been killed. I took him home and fed him with a baby bottle and spent every minute loving him, playing with him and bonding deeply with his soul. He heard the mantras chanted every day as he grew into a huge tiger. He was a large cat in two lifetimes, which is why he was never intimidated by human beings!

Lately when I go into deep states of meditation, he goes into them right with me. In the past he has wanted to go outside, but now, if he knows I'm going into deep states of meditation, he'll lay right next to me. Bodhisattva listens to chanting, meditates when I meditate, and is evolving at the speed of light.

We are helping our animals evolve tremendously, and they will Ascend also. Some animals are already high on the evolutionary scale, and will go into liberation, as Ramana Maharishi showed with Lakshmi, the cow. They are here to evolve and we have a tremendous responsibility to them. Anyone who Ascends and wants to bring their animals with them, can.

MEETING THE DIVINE MOTHER KARUNAMAYI

One day I was in a Santa Fe bookstore, and noticed a flyer announcing an upcoming local program for Karunamayi, the Divine Mother. I could tell by her photo that she was very sweet, so I decided to call the contact number. The woman who was sponsoring Karunamayi answered and said, "I'm scared to death! I've never done anything like this before. A saint is coming to my house, and I have no idea of Indian protocol." I enthusiastically replied, "I do! I'll help you!" And I just took over.

The day of Karunamayi's arrival, we drove to the airport to pick her up. About a half hour before her plane landed my friend and I started crying uncontrollably for no apparent reason. It was the same kind of deep longing I had felt in India, when I cried for the Divine Mother. The plane arrived, and out walked a beautiful little Indian woman, Karunamayi. She warmly greeted and hugged us. She looked into my eyes and said, "You have been waiting so long for your mother." It really hit me. I told her I didn't know why

I couldn't stop crying, and she said, "You're crying because your heart is longing for the mother, and when you can cry like this, much karma can be released. It's devotion, baby."

I said, "Is that what I was feeling before you came?" She replied yes. It was a beautiful meeting, and I just loved her. She was so sweet. Her eyes were like pools of compassion. She was carrying a bag, so I grabbed it in order to carry it for her, and she grabbed it back; then I tried grabbing it again. We both laughed. We had an immediate close and playful connection.

The next morning, I went to the sponsor's home where Karunamayi was staying, and was invited into her room. Karunamayi told me I was from the angelic realm, and she saw huge angel wings on me. I felt very comfortable with her, and asked many questions. "I have been on this path a long time and have really worked hard. I don't know where I am on this path, but I'd really like to make it in this life-time. I don't care what I have to go through, I just want to make it." She interrupted me and said, "Very little karma left. Very little karma, baby. Come and sit at the feet of your Amma and we'll work it out."

Then I asked, "Will I make it in this lifetime?"

Karunamayi looked at me with her deep brown eyes and said, "You will make it in this lifetime." What incredible grace to hear this directly from her!

Karunamayi became my teacher and initiated me into the Saraswati mantra by inscribing it on my tongue with a Tulsi twig. I had been reciting a Durga mantra for years, and Mother said I could still use it and would empower that one too, but I wanted to try the Saraswati mantra to know this aspect of the Divine Mother. I knew of Saraswati, but I hadn't been drawn to her before. After Karunamayi initiated me, I chanted the Saraswati mantra day and night.

It was an incredible blessing to have Karunamayi in my life, and a high honor to serve her for eight years. I was part of her staff in Santa Fe, then in Sedona when I moved there. I wanted to sponsor her in Sedona when I first moved there in 2000, but her national program schedule was already full. My persistence and deep desire paid off, because one of the other programs was canceled and she was able to add Sedona to her schedule! She allowed me to be very close to her, which was a privilege not extended to all. When she came to Sedona, I drove her around and showed her holy places. I held her hand to guide her as we walked over the sacred red rocks, and was able to share personal moments with her.

One day when I was sitting with Karunamayi I noticed a Ganesh[37] in her hand that was not there before. I didn't see her reaching to get it, and wondered where it came from. Karunamayi sweetly reached over and handed me the *murti*. Later I asked her cousin, Swamiji, "There was a Ganesh that appeared out of nowhere in Amma's hand. Can she materialize things?" Swamiji nonchalantly replied, "Oh yes, she's been doing that since she was young." Karunamayi

---

37   Ganesh is the Hindu Elephant-God who is the Lord of success, wisdom and the remover of obstacles on the spiritual path.

also gave me a beautiful note that read, "Mother is always in your heart. Mother cares, Mother shares, *Amma.*" The Ganesh and note from her are among my most cherished possessions.

My time with Karunamayi was very powerful, sacred, close, and extremely evolutionary. She worked out tremendous karmas in me. I spent as much time as I could with her because to be with a great one personally, and meditate in their presence, is an incredible opportunity to mirror any imperfections we have left in us, and is a fast route to God. She speeded up my karma a hundred-fold, and gave me much encouragement.

I didn't know if I would ever go back to India, but after seventeen years Mother pulled me there in 2002. When I

Sri Karunamayi holding my beloved cat, Bodhisattva.

arrived at her meditation retreat in Penusila, all I did was cry. I put white netting over my head to protect myself from the mosquitoes, and felt like a bride of Christ, crying for hours on end, blowing my nose! Karunamayi was working out karma after karma, pain after pain, lifetime after lifetime. I didn't even see all of what it was. It was deep grief that had been lodged in my soul, which she brought up in such a beautiful way. I didn't have very high experiences that first retreat, but later experienced a total love union that went from being into my head, to dropping into my sacred heart. She transmitted lots of bliss and peace, but most of my time with her was very hard work. By her grace she released a great deal of karma to make sure that I would make it to God realization in this life.

The Saraswati aspect of the Divine Mother is wisdom, and Karunamayi taught me a great deal about it. I learned about correct speech, to filter everything through my heart, to not speak to anyone if it was coming from reaction, anger, or from anything but love. Of all the women Masters I have met, Karunamayi was definitely the aspect of total compassion. Her eyes were pools of compassion, and when I looked into them I knew there was nothing that she didn't know about me, and nothing that she didn't understand. The compassion that flows into her devotees makes them want to do their best sadhana for her, not for just themselves but because they love her and want to fulfill her desire for us all to be free.

Karunamayi was one of my great teachers, who took me to a higher level, and gave me the courage and strength to go through the incredible karma she was bringing up in me. I was also able to be very human with her as well as divine. Every time I was with her I would come to a new level. I never knew what to expect, and eventually learned to have no expectations. Every mirror I needed, in order to clear the karma I hadn't yet worked through, would appear, and any person I had not forgiven would be there in front of my face. It was a beautiful, delightful, encouraging, and fabulous way to grow.

The second year I returned to India for Karunamayi's meditation retreat, my friend, Art, wanted to take me to Chennai to have my Nadi leaves read. Art had his Nadi leaves read by an Indian family, and highly recommended them. Nadi leaves are ancient written records from the Akashic Records, which describe in minute detail the lives of individuals who are living in this day and age. They were written in Sanskrit by the great sage Augustiar. Several thousand years ago, they were translated into Tamil by the Maharajah Seerfoji II of Tanjore and were stored in his palace library. During British rule sixty percent of the scrolls were burned and the others were auctioned off. Some families still own them and have preserved these sacred records over the ages. I first heard about Nadi leaves from my friend Kriyananda, who founded the Ananda Ashram in Grass Valley. Kriyananda had his Nadi leaves read with incredible accuracy.

Art was very excited about his Nadi leaf reading, but before I agreed to go, I wanted to get permission from Karunamayi. After the retreat I was able to spend time with

Thea showing Sri Karunamayi some of the sacred rocks in Sedona.

her, so I asked if it would be a good idea to have my palm leaves read, and she replied, "It would be a very good *darshan*, baby. You go."

When Art and I arrived at the Nadi leaf readers' home, they took my thumbprint to establish if it matched any of my hereditary lines. If it did, my reading would be there. My thumbprint was a match, so I was seated before a young Brahmin priest who chanted in Tamil. While they searched for my Nadi leaves, an English interpreter began asking me some preliminary questions, such as my birth date, time and city of birth. The Brahmin priest continued to chant in

Thea, Sri Karunamayi and Brian in Santa Fe, NM.

Tamil, and suddenly, the interpreter started spouting forth facts about me... *"Your name is Theodora, your mother's name is Stella, your father's name is William, you were born in a good Christian family, you were born..."* and on and on! I was stunned. This was all on the palm leaf? There was so much thrown at me that it was fortunate the session was tape-recorded, otherwise I never would have remembered it all.

Every statement was accurate, including the part about Brian renouncing the world, and going to the Himalayas, which he had done a year before. The Nadi leaf reader continued, *"You could not have come here until your husband renounced the world. If you tried to come earlier, it would not have worked out."* The leaves also said that Lord Shiva and Parvati were very pleased with Brian because he was going for total realization like an Indian *sadhu*. They said he had tremendous grace, and would always love me and look after me even though he was in the Himalayas. My heart had been broken on one level, but it was destiny and everyone was in complete alignment with their own destiny.

I inquired if I had past lives in India, and they confirmed I had had many. In one, I had been an Indian doctor and a natural healer. I inherited a great deal of money from my family, became quite the playboy and gambler, and as a result my healing practice suffered. I performed abortions on two women and assumed they were looked after by my nurses. And because I was too distracted with my less than *dharmic* lifestyle, I didn't follow up and they died from complications. It was a deep blow, and later in that lifetime I turned to God by giving money to build temples. The karma had already been accumulated; some of it was coming back to me in this life, and being worked out in the form of losing large amounts of money.

The leaves said in this lifetime that I would become a realized soul, and teacher to many. I would write a spiritually awakening book that would be a household item, and would found an ashram for enlightenment for a select few. I was also told about the people I'd meet in this lifetime, and the exact time of my death. They also said that I would have many spiritual teachers and that Karunamayi was my current master and would take me a long way on the path. They went on to say that I would have the *darshan* of Shiva and Parvati.

I was also told that Augustiar, who wrote my palm leaves, was an Ascended Master from the Himalayas, and had been the guru of Mahavatar Babaji. Augustiar foretold everything that would happen to me, and in order to overcome particular sins and karma, he prescribed that I visit temples in India, feed the poor, and do various *pujas* or spiritual ceremonies. Art and I were excited about my assignment, but when we went into the temples we felt like hell, because it brought up so much karma. I was glad we were together to support each other.

PILGRIMAGE TO HIMALAYAS WITH BRIAN
AND SHIVA'S DARSHAN

Brian felt a calling to go the Himalayas and to experience solitude. It was something that had been with him for years, but it wasn't until that timeframe he felt he should actually go. I wanted to go with him, but it wasn't my direction. So we separated with great emotion and pain, not knowing when we would see each other again. He had been in the Himalayas for three years when he called me to come join him.

He said, "I'm planning a pilgrimage for us in the Himalayas and am sending you money to fly out." It was a golden opportunity and of course I would go! I decided to also sign up for Karunamayi's annual meditation retreat in Penusila. To get in shape for our trek through the Himalayas, I hiked every day in Sedona's red rocks.

Wearing blue jeans, hiking boots, and a good backpack, I boarded the plane to India. Brian said that Babaji was planning our whole trip, and I thought, "Babaji is really letting me go back to the Himalayas? I thought I wasn't supposed to go back again." I was beside myself with excitement and anticipation to be with my dear Brian again, and near beloved Babaji in the Himalayas.

Brian was there to meet me when I arrived in New Delhi. He was skin and bones, his hair had grayed, and he looked like he had aged fifteen years. I said, "Oh my God, buddy, you're not well." We later found out he had lymphatic cancer, which continued to worsen some years later.

It was so good to see him, and it was as if we had never been apart. Our goals have always been the same: our love for meditation, and to become realized. After a few days in New Delhi, we started our trek to the Himalayas on an overnight train to Almora, then rented a jeep for the drive to Kasani, high in the Himalayas where Brian lived. The beauty and high vibration of the Himalayas were indescribable.

After two days we arrived in Kasani. We had to carry our groceries and luggage on foot as there was no road to Brian's house. Brian rented an independent portion of a beautiful home that had been built by the Nagy's, a family who owned most of the village. The apartment was furnished with its own kitchen, bedroom and living room, and Brian had done a lovely job decorating it western style. The minute I walked into his place it felt like heaven. I was so accustomed to his vibration, from meditating and growing with him for 17 years in married life, that it was a welcome sanctuary after my long journey.

The journey and heavy pollution in New Delhi had taken its toll on me and my sinuses were draining like a leaky faucet. Brian told me the same thing happened to him when he first arrived, and added, "Welcome to India!" After a few days of solid rest, my body strengthened and I started meditating nonstop. Brian was used to me meditating all the time, so he completely understood when I told him I needed to use every minute to go inward. I knew there was a big story in the Himalayas waiting to be told, and only by concentrated meditation could it unfold.

Not since my days at the ranch had I been able to meditate without interruption, going deeper and deeper, stopping only to sleep or eat. It wasn't long before all the great ones started to appear to me. I received the *darshan* of a pantheon of Gods. I saw Lord Shiva, the Divine Mother in many forms, Sri Ganesha, Hanumanji and Babaji. They were always with me, but it wasn't until I reached a quiet state in solitude that I was able to see them. I knew I had spent many lives in India because I felt so at home, and didn't care if I ever left Brian's apartment! Everything I wanted or needed was right there, but destiny had other plans.

Just before the snows come in October and November, there is a narrow window of time when the mountains clear. It was then we boarded a local bus to our first stop, Gangotri, a place sacred to Lord Shiva. According to folklore a great king who had performed great austerities to Lord Shiva resided there. The villagers were without water, so the king prayed to Lord Shiva for his divine help. Lord Shiva appeared, hit the ground with his staff, and water spouted up from Gamuth, the very beginning of the Ganga River.

The bus was old and rickety, and the narrow road that wound up the Himalayas was absolutely treacherous. And it didn't help knowing that many people died every year going up that road! I wondered if the other pilgrims on the bus knew this bit of information as they sang to Lord Shiva, oblivious to the danger. I briefly looked down the steep drop at the sparkling waters of the sacred Ganges River, but quickly decided to keep my eyes closed and chant the mantra.

We arrived in Gangotri at night, and it was freezing. Brian and I rented an unheated room (the only type available) for the night, with just our outerwear and a four-inch-thick blanket to keep us warm. Shortly after Brian went into the bathroom, I heard him yell, "AHHH!" The icy cold water from the European-style toilet apparently squirted upward when he flushed! We had a good laugh over that.

The next day we searched for a nice place to rent, where I could stay while Brian hiked up to Gamuth, the source of the Ganges. I had planned to go with him, but between altitude sickness and the head cold from which I was trying to recover, it didn't seem like a good idea. Brian's plan was to do a ceremony of renunciation at Gamuth, to release all our desires, and to ask for Lord Shiva's blessing for Brian, me, and of course our cat, Bodhisattva who was still in the States.

As we looked at available rooms, we walked past many

sadhus, or Naga Swamis, who had conquered the cold and wore only loincloths. I knew I had a long way to go to get to that state.

We found a beautiful apartment with a large picture window overlooking a bridge across the Ganges to the temple. As I watched the pilgrims walk across the bridge, I had a strong feeling I was going to be blessed by one of the sadhus. The barefoot monks were initiates of Shankaracharya, a great master who was an aspect of Lord Shiva. They had the three lines of ash on their foreheads and carried a staff, or trident, representing Shiva. Some of the beggars could have been mistaken for sadhus, and sometimes we really didn't know who was who unless we tuned into their vibration. Suddenly it occurred to me that I needed to know who's a saint and who ain't! I felt I was going to get blessed by someone who was really beautiful, but I wanted to be sure they were higher than me.

I can see energies, but I need verification of where people are spiritually. I prayed to my Masters for help, and was given a number system or "enlightenment chart," and was shown where I was on it. I began testing this new enlightenment chart on the people walking across the bridge, and the information came to me through my third eye. I was certain I would receive a blessing from a higher being, and didn't worry about it any more.

After Brian left for his journey, I walked across to the temple to take in the powerful energies of the area and to go deep within. There were many beautiful people there from all over the world. I met an American *sadhu* who had been raised around Muktananda, as his parents had been devotees. The American was installing solar panels to the temple so there would always be light.

The beauty and feeling of the place was beyond description. The waterfalls, the trees, the huts of *sadhus* meditating day and night, all emanated an indescribable energy. Many in India knew that going to Gangotri just once in their lifetime would be the greatest blessing they could receive from Lord Shiva. Poor people would miss meals to save their money to travel to this holy place.

I had gotten into the daily habit of going to the Ganga, which was right below me. I spent hours picking up stones, meditating, looking into the radiance of this river so alive with *Shakti,* and becoming attuned to that beautiful aspect of the Divine Mother.

One afternoon I was meditating in my apartment, when suddenly my eyes opened and I saw a stout man with matted hair walking across the bridge, holding a big Shiva trident. It was an immediate recognition. I knew he was the one who was going to bless me. After I quickly checked him out on my enlightenment chart to verify he was much higher than I was, I sprinted out of the apartment and followed him across the bridge. By the time I reached him, he was sitting outside the temple waiting for me! I bowed before him and said, "Swamiji, may I have your blessing?"

He looked at me and said, "Are you willing to die?" I realized it was the death of my ego that he referred to, and

I nodded yes.

He took his staff and gently hit me on the head and on each side of my shoulders and said, "This will be a delayed blessing. Go back to your room and meditate. It will not happen right away, but it will happen."

I returned to my room, went straight into meditation, and about four hours later felt a power I had never felt before. I opened my eyes and there in front of me was Lord Shiva covered with ash from head to foot, riding his bull, Nandi. This was not a vision, but an actual materialization. I was in complete shock, and all I could do was cry. I bowed down to him in complete reverence, and offered my total soul to him.

All the worries my heart had been carrying spilled over as I said, "Lord Shiva, America is in big trouble. *Please* do something with our politics in America, and bring it back to what it represents. You are the destroyer of all ignorance, you can do anything and I give it to you." Then I started crying again, and continued with a personal plea, "I've been in America many years and have gotten into delusion. I was so high when I was young, being with the Masters and going into *samadhic* states. I know I've grown a lot, but I want to get back to those high states. We have to make up for lost time. Please help me."

These prayers were coming from the center of my being. I had no idea I would talk to Shiva, and didn't plan or meditate on what to say. I gave him everything. The power— I have never experienced such power, compassion and love in one being in my entire life. It was emotional, shocking, purging, and wonderful; it was anything you want to call it in one big experience. After Lord Shiva dematerialized, I went into a very deep meditation and felt continual clearing. He released so much karma from me in such a short time, that I went from a state of trying to meditate to a state where meditation just overtook me.

Before our trip, I told Brian these were Lord Shiva's mountains and that he was the presiding deity of the Himalayas. And indeed, after Lord Shiva's *darshan,* everything became Him. Every place I looked I saw Shiva, even tridents on cars. Everything to do with the Himalayas was Shiva, except for Babaji, who I knew was guiding us to every place we were to go.

When Brian returned it was as if years had passed. So much had happened. I shared my powerful experience with him about Shiva, and he told me about his experiences in Gamuth. He said our renunciation ceremony was incredible. It came alive and he knew everything he asked for would be granted. The *Shakti* was so intense he didn't know how he would make it back to the guest house in Gamuth, where he was staying. For a long time he lay on the rocks until he regained enough strength to walk back to the lodge just before dark, then fell into his bed and slept.

It was so hard to leave such a holy and beautiful place, so we stayed to meditate an extra two days past our original departure date. There was much to do before the snows came, however, so we reluctantly boarded a bus back down the mountain. Unlike the ride up when I had more than a little trepidation about the dangerous route, on the way down I felt the presence of Lord Shiva and Babaji everywhere. Certain memories started to open up, of an ancient lifetime in the Himalayas with Babaji, and there was great emotion and feeling associated with it. I knew eventually I'd get the whole story but for the moment, I put on my sunglasses, cried, and surrendered to the purging.

Many people thought I was crazy traveling on Indian buses, but I liked it. The colorful people were always sweet to me, and I enjoyed sitting next to a window. What I was getting tired of, however, was the bumpy ride. So I prayed to God, "Could we take a really good bus to Badrinath?" About a half hour later we came upon a stopped tour bus with Westerners. Our bus stopped behind it, so Brian and I ventured over and talked to the driver. We told him we planned on visiting the famous banyan tree where Shankaracharya became enlightened, and then to Badrinath. To our delight, the tour bus driver said they were going on the same route and invited us to ride with them! As we rode in total luxury, I silently thanked God for honoring my prayer.

Our next stop was Shankaracharya's place of enlightenment, another incredibly holy site. Brian and I sat there for a long time and learned that Shankaracharya was an aspect of Lord Shiva. The year before at Karunamayi's retreat, she had given us the history of Shankaracharya, the monist saint and aspect of Shiva who originated the teachings of the non-dual path.

As we rode to Badrinath I knew we were going into Babaji's territory. Above Badrinath is where Babaji's subtle ashram is located, and is an extremely powerful place. I had heard stories about the hot springs at Badrinarayan Temple in Badrinath and how the ancient Shankara had visited this temple. While in meditation, Shankaracharya was shown in a vision that the statue of the main deity had been thrown in the Ganga, so he dove into the river and retrieved it. The statue still stands to this day, and it is clearly an image of Babaji who is Vishnu.

Brian and I went to the temple and received offerings, then I enjoyed bathing in the hot springs with the Indian women. They were giggling and laughing, and splashing water at me and offered me their shampoo to wash my hair. It was delightful!

Badrinath was much colder than Gangotri. From here on we began our long trek to Vasundhara Falls, ten miles from Babaji's subtle ashram called Gauri Shankar Peetam Ashram. As we walked up the rocky pony trail, I had a tough time keeping my balance, which wasn't that great to begin with. It was a miracle that I made the hike up. The trail was steep and uneven, and I felt weak and dizzy from altitude sickness. Hanumanji[38] was constantly by my side holding and balancing me by the arm, and literally giving me physical and mental strength to accomplish this incredible feat.

Many times I just wanted to sit down and say, "I'm sorry Brian, but I just can't make it. I want to go back." But something kept me forging ahead. I carried a red, heart-shaped rock from Sedona, into which more than 50

38   Hanumanji is the Monkey God, the greatest devotee of Lord Rama.

people had anchored their prayers for world peace. It was my mission to bury it at Vasundhara Falls. If that's all I did, I knew the trip would have been worth it. With every step I chanted *Om Kriya Babaji Nama Om*. Also, we were in danger of the snow avalanching from the steep slopes on either side of us. I thought of death a lot going up that mountain, and later remembered that in a past lifetime, I had died in those very snows, trying to find Babaji.

We finally made it to Vasundhara Falls and I cannot say how relieved I was! Completely exhausted, I fell to the ground and let the earth and mountains recharge me. I admit there was an expectation that Babaji would be there after my huge *tapas* getting up the mountain. I was disappointed that he didn't materialize, or do something special for me. But I also knew he'd sent Hanumanji to me. Babaji wasn't about to let me go to my death again! And I also knew he was with me in my heart, every step of the way. Babaji guides us, but he is very elusive and comes when we least expect it.

Brian and I crawled out onto a ledge where a beautiful, natural rock altar stood, and where other pilgrims had made rock offerings. As I put the heart-shaped rock on the altar, into which so many people had poured their hopes and prayers, the Himalayan breeze wafted over the rock and us, and I knew we had been given a tremendous blessing. We sat in meditation for quite a while, and it was very beautiful. Part of me was still in survival mode and feared that if we didn't get back to the village soon, we'd be killed by an avalanche. We had witnessed a few snow slides very close to us so my fear wasn't unfounded. Brian must have felt the same because he urged us to head down to the village before dark. I'm a good hiker but my balance isn't great, so Brian balanced me the whole way down. I did manage to look up from time to time, and feast on the breathtakingly beautiful valleys and meadows, unlike any I had ever seen before.

We made it to the village in the nick of time, and the first thing we did was savor a hot cup of coffee. I seldom drink coffee, but boy, it sure tasted great! When we went back to our room, I told Brian I felt we were complete with Badrinath, and I wanted to go back to his apartment in Kasani.

It felt so good to return to Brian's village and his apartment, where just by going within I had experienced the *darshan* of the pantheon of Indian gods! I was also grateful for the warmth, comfort and safety of his home. The first thing we did when we got there was to make a good home-cooked meal. Then I enjoyed a hot bath and crawled into a warm bed.

For the rest of the visit I focused on Brian. To distance himself from the traumas incurred through many past lives in battle, he had placed shields around his heart, and through meditation and prayer we were able to lift them. I knew my time with Brian was coming to an end, and I was very sad. My next adventure was to travel to Karunamayi's meditation retreat in the south of India where I had been four times previously. I left Brian with deep sadness, not knowing when if ever I would see him again.

—

My friend Mary from Sedona also planned on attending the meditation retreat. She had made arrangements with Gary, a young Sikh, to meet in Kasani, and drive in his Indian Land Cruiser to New Delhi. What a treat it was to ride in luxury! Gary was a beautiful, high soul and we became very close. He wanted to take me to the Golden Temple, the holiest place of Sikhism, and to Kashmir to meet his family. Mary and I kept to our schedule, and took the train from New Delhi to Chennai. I had known Mary for about a year. We always had fun in Sedona whenever we would get together, so we spent much of the train ride laughing. Once we arrived in Chennai, however, she reverted to an intense aversion mode, and was just miserable. I knew old tendencies were being stirred up by the fire of the guru, Sri Karunamayi.

Two days later we commissioned a driver and car, and were on our way to Karunamayi's ashram in Penusila, a five-hour drive northwest from Chennai. Being at Mother's ashram was like coming home. Situated on seventeen acres of remote forest and nestled at the foothills of the Garudadri mountains in Andra Pradesh, the ashram is incredibly pristine and beautiful.

The area is permeated with *Shakti* from the ancient rishis who meditated in those forests and mountains. As a young woman, Karunamayi meditated there for ten years. She went to one of the forest's many sacred groves, and remained absorbed in meditation for hours, days, or even weeks at a time. Local villagers who spotted her sometimes mistook her for a statue, as they could not detect even the movement of breath in her perfectly still form.

She later founded her ashram in the 1990's. There are beautiful white temples with hand-carved and painted sculptures and reliefs of Hindu deities, a large open pavilion for *yagnas* or sacred fire ceremonies, and an enclosed meditation hall. Mother's personal quarters are situated on lavishly landscaped grounds, not far from the sleeping quarters for retreat participants and ashram staff. The complex is surrounded by a white stone wall with a pillared entry and a twenty-five foot high Hanumanji statue welcoming all who come.

I realized that Babaji had led me to all three places of the Hindu trilogy: at Gangotri, the place of Lord Shiva and Parvati; at Badrinath, the place of Vishnu and Lakshmi; and at Penusila, the place of my teacher, Karunamayi, who is Saraswati, the consort of Brahma. As usual, there were tremendous realizations, depth, bliss, love, surrender and clearing for me at Karunamayi's meditation retreat. At the end of the two-week retreat, which passed all too quickly, Karunamayi asked me to go to Peace Village, located in a remote area north of Bangalore and where cottages are being built for devotees to stay and meditate in solitude. She said she was planning on going there in several weeks with a small group and asked me to accompany her. I was thrilled that she invited me, but I also had some trepidation because I had a feeling Peace Village was still under construction, and wouldn't be ready for some time. Enduring more rugged conditions would be hard on me physically, but I also knew I should follow my guru's instructions, so I agreed to meet her in Bangalore.

I had several weeks of free time, and visited Arananchala, the powerful place of Ramana Maharishi and sacred mountain of Shiva, and then to Sri Aurobindo's and Mother Mira's ashram in Pondacherry. It was my second trip to Pondacherry and it was such a treat. I loved the people there and met a wonderful English lady who was staying at the same guest house on the beach. We walked to the shrine where Mother Mira attained *mahasamadhi,* and sat for hours feeling her divine presence. The ashram food was great. We had fresh yogurt, curd and even eggs, all of which my worn-down body needed and savored.

REMEMBERING THE LIFETIME OF JESUS

When I was 23 years old, I started having memories of the lifetime of Jesus, but it wasn't until recently that I met Mirabai, a spiritual teacher from South Africa, and the complete story opened up to me. I understand now why it took 2000 years for me to face that life, because the grief and loss were beyond comprehension.

I was Mariam, the daughter of Rebekah, Mother Mary's sister, and was born a year before Jesus, who we called Yeshua. When I was about nine years old, my mother died of leprosy. She was a very high, sensitive angelic being, and her fragile body could not fight off the disease. The same being who was Rebekah in that life was my mother in this life, too. She was a very high angel and way ahead of her time. She was almost too sensitive and fragile to be here without the right people around her, people who understood her. I can see my beloved mother on the other side, and that she's with Archangel Gabriel, and is doing tremendous work with the holy family and the great ones.

233

After Rebekah's death, I was adopted by my Aunt Mary and Uncle Joseph. I recalled joyfully playing, and being at Mother Mary's house with other Essene children, most of whom were my cousins and close souls. There were many women in her kitchen cooking and laughing and it was a secure, loving and spiritually close-knit community. These women were the disciples of Yeshua, and were closer to him than anyone.

I was a very precocious child, and always loved adventure and challenges. I had a special bond with Yeshua, because I understood his soul and was his best friend growing up. We always confided in each other, and even did a child's blood ritual, swearing we'd never be apart. Yeshua was very fiery and sensitive even then, and was awakened in degrees. I remembered the joyful times we had playing with each other. He hated injustice, and was such a good friend to all of us. How loving, giving and beautiful he was. I remember building hideouts then, as I did as a child in this lifetime. I loved nature, and collecting branches and twigs to make houses. I'd make the frame and fill it in with the branches. We had a lot of fun growing up as Essene children. We had grandmothers, aunties and everyone around us who loved us. It was very secure. When my mother died, we were raised with many parents and children. We were all prepared and trained for the coming of the Messiah, who was our friend, both human and Divine. Later as He went into his initiations He became more and more detached from us as human, and more into his divinity, yet He always loved us as much as ever. That was never lost. As his states became higher, He became increasingly detached, so He could accomplish his mission.

Mother Mary homeschooled all the children and taught us the fundamentals of reading and writing, but more importantly we learned about truth, healing, surrender, and love for one another. When I was of age it was decided I would be educated at the Essene temple, as Yeshua was, and I was brought to the wisest teachers of the Essene community. We all gained in wisdom, but it wasn't easy. We learned to release our attachments to everything outside of ourselves, anything that we clung to. I never could release Yeshua, my close friend and blood brother.

Mother Mary also went to the Essene temple when she was three years old, where her parents, Anna and Joachim also lived. Mother Mary was one of twelve candidates chosen by the Essene elders to be the mother of the Messiah. The elders knew Spirit would reveal who was to be the mother of the Christ. Little Mary was in total joy as she attended the Essene school. She loved wandering, singing in the fields and communicating with the nature spirits. She could see the unseen from an early age. At the opportune time Spirit shone its light on her, and it was revealed to the elders that Mary would be the mother of the Messiah. She had been groomed for this post, as the other eleven girls had, and they became her attendants and friends to help her prepare.

Beloved Joseph was one of the greatest beings of the

Essene temple, and was known for his humility and dedication in serving the Essene community in whatever way was needed. The Essene council looked for signs from the Holy Spirit as to who would be the parents of the Messiah. Joseph was chosen as the father and protector. It was later revealed to me that beloved Joseph has reincarnated many times as great masters, including St. Germain.

As we got older and understood meditation and the Essene principles, we were taken to Egypt and India to study under the greatest teachers of that time. The training required tremendous discipline. The girls and boys were taught separately, and Yeshua was always ahead of the girls in his initiations. Even though He went to higher levels, I always knew it was where I wanted to go too. He was paving a way for all of us to arrive at that consciousness. I attended the schools with my cousin, Mary Magdalene. Because of her fiery disposition, I was one of her few friends; we both shared the loss of our mothers at an early age. Mary Magdalene and I were always together holding hands as we faced our deepest fears, went through our initiations, and all phases of our training. I don't remember everything we were taught, but it was intense. We were taught entity release, with which I am now an expert, and how to hold energy so that pure and high souls can come in at the time of conception when the parents are in a *samadhic* state. Before we learned the animal way of procreation, we merged spiritually.

During my recent trip with Brian in the Himalayas, it was awakened in me that a group of Essene women, including Mary Magdalene and I, went to the Himalayas soon after Yeshua, to meet the great Babaji. In order to be with the great Babaji one has to be lifted to another frequency, otherwise there is no way the physical body can survive the higher altitudes of the Himalayas. I remember the astounding beauty of the Himalayas, and doing simple tasks, such as gathering herbs in the fields.

Yeshua went through many years of training to prepare Him for one of the greatest and darkest times in earth's history for an avatar to embody (which my teacher Karunamayi also had told us). Judith was commissioned to be one of Yeshua's primary Essene teachers. Later, his father Joseph, an adept of Babaji, took Yeshua and his brothers to India to be with this great avatar. It was under the training of Babaji that Yeshua learned to bi-locate, and to go into deep *samadhic* states, in preparation for the crucifixion. Yeshua's father stayed with Babaji in the Himalayas. Later, the news was given to Mother Mary and the Essene community that our beloved Joseph had made an incredible Ascension transition.

Babaji, Krishna, Rama, St. Germain, and all the Masters and siddhas that have Ascended from the Himalayas, are tenaciously working together to bring this earth to completion, and to help her Ascend. It was a destined plan from the beginning of time. It wasn't just about Yeshua; it was about a world mission, involving all the great Masters who have agreed to bring this Earth, which is also a great being, to completion.

Yeshua spent time in Buddhist monasteries, and in

fact, there is a record in a Kashmir monastery about a man called Issa, our Beloved Yeshua, who came and stayed with them. He mastered Buddhism, Hinduism and all the world religions, and learned to love the Divine Mother in all her forms.

It was always wonderful to have Yeshua come home after his jaunts. We were always on the move also, but when we all met back at the holy land in our beloved Jerusalem, it was so joyful. We had family celebrations at the home of Joseph of Arimathea, where Mary Magdalene, Lazarus, and Martha lived. Their home was a large, sunny and bright house with wisteria vines on lattices. We and the many children, and Essene community, gathered here when Yeshua came home. How heartwarming it was to be with Him again. We could feel He had moved to whole new levels of consciousness after his initiations with the Masters. Yeshua was so playful and joyful, and when He came into a room, the whole space would brighten.

Jewish weddings are the happiest occasions one can imagine, because of the dancing and celebration. Yeshua danced, celebrated, and was the light of everyone's heart. It was Jewish tradition to marry, so of course Yeshua married. I was one of the twelve candidates chosen to become Yeshua's wife, and it was extremely stressful, because it was not determined who was to be picked until much later, when the Holy Spirit would reveal it. Mary Magdalene was chosen, and Yeshua married her under Jewish custom. Their relationship was beautiful and divine. It was like the relationship of Krishna and Radha. Divine relationships are not based on the fear of losing, but on merging together in divine love in *samadhic* states. Mary Magdalene was his twin flame, his counterpart, and was an incredible being. She was very feisty, which she had to be, for she needed to be strong for what she had to do later. Mary Magdalene was closest to his level of consciousness, and therefore was the one who completely understood Yeshua.

I always loved Yeshua. It wasn't the "in love" or magnetic love, because we were too high for that; it was the soul love that was deep of understanding. When we were young we vowed to be unconditional friends and to marry, but I realize now it wasn't a physical marriage. It was the marriage of the soul, because anyone who is close to Yeshua and goes into Oneness, goes into marriage with Him. Because I couldn't marry my beloved Yeshua, I married Nathaniel, whom I deeply loved and respected. We brought in a beautiful son and daughter.

Yeshua needed the love of his own people to help him get through his travails. Even though he was a very high master, and could go beyond illusion in samadhi, He was still very human. The incarnation of Yeshua was one that took the bravest of avatars to go through. Being in the physical body is a tremendous sacrifice for an avatar because they are subject to the same fetters of suffering, disease and old age, and in his case, being brutally crucified. As the twelve women disciples, we were able to serve Yeshua unconditionally and he gained tremendous strength from us. He loved us very much for our hearts were porous and He could enter in. We supported Mother Mary, cooked in her kitchen, administered healing when the Holy Spirit came in, and were Yeshua's assistants, but most of all, we were his deepest friends. When we were with Him, serving Him, it was a time to revel in his divine presence and joy and to receive the divine energy He would transmit to us. Everything He did was a teaching.

The male disciples were pretty rough guys before they met Yeshua, but they had to be in order to survive in the world. When Yeshua came into their lives they were totally softened. The men were beautiful, loyal, and awakened, but the twelve women disciples were much closer to Yeshua, because we felt Him with our whole hearts. We also understood his spirit and held a strong energy for him. The men, particularly Peter, were jealous of the women disciples. They were especially jealous of Mary Magdalene as well, because Yeshua wanted her with him almost all the time. She was the only woman allowed this great privilege because, after all, she was Yeshua's twin flame and her consciousness was one with his. She was one of his greatest disciples, because she completely understood his teachings. Her mission was huge. She was to carry, protect and preserve the secret teachings.

When the patriarchs took over, the writings of the women disciples were removed from the biblical texts, but their contribution of love, understanding and selflessness remain in the Akashic records. They will be revealed when humanity is ready for the truth.

Yeshua could read every situation, every mind, and knew exactly where everyone was coming from. He was from the Truth Ray, the same as Lord Shiva. With right speech and love, He cut through ignorance and illusion to bring forth the truth of the ego in each person. Those who didn't want to grow, hated Him. Those closest to Him could feel the buildup of hatred in Jerusalem, of the people who didn't know Him, and who were not ready to have Him mirror their darkness.

Many of the priests of the Sanhedrin, a religious assembly of the highest Jewish legal-judicial tribunal in the Land of Israel, were stuck in Jewish dogma. Except for Nicodemus, who was very close to Him, few priests understood Yeshua. As Nicodemus became aware of the plot to kill Him, he spoke up to the Sanhedrin, but their lack of true understanding made them complacent, and they did nothing to avert the scheme.

We knew what was going to happen. It was well known among us that the Messiah would come and that we were holding the energy for Him in preparation for the dark times ahead. We knew the prophecies and scriptures well, and knew that it was written in the Old Testament that the Messiah would be crucified at the hands of the evil ones. But living through it was another thing indeed. We lost so many loved ones, including my mother, and of course, Yeshua. Memories came flooding back from Yeshua's crucifixion, from the time they whipped Him, accused Him of being a thief, and placed the crown of thorns on Him, to seeing his body hanging on the cross. Nearly catatonic, we watched as our beloved Yeshua endured tremendous physical suffering, felt the people's ridicule, hatred, and complete lack of understanding of who He really was. We stood watch with our best friend, our beloved, the purest of all lambs, being sacrificed by hatred. We knew that at any point, any one of us could have the same fate because we were his family.

Even though we were all falling apart at the crucifixion, Yeshua glared at us with incredible power that insisted, *"Remember your mission!"* Mary Magdalene, Sara (Mother Mary's sister) and Mariam were trained to hold energy during his Ascension, for everything was always mapped out. We knew what was going to happen; we just didn't know that when the time came, it would be so intense for us. We felt all the human emotions and terror of the times. Mary Magdalene was in shock, and with child, and we were trying to protect her. Everything that happens in pregnancy is felt by the being that is carried, and it was a terrible trauma for her unborn child.

As we struggled through the crucifixion, at one point, our Beloved, after transmuting his earth karma, lifted us to where He was. Even though He was in a *samadhic* state when He took on the karma of the earth, it was very intense as it passed through his body while transmuting it. Those of us who were able, also took on some earth karma to the extent that we could. Mother Mary took on a lot. So in his darkest moment, Yeshua lifted us up to another level where we could see that it was all illusion, and that we were both human and divine at the same time.

After we received *the look* from Yeshua, I prostrated in the dust in total surrender. My heart was aching, yet so filled with love that I knew I would do anything for this being. He said to me, "Mariam, as you love me now, always love me." As He was on the cross and in a *samadhic* state, He would look into each of our eyes with beautiful grace, giving us energy and strength to go through his incredible transformation.

After the crucifixion, Mother Mary, Mary Magdalene, Sara and I took Him to the tomb. We prepared the body according to Jewish custom, cleansing his wounds and body with frankincense and myrrh. As we had been trained in the Essene school, we tenaciously held the energy through constant prayer and meditation. The time in between death and Ascension was very critical in order for Him to accomplish this state. Dark spirits will try to stop an Ascension during this interim period of time, because the fallen angel's job is to keep us from this state. They are jealous of those souls who can Ascend, because they cannot reach that state after their fall. This is what we were trained for: how to bring in souls and to help them Ascend by holding the energy. We were totally attuned, holding the energy in the tomb, and we were lifted above the delusion of his death. At the time of his Ascension, we were lifted very high into a glorious celebration with Masters, angels, and beings of light. Then Yeshua appeared to us in his Ascended body and we knew He had totally succeeded in his mission.

After the crucifixion it was dangerous for all of us—the disciples, Yeshua's family and especially Mary Magdalene. She was pregnant with Yeshua's child, and would carry on the Christ bloodline. We needed to go to a safe place where we could protect her, the bloodline, and the teachings. The Essene council decided that a large group, including Sara, Ruth, Mary Magdalene, Mother Mary, myself and others should flee to Southern France by ship. Joseph of Arimathea, Mary Magdalene's father, funded our escape. He was a very wealthy man, and paid for all the initiations and trips for everyone. We were grateful for our kind and generous benefactor, who always supported us in our time of need. My son Benjamin and my husband Nathaniel were with me.

Once in France we connected with other Essenes already there, and formed a very close, underground secret society. Even in Southern France there was tremendous hatred, and although not as intense as in our homeland, it was no picnic either. The dark forces were always trying to find us, and every step we took was beset with the challenge of survival. The Holy Spirit gave us incredible inner strength and focus, and a knowing we would make it and win. No one would be killed who didn't need to be, at least not right away.

The Essene way had taught us how to worship the Divine Mother, as Joseph and Yeshua had been taught in India. We adored Her as the *Shakti*, and Holy Spirit herself. We secretly kept up with the *pujas*, the rituals and mantras in Hebrew and Sanskrit. My son Benjamin was a beautiful child, and grew up to be a wonderful healer and Essene in France. When he was a teenager he was doing a ceremony to the Divine Mother when the Romans came in and killed the entire party. At least he died in service of the Divine Mother. Benjamin incarnated again in this life as Timothy, who is a healer and my good friend. I trained Timothy to be a healer, but didn't have to work very hard, because he remembered skills from his past lives just as Brian and I had. As I have relived my experiences during that life, Timothy has been right behind me.

Many who were closest to me were killed, and I had to feel the pain and the sadness of not being able to prevent their deaths. That lifetime was full of grief, and we had to be very brave. We had to live in the present and couldn't allow ourselves to get emotional because we were holding a very powerful and crucial energy. Those souls whose lives were sacrificed went to very high and beautiful realms to help us and our mission, as they could do so as powerfully in the angelic realms above.

Mary Magdalene found wonderful caves in Southern France, and spent hours meditating there. Everywhere she went, Mary meditated, because that was the only way she was connected to Yeshua. He would talk to her, as He would talk to all of us if we became quiet and still.

Surrounded by the love and protection of a small group of Essenes, Mary gave birth to the most beautiful light child, Sarah, in one of those caves. It was such a happy occasion. The child was a very high being. We stayed in Southern France as long as we could, but it became too dangerous, especially after Benjamin and the others were killed, so Mary Magdalene and our small band went to England.

I believe that the secret teachings of Christ were given to Mary Magdalene to take with her to southern France for safekeeping, and later, to his disciple Paul. These got away from Paul, somehow, and ended up in the Library of Alexandria, or in the hands of the Roman soldiers. I'm not sure, but my intuition tells me they are in the Vatican. I believe the real teachings of Christ will be revealed within the next few years.

The teachings in the Bible are extremely limited compared to what we learned from Yeshua. He knows that his own teachings have been distorted and used as dogma. There are beautiful parts of the New Testament that are his true teachings, but the bulk of it, such as universal truth, reincarnation and the closeness of the women disciples, were left out, so that the patriarchy could control the belief systems of the Christians.

Many Christians will be taken aback when they learn that Yeshua studied all religions, and taught that all religions lead to the One, as all the great Masters teach.

Yeshua was the Christ, but He is *not* the only way. We are all potential Christs. All the avatars, under whom Yeshua studied, knew their Christ Consciousness fully and completely.

During this time and age, the Return of the Christ is about remembering our Christhood, something we have lost since the time of the original "Angelic Fall." I also believe that Yeshua and all the Ascended Ones will literally walk with us in this great time. But before the return of the Great Ones, the earth must Ascend.

MOTHER MARY'S ASCENSION

After traveling to different places, Mother Mary returned to Great Britain, Avalon, and John the Beloved was her constant companion. They lived in a beautiful cottage surrounded by flowers. Mary was a pillar of strength and light to all the disciples of Jesus and an inspiration to all of the women of Christ. The Essene community and many of the disciples went to her to be healed, and she was available day and night. Mother Mary worked tirelessly with divine healing, and had a special focus of working with children. She had the same healing power as Yeshua; Mary is the split, or Twin Flame, of Archangel Raphael, and they are in charge of the Healing Ray.

In previous lives Mary was trained in the Egyptian temples and in Lemuria. All the teachings were given to us from the beginning and we used different forms for healing, whether it was in oils, light, color, or sound frequencies. Regardless of the type of practice, we were the instruments of healing, to allow the higher beings to come in and work through us. Mother Mary taught us this method in her home-schooling course, and we continued to learn healing in the Essene temples. We learned how to get ourselves out of the way, and let the high beings come in. Our faith was empowered through our healing work, as we could see the angels come in to help us. We were the anchors between the heaven and earth; higher beings needed our prayers, but they did the work.

It was the same with Yeshua. He was a master healer and could do anything, including bringing the dead back to life. The higher He went in consciousness, the more angels and beings of light were assigned to Him. When He merged with the Divine Consciousness in *samadhic* states, He saw all as perfection, and knew all was illusion.

John the Beloved also came from the angelic realm, and out of all the male disciples, it was he who understood Yeshua at the heart level. He was the natural choice to be with Mary, and he benefitted greatly from his years with her. The secret teachings were also imparted to him. He took them to Greece, then to the Himalayas, where they are being kept in safety by the great Masters guarding the Akashic Records.

I had been away from Mother Mary for four months. I had great intuition that she was getting ready to ascend and and I didn't want to miss out on that great event. I longed to be with her. There had been a great persecution of the disciples of Christ who stayed in the Essene communities throughout Europe, for the Romans were becoming more aware of these high vibratory places and they tried to destroy them and ridicule the people. Many Essenes were killed and tortured as their beloved master had been. Mary and John were pillars of strength to the Essene community with a fearless energy they held by their presence. Mary brought forth her wisdom, realizations and healing abilities, and gave tremendous strength and hope to everyone. She offered her healing and soothing words until the end, with her kind and loving heart.

When I arrived back in Great Britain, Mother Mary was ecstatic to see me. She was more beautiful than ever in her divine radiance. When Mary became ill, we kept a close watch on her, because we knew her time of Ascension was near, and we didn't want to miss a thing. We knew it was going to be a powerful event and we all wanted to be there. Rather than a *mahasamadhi,* when the body dies and the soul becomes realized, hers was an Ascension of the physical body and spirit. Mary was going more into *samadhic* states, and becoming more detached from this earth, and from the healing work she loved.

One night, news spread that Mary was walking to a beautiful grove in Avalon, near her home. The devotees intuited the great event that was about to take place. People came from every direction to be a part of this including her beloved nature spirits and devic friends. Mother nature had always helped to transmute many of her sorrows and heartaches throughout her lifetime, renewing her, no matter what trial she was going through. It was natural for this site to be her point of Ascension.

Mary's face was transcendent, emanating an incredible vibration of *samadhic* ecstasy and we knew she was communicating with the Archangels and Yeshua. Joseph and those who had been killed or Ascended were there. Archangel Gabriel, her dear friend, who had always guided her through many transitions, was present as well.

Mary had endured the loss of many loved ones—her son, her husband and others—and had always remained a pillar of strength, as an aspect of the Divine Mother. She knew the illusion of life, yet she was human, and felt the deep bonds of mother and child, wife and husband, and of friendship.

We knew Yeshua was going to help her Ascend. He then materialized in the form of light, and gradually resurrected into the physical body. The communion among all of us- Yeshua, Mary, the angels, all of the Essene community was not only about Mary's Ascension, but a celebration of our reunion with Yeshua, now in his Ascended body. Now He was present to reward his beautiful mother, who had endured a life of much suffering and heroism, and to promise her that she would never have to return to earth, except by choice.

As she stood there before the pantheon of Angelic and Ascended Beings, she asked Yeshua to help us understand how her incarnations had prepared her to be the mother of the Christ. She was shown her many lifetimes with Yeshua and her many lessons. She had been the wife of Buddha and suffered the loss of her husband when he renounced his worldly life to find realization; however, she later became enlightened too. Those of us there could also see our karmic connection with her.

With one touch of our beloved Yeshua, she would be transformed into the Ascended body to be with Him. It was a very joyful time, yet we were sad because we loved her dearly and would deeply miss her physical presence.

Everyone present was lifted to an elevated and ecstatic state, our reward for that lifetime of constant duty. After Yeshua answered all the questions, He touched Mary's forehead with his right hand, and her body transformed into the subtle body of light. Unlike Yeshua's Ascension, Mary's was instantaneous. She became young again, totally radiant as her gray hair turned to brown. We were so uplifted and above the delusion of the physical plane our sadness dissolved at that point. Before she left, Mary said, "Think of me and I will always be with you." Then she disappeared in her Ascended body with Yeshua, Joseph and the Angels and all the Great Ones. Another Ascension had been completed. Our group remained for a long time, deep in meditation.

I lived to be about 69 years old as a healer and counselor. In that lifetime I had known nothing but danger, and was educated even from childhood to always be on guard. When I finally passed, the Divine Ones were all there for me, too, and it was such a relief. The interim between lives, with Yeshua and Babaji, beyond the delusion, was ecstatic.

SOUL GROUPS ON MISSION

We came together as soul groups in Lemuria, Atlantis and in Egypt, and many of us were separated, some coerced into the dark. Of all the times the soul group came together in our training, we came in on the highest mission during the Essene lifetime with the Christ. We weren't able to savor the joys of being human because the training was so intense. There were certain things we had to do and learn for that time. As Essene children we were taught truth principles at the home-study schooling. Some children went on to marry, and others went on to the temple schools, but then, as now, we all were holding a post in a very important time. It was the divine Master Plan that Yeshua transmute for humanity, not for individual karma, but for Earth. As He hung from the cross, He lifted and transmuted tremendous karmas from Earth. Even now we are transmuting our individual and collective karma from past time periods, so that we can also Ascend. The Earth changes occurring now, and others destined to happen, are because Mother Earth is kicking off illusion. For eons people have refused to look at their karma, which has held back evolution for both the Earth and the rest of humanity. This is "Kick Our Ass" time. Last year, when I saw Lord Shiva, he showed me many Earth changes. They will be drastic! Souls that will be taken want to transition, and will go to another slower place to evolve and grow.

Our planet would have been destroyed long ago if not for the Brother/Sisterhood of Light, made up of all the Avatars, Teachers and Great Ones. Within this Confederation of Light are space beings in their Christ Consciousness, who are monitoring, and working for the planet in "Christed Ships," strategically placed all around Earth. The plan is to help the Earth ascend to a very high frequency, and in the process, darkness and illusion are also being heightened. We must go through this course of action in order for Earth and all of us to go beyond delusion, and into the Fifth Dimension. For those whose destiny it is to Ascend and stay with Earth, it will be so. Those who cannot take the frequency of the Earth will be taken off, and they are choosing to leave through Earth changes and other means.

All the souls who have recently died in hurricanes, tsunamis, 9/11, war in Iraq, and so on, left because they no longer wanted to be here and had made a prior agreement to leave. As futile as the war in Iraq may seem, many of the soldiers who have died there have evolved. Many other beautiful realms exist, where souls can transition and evolve at a slower pace. Ours is a fast-track course on Earth, and those who can't cope will want to leave. All that happens in this universe is done out of love. For those diehards who want to go all the way through, karma will be speeded up in order to Ascend, not simply dying and passing into the Light Body, but resurrecting the physical body and cells. It is important that at this time our karma is released all the way through the body and cells.

The cells carry memory of tremendous karma, and as we release karma on the subtle levels, the physical body must release it too. It takes longer to release karma from the physical cells. For this reason we are being given much help to lift it, such as healing through prayer, and by the grace of realized spiritual teachers and avatars who are embodying in this time.

The dark forces will be revealed; it is starting now. The truth is slowly starting to come out and everyone will be accountable for their actions. There again, it is not judgment. Everyone has their parts to play and those who played the darkest and most stuck parts also need to be validated. Many who chose a destructive role will have to face their karma. They chose to be a mirror so that the collective can finally see through the illusion and wake up. This universe is held together by love, and will be raised more and more into the frequency of love. Those who want to go with it will, and those who don't won't. It's that easy. We always have the abilty to choose.

When I first heard Princess Diana had been killed in a car accident, I took the time to go into solitude. I wanted to find out what was happening with her, if God allowed it. I saw that the dark forces had killed her because she was a high angel. I believe she was carrying Dodi's child. The dark forces wanted her out of there. Princess Diana was an aware being. I saw her become a huge archangel in her causal body. Because I was able to witness it happening, she said to me, "I can now help you with your healing work. You can now call on me." After that, I called on her for my healing sessions and she would come in with Mother Mary and my own mother, who had passed away by then. At the time I didn't get the connection and wondered why they were all coming in together.

Then a book fell into my hands, *Celestial Voice of Diana*, written by Rita Eide, who channeled Princess Diana after she left the body. According to the book, Diana was an aspect of Anna, the mother of Mary. I didn't know at that time that my mother was Rebekah, the sister of Mary, the mother I had lost during the lifetime with Yeshua. My mother in this life was sweet and beautiful. Everything I went through with her was to help me get to India and into my healing work and to understand "why?"

Princess Diana's role on Earth was to hold high energy in the middle of the dark reptilian energy of the British hierarchy. Princess Diana saw a lot, and after she passed away, she kept coming to me in sessions, asking me to pray for William and Harry. She was very worried something was going to happen to them. She has watched them tirelessly from the other side. I think the children were aware of her presence, and could communicate with her. They are also very high beings, and part of the plan to bring in light and bust up the darkness. During her life, Princess Diana had one heartbreak after another; however, she became an angel of mercy by doing an incredible amount of good work for humanity.

There are many many aspects of God in all hierarchies that are tirelessly working on the other side to help us. Yeshua, Mary, Princess Diana, my mother, and all the unseen angelic beings are connected, and continue to help us from the other side. These selfless beings have gone beyond ego identity, and have no need for receiving gratitude or honor.

So, once again, we are all here for the big show-down, holding the energy, waiting for the truth to come out, while watching our government literally get away with murder. We know it's a matter of time, and we're not fighting back. Our goal now is to transcend delusion, and remain positive. Last year I asked Karunamayi, "What do we do with the American government?" She said, "Go beyond the illusion."

We can be more effective as a divine aspect of God. Karunamayi said, "I want 10,000 Karunamayis out there!" We can only help when we are beyond the delusion. Every bit of karma that we release helps, because we are becoming increasingly aware, and realizing who we truly are.

The soul group that incarnated with Yeshua as his disciples and the Essene community has been clobbered by the dark in many lifetimes. It's okay though, because every bit of karma is being released in this lifetime for those of us who are destined to transcend.

Once when I was on Maui, I had a particularly bad day. I was feeling fed up with the delusion, and the innumerable lifetimes of holding the energy. I was so angry at Mother Mary and had no clue why, but I allowed the feelings to come up. I didn't want to be here anymore and cried, "Why did you get to leap out and we were left behind in this hell! You are floating in your bliss after Ascending!" She came to me and said, "Don't you remember?" And I said, "No! I don't remember."

Mary said, "During the lifetime of Yeshua I projected the future so that you could see the story, and understand it when it occurred. It was my time to leap out with Yeshua into our Ascended forms, for we do it in degrees and in groups. You are here to hold the energy longer. The time for you to transcend is now. You couldn't leave sooner. That was not in the divine plan that was formulated from the beginning. Many souls will be leaving now, having worked out much of the collective karma, as well as their own. A time is predestined for you, for you too will leap out with all the great ones who are here now, holding a tremendous energy. You and your soul group are needed on the physical plane now. Without these groups holding the energy, we couldn't achieve the goal."

I understood then why many of us couldn't Ascend at that time. It was simply timing. From the very beginning as angelic beings, we saw the whole history of Earth and we were all in agreement. If everyone had leapt into the Ascended state at the same time, no one would have been here to hold the energies for the future. We are holding the energy whether in or out of the body, but when we are in the body, we anchor the divine to the physical. Legions of Masters and angels who work with us from the other side need our human body to anchor in what they do with us, so it is teamwork. Many light workers who didn't get to leap out with the Ascension have reincarnated to make sure we succeed at this precious time. I have never had any doubt we would win. We win by going beyond the delusion.

Apparently there is a board of angelic beings— karmic board, call them whatever you want— that monitor our agreements, which we cannot break. Certain things can be altered somewhat, but the original contract is there. At this time, an entire group of us are here, who have been here longer than the others. From the other side, it is much easier to see the Earth plane as an illusion. We have to be in the illusion in order to stay here. As Mother Mary said, every-thing is timed and is released in groups. Some leap out of the illusion, others stay. Then the next group leaps out, and another group stays. These are the first, second and third waves. We're the first wave.

It has not been easy to tenaciously hold the energy and be human too. We haven't always connected with the guru or lived with the support of spiritual community as in the Essene life, which was so beautiful. We've been scattered and have had to become very strong within ourselves and pass the initiations we hadn't totally completed in Egypt. As all the karma, attachments and aversions are resolved and released, we leave it all behind, and go beyond in spirit like Yeshua did. The Ascended Masters have paved the way by their incredible work and sacrifices for this planet and for us.

As part of the original soul group we have reincarnated many times with these Avatars and Great Ones, to hold energy in different dark periods. It's all part of the play, the illusion, and it has not been fun being tortured, raped and killed because we held to the truth. In one life I was a simple and innocent herbalist believing in all ways and religions, and was accused of being a witch and burned at the stake. Death itself was never bad; it was simply the vehicle. To be ridiculed, dishonored or killed was simply the karma I have had to work out through many lifetimes. What I didn't work out before, I've had to face this time around. And, it is the same for others whose time it is to Ascend. We have been given the karma in this lifetime we didn't see before, in order to be free. We want to go beyond delusion and all suffering, and to be in joy and spiritual Oneness again. As we come back to that unity, we will be much higher angels than we were before, because we will have gone through every human experience. We'll be able to look from heavenly realms without judgment, and say, "Sure, we'll go in and help this guy, because that's where we were once."

In the scale of evolution everyone is within a certain hierarchy; there is no stopping us. We continue to evolve. It's interesting to see the same souls return again and again.

Yeshua was Amelius in the Atlantean temple and many characters in between; He returned as an avatar 2000 years ago. Krishna and Rama were the same beings as Vishnu. Krishna was one of the ancient avatars who came to India soon after the Lemurian period to clear the dark forces and energies. Looking back even further, these Great Beings are all on a council of original Earth planners, and are now working together now to uplift this planet. What an intricate story this is! And what an opportunity to be with the Masters over and over, and have them influence our lives and our actions on our remarkable journey to enlightenment.

The Yeshua story continues to unfold. Many people in my life now lived during the time of Yeshua, and they have provided me with their memories. I have also had the revelation that the original teachings of Yeshua will come forward.

The soul family is back again, and we are all starting to come together. We were not meant to go into the total Ascension at that time; we needed groups to keep reincarnating for certain times. This is a key time period. We are just now seeing what could be the collapse of our United States government. The light workers have closely watched the escalation of deception in our government during the present administration. Holding the energy, waiting and watching, has been difficult because it appears as though we're losing again, with a reptilian government coming into power and repeating the plan to take over the Earth. But all the work we have done through innumerable incarnations holding the light and being killed, raped, tortured, ridiculed and sacrificed is now coming into its completion. Karmas are being released so that we can transcend and be with the holy family forever. Over the next several years all will unfold, as it was intended.

RELEASING CELLULAR KARMA
AND ASCENDING

We are undoing the entire history of the Earth through our cells right now. The karmic time periods we've lived through were very powerful and intense. There were many elevated lifetimes in Egypt that included initiations with high Masters and worship to the great Isis, the aspect of the Divine Mother whose life was very much like Mother Mary. Isis also had a virgin conception and gave birth to Sirius, a Christed soul. I remember when Atlantis went down. Many of us were reincarnated in Egypt to be healers in the temples in order to release the animal people, who had been genetically engineered in Atlantis. The dark forces mated animals and human beings to form different species, all genetic experiments that were so bizarre and traumatic for everyone involved. I had many good lifetimes in Egypt, but the most difficult I have had were during times when the fallen angels and reptilians came in and took power.

The plan for the Earth is for the Masters and Great Ones to continually amp up the divine light so that the dark forces cannot maintain, and they'll either leave the planet or transform. Many dark forces have been transformed, and are extraordinary, powerful beings. By combining that knowledge with love and surrender, they can become tremendous instruments of the light. Milarepa, a great Tibetan realized master from the 12th century, started out as a black magician, but later repented. His guru, Marpa, made him build houses and tear them down, to release some of the karma Milarepa had accumulated through his dark actions. After Marpa worked him over, Milarepa renounced everything and went into the mountains, where he remained in meditation for many years and became realized. Maha Kala, who is one of the greatest protectors of *dharma*, was a demon that was transformed into the light. Karunamayi tells us the Divine Mother never slays demons out of anger, but through divine love, so they can be liberated.

Throughout history, avatars have incarnated during dark periods to teach the truth, and the light workers have been coming with them. Akhenaten, the great pharaoh of light in Egypt, went beyond the dogma of the old beliefs of multiple Gods and created Atenism, a monotheistic religion based on one God. He built the City of Light and was a powerful being. It is said that Akhenaten fathered a Christ child, but the child was killed. This was another time when the dark forces totally took control. Most of the light workers were killed, and the City of Light was destroyed. I know that story, because I was Akhenaten's daughter from one of his many insignificant wives. We lived inconspicuously, but he loved us both very much. I knew Akhenaten was going to be killed. He pleaded with me to leave, but I was a diehard and a martyr, and stayed with him to the end. They dragged me behind a horse through the desert to my death. I'll never do that again. I have had enough martyrdom on my time track!

Many of us have gone through remarkable periods in his-tory, and now the boil is going to be popped. In our very time we'll see great changes, not only in our government, but all governments. The truth of what has been hidden, and the deceptions of men and women of power will be revealed. In the Himalayan scriptures that Brian was documenting, the Illuminati's plan to control was again predicted. We are all here again, only this time they will not succeed. We will prevail. In truth, there is no winning or losing, but it seems, in duality, that it's been one hell of a battle. As Mother said, we have to go beyond the delusion. We're getting there. The dark forces have driven us beyond the delusion. If we had become too complacent in this delusion we wouldn't have grown, but because of what we've experienced,   every situ-ation we've encountered gives us incentive to transcend. We want to go farther than we've ever gone before— we want to be free of pain and suffering, which only enlightenment can give.

During these powerful times, it's been difficult for the

light workers. Many of them have struggled financially. We've had to support ourselves and others, and also try to grow spiritually. Many light workers whom I know are weary because they have been working and holding energies on many planes. I've been waiting a long time for positive changes to take place, in our government and in our financial system. I believe that one of the changes to take place will be that the treasury bank will return to the intent of our original Constitution, by returning to the gold standard, a previous attempt that got John F. Kennedy killed. The Illuminati violated the mandate of the original Constitution in 1913, when the Federal Reserve was introduced. Our money was no longer backed by gold, as per the Constitution, and credit was introduced. Previously, homes were never paid out of escrow, and credit was not allowed. The new plan was the Illuminati's way of controlling and redistributing wealth to the powerful. This is nothing new. The Illuminati have been in charge of the monetary system since Lemuria. In our time it will change. Many groups working behind the scenes are attempting to bring us back to the original constitution. Many White Knights in our government have been working tirelessly to reinstate the system of treasury banks backed by gold, and to stimulate the equitable distribution of monies among all. The Bible reads, "The meek shall inherit the Earth," which refers to those humble souls who know and follow God's will instead of their own. They will be the bankers and stewards of this new world. Many are innocent and detached from the world, and will get direction from

God on what to do with these huge amounts of money. The plan will be a rebuilding of Earth. Earth changes will continue, and many souls will choose to transcend. Many will stay and go through the Ascension with our planet.

Many strong-willed beings called the Indigo Children and Crystal Children are coming in at this time. The Indigo Children are from special planets that can handle this technological age. They are bright, determined, and can see through illusion. The Crystal Children are gentle and surrendered souls, but have tremendous wills to withstand the incredible challenges and trials of this time. They will be the Christs and leaders of our countries. What I was told by my Masters, (I don't know how I get this information, but it just comes in as intuition and a knowing) is that they are trying to speed everything up by 2008, because by 2012 we have to be at a certain vibrational level. Every planetary system has been watching the great experiment on planet Earth. Every eye is focused here. Will we, as a mass consciousness, be able to go beyond delusion? Will enough people reach the level of awareness needed at this time? I have no doubt we will make it, because many of us, light workers all, have been tenaciously holding the energies, and working to become enlightened. We sacrifice personal desires in order to create a livelihood in service to others. Sometimes we're afraid we'll fail, but we always take time for our spiritual practices on the path, because we are committed to the goal. As I see it, the time of the reptilians and fallen angels is almost up. They've served their purpose of being great mirrors in the duality, and as we go beyond duality, we can't even see the dark. Mirrors to our fears, illusions and darkness within, as darkness is eliminated, these beings will no longer need to be here. Many of them will be embraced by the Divine Mother and become enlightened. As my father taught me with snakes, neither we nor they will be fearful. Love will dispel all fear, and all duality.

SHIVA'S SPEED COURSE AND THE DARK
NIGHT OF THE SOUL

Last year when I came back from India, I worked to integrate the incredible experience of Lord Shiva's materialization by meditating as much as I could. Since that time I've gone through about ten year's worth of *sadhana* because of my agreement with Shiva. It hasn't been easy. Many times I felt like reneging on my deal, but then I'd surrender and say, "No, no, no, I don't mean it! You know how much I can take." After tremendous purging and going through a week of *samadhi,* I quickly realized that to be recalibrated into the high states of bliss and Oneness was just as important as going through the muck. I looked back on what I had done in order to get to these states, and realized we really have to work hard and have to want it more than anything else in this world. When we go into Oneness and the absorbed states, we can't move or eat or do anything, because we are so inward and deep in bliss that we don't want anything else. It's what we have been seeking all of our lifetimes, and is where we were before the original fall and separation in Lemuria.

One day I was driving to a friend's house and suddenly I saw all as perfection. I had to stop the car because my mind just went blank. I didn't know where I was, or how to get to where I was going. I wanted to stay in that state where everything was perfection, but I thought, "What is going to happen to me? I can't be in these states and function at the same time." I remembered that my good friends, Naomi and Ehrton lived close by, and I knew they would understand. When I arrived, they gave me a safe refuge until I returned to my normal state of mind. The next morning I woke up in total Oneness and bliss, and although I loved it, I also wondered who would take care of me. Brian used to look after me when I'd go into these states, because I'd get so far out. I knew I needed to function and be grounded. Lord Shiva took me beyond duality for about a week, keeping his end of the deal in response to my plea while in the Himalayas. I had been in the west for years, and yes, I had grown, but not as if I had done non-stop *sadhana* in India.

From that point on, everything was so accelerated, I didn't know what hit me. On one hand Shiva gave me incredible experiences of bliss and Oneness, and on the other, He gave me experiences of death. I remembered lifetimes of being tortured and killed, which brought up the fear of death and the cruelty of this Earthplane. How many times have I been tortured and killed because I was a good person working for the light? In one life, which I previously mentioned, I was accused of being a witch and burned at the stake. I could hear the people yell as the flames crackled around me, "Witch! Witch! Witch!" When we are traumatized, the shock travels deep into the unconscious. As we recall karmic timeslots, we have to experience the states of shock, or catatonia, and other emotions. When I relived the time I was raped by the twelve men in Atlantis before they lasered me down, I went into such deep states of shock, I couldn't even function. I went into shock recalling the lifetimes in Egypt where I was a high priestess and was poisoned to death. I didn't try to relive these traumas; they just came. Apparently it was necessary for my own evolution to go through them. Now I can understand what every client who comes to me has experienced, because during some lifetime, I have gone through it as well.

The duality of the light and dark is such an incredible play, and I wish I could have seen it that way when twice I went through what Christian's call "the dark night of the soul." During this intense state, I felt as if I were going through a dark tunnel and couldn't get back into the light. I felt cut off and alone, and betrayed by God and everybody. The only way I got through it was by praying, meditating, and having the support of dear friends who had already been through it.

Glenn Maxwell was one of those friends who helped me. He is a beautiful man and great healer, whom I met about five years ago through a mutual friend. Glenn was a barber in Newport Beach in the 1950's and became good friends with Dick Powell, who was married to June Allyson. Dick and Glenn were avid sailors, and spent a lot of time on Dick's yacht and became very close. Dick had a premonition he was going to die, and one day on the yacht, he said to Glenn, "If anything happens to my family, would you look after them? You are my best friend and one of the few people I can trust." Glenn promised him that he would.

Dick's premonition was right; shortly after their conversation, he died. Glenn and June Allyson later fell in love and married, and he helped raise her children. June was wealthy and lived a lavish life. Hollywood's elite, the movie stars, often hit the party circuit, and Glenn and June were no exception. Cocktails flowed day and night, and not only did Glenn become an alcoholic, but quite the playboy as well. He knew all the movie stars and directors because that was his world. I remember reading about Glenn Maxwell in some of the movie magazines; everybody loved him. Glenn said he would drink until he passed out, and hours later, wake up on the floor next to a movie star. It was a heavy and ongoing drunken scene on one level, but on another, there was a certain amount of love and unity. Glenn was with June for many years, but the relationship eventually fell apart and they divorced. He returned to his old profession as a barber in Newport Beach and later married Sally, a wonderful woman. She helped him battle his alcoholism, which is why he knew about the dark tunnels

– he said he had to go through many dark tunnels in order to get out of all the things he created in this lifetime.

Years later when Glenn had a heart attack he had an out-of-body, or near-death, experience. He wrote the book, *Glances at Eternity: A Memoir to Remember,* describing his astonishing life after death experience. He was taken to an Emerald City of Light where he was able to look down upon the heavenly realms. He saw realms where Native Americans were chasing buffalo, and where thoughts instantly manifested into reality. The higher the heavenly realm, the more subtle it gets, and the more we identify with light and the causal body. He ended up on the highest heavenly realm where he was surrounded by archangels, Jesus and Mother Mary. In front of him was a huge throne emanating a tremendous body of light, and a booming voice from the heavens that said, "Well Glenn, by now you wonder why you can't land." The Heavenly Father continued, "We have work for you to do and need to send you back, but before we do, I want you to ask me any questions you want, whatever is on your mind." So Glenn did. He asked Him about reincarnation and karma, and his inspirational book is full of information about this experience. He also said the Heavenly Father has a great sense of humor and that He is a cut up!

When Glenn came back to his body, the awe-inspiring state of Oneness dissolved and he began to sob. He didn't include this in his book, but Glenn screamed at Jesus, "This is one hell of a dirty trick! You let me experience the Oneness and go to the highest realms, then You bring me back into total limitation in a broken body? You have to compensate me! I don't want to be here after what You have shown me." So Jesus did compensate him and sent him Angel Ruth, a great healer from the heavenly realms. After that experience he continually worked on himself, and has become a very humble man. Angel Ruth works through him, and together they are one of the greatest instruments of healing I know.

In the Essene lifetime, Glenn was Jesus' cousin Zacharias, the husband of Elizabeth and father of John the Baptist. Zacharias and all the other beings during Jesus' lifetime were great souls, and have come many times in the same group to hold the energy. If there is one attribute to describe Glenn, it is kindness. I've never known such a kind, loving and patient person. Glenn is a man who had great wealth, could buy anything, party on yachts, hang with movie stars and directors, and sleep with any woman he wanted, but it did not give him happiness. When he left that life, he didn't take a penny with him.

Glenn is very evolved and selfless, and everything he does is for God. He lives for, and loves the healing work, as I do. A couple of years ago, we worked on an assignment together for a shaman from the South African Zulu Nation. The shaman's daughter was in the hospital dying of AIDS, so Glenn called me to help. Shamans cannot work on their own families because they have to be detached in order to be an instrument of healing. Glenn and I called in the angels and worked on the girl day and night. We saw from the beginning that she was absorbing the energy, and that our prayers were really going in. Within three days she walked out of that hospital free of AIDS. The shaman was absolutely blown away. We knew she was being healed because of her incredible receptivity. Sometimes people don't want to be healed, and in other cases, there is a timing or "karmic rightness" when the energy goes in and we know they are going to be recover. It may be that something in the person releases.

When I went through the dark night of the soul, I was in touch with only a few people; Glenn was one. He said that to get to the light, everyone has to go through the darkness, which happens more at the end of the path. We feel abandoned, betrayed, and rejected by God, totally alone, with nobody there for us. It is a very difficult state of consciousness to endure.

For me, it began around the time of Shiva Ratri last year. There were no formal celebrations to attend, so I went into silence for the day, chanted to Shiva and meditated. Suddenly, I started feeling cut off from God and everyone; it was horrible. It was a contrast from the high states of bliss I'd experienced the week before. After speaking with Glenn, I remembered a book by Mirabai Devi that explained these dark states, so I opened it and read more carefully. After Mirabai went into *samadhi,* she also went through these very dark states. She said out of the original creation was brought darkness and light, and when one experiences

275

the bliss and light of a *samadhic* state, one also must pass through the dark periods or hell realms. These realms are endless tunnels, from which we think we'll never emerge. It made sense to me that darkness and light must be co-creators of the same energy; why else would I go into such high states of *samadhi,* and then pass through these deep states of darkness?

Thankfully it didn't last— maybe a week— but it seemed like an eternity, enough to almost push me over the edge. I was tired of this journey, of always being on the front lines and holding the energy. I was tired of knowing what was happening behind the scenes: the corruption in our government and world, and not being able to tell people. Sure, I had clocked a lot of bliss and often went beyond the delusion, but I also struggled to go through these karmas. So on that day of Shiva Ratri I said to Lord Shiva, "I think it's time for me to go now. I'm complete and I don't want to be here anymore. I've lost everything-my husband, my money— and I have nothing but you and God. I've only wanted to be here to experience God and I don't want to drop this body until I do. I wouldn't mind if you'd lift the rest of my karma so I'd be done."

Karunamayi had said I would succeed in this lifetime, but I didn't know what I would have to go through to make it. When I went into *samadhic* states in the beginning with Papa Ramdas, I just thought "this is a cinch." I had no clue! For someone whom the Masters adored and told that very little karma remained, well, for very little karma, holy mackerel! I was reliving the whole history of the Earth! My beloved Karunamayi said if we make it in one lifetime it's because we have been going for God many lifetimes with complete sincerity and have already released a lot of karma. So I pleaded with Lord Shiva, "I am tired and I don't want to continue. The more I let go of desire, the less I want to be successful or do anything in this world. I don't have desires for the world like others. I don't want a big house or a fancy car anymore. I just want a car that runs! I want a simple place where I can meditate privately and be with you. Please do a tape release on me!"

I had seen Lord Shiva do a "final release" when I was in Banaras. When I was in a rowboat going down the Ganges with Swami Prem, I asked the swami if people get liberation in Banaras. He said, "Absolutely! Just ahead we'll be going by a burning ghat [where bodies are cremated.] I want you to meditate, and tune into what is happening." As we passed in front of the burning ghat I meditated and observed. I saw a vision of Lord Shiva and many Masters raising the subconscious of the soul who had just passed and doing a final release for liberation. I called them Shiva and the Cleanup Crew! They brought up karmas, one bit after another, and instantly released them through light. The karma was released so fast, I could hardly discern what they were. Many pilgrims travel to Banaras in total sickness to die. If they make it, it is their destiny and they will get liberation because of their sincerity.

As I went through the dark night of the soul I continued my petition to Lord Shiva, "Get me out of here! Do a final release, because I don't think I have a lot of karma left. It would be real easy for you. I'm not in Banaras; this is Sedona, but I'm ready to go!" I said that I had enough. "I've done a good job on this Earth, so just take me now." Well, my pleas didn't help! Nothing happened. I was still in the dark.

The next morning Glenn called me and said, "Angel Ruth has the strangest message for you, and I don't understand it. Maybe you can throw some light on it. Lord Shiva came to her and said you want to release your body and don't want to be here any more."

I said, "Yeeesss... that was between Lord Shiva and me. And now Angel Ruth and you know?"

Glenn continued, "Lord Shiva said you have to learn to love the Earth because you are going to be here a long time. What you are going through is just a passing phase. You now have to learn to love the Earth with all your soul and love being here. You don't have a choice. You cannot get out of here right away."

And that was Lord Shiva's reply. I got over the dark night and was able to function again. I wasn't in a high or a low state, but somewhere in between. I could talk to people again, understand their problems, and be more human and grounded. I also knew that I wasn't the doer— I could never take care of myself anyway, and it was God who sent the people to me for healing. In fact, this whole last year has been orchestrated. Shiva was putting me through fast *because I pleaded with him*!

As I got through the dark night after my trip to India, I became normal and grounded; the phone began ringing again, and my healing sessions became more enjoyable. They always have been, but with every step forward, I could help my clients even more.

This past year I've taken a lot of time out between teaching workshops and working with clients, just to get through to the next level. Shiva was definitely keeping his end of the deal and I definitely wanted to keep mine. I realized in one year's time, I'd probably gone through ten years of karma. I asked for my karma to be speeded-up. I really have to be careful what I ask for! But, I'm glad I did; it's what my soul wants. I look back and say, thank God it's all behind me. I feel very detached at this point. I can't cling on to anything, even a guru. It's a state of freedom. Clinging is actually a state of fear that creates separation.

HUMAN LOVE

I realized everything we have as a desire is idol worship because we are looking outside of ourselves for happiness. If we would just spend time looking inside, we could progress faster, because when we are not attached to the senses, we can enjoy them fully.

Most Great Ones are disinterested in the sense pleasures when they go into Oneness. Sex loses its charm when one is identified with spirit rather than the body. Not only have Masters controlled the senses, but they have gone beyond them. When Brian and I met for the first time, I had been in solitude for eight years of intense meditation, and had transmuted my sexual desire. I watched it arise with non-judgment, as energy caught in the second chakra. Then, the energy rose up my spine and was transmuted into intense bliss. Why would I then want a sexual experience? If I had explained this to a psychiatrist, I probably would have been told I had all sorts of hang ups. Try sitting down and transmuting your sexual desire and see where it leads you! All psychiatry would change if they understood that.

There is great illusion in this world. We believe we need everything on the outer, such as sex, wealth, beauty, or material possessions, but we often neglect the inner- we fail to go within and feel the spirit of who we really are. We go through lifetimes of attachments and aversions. As my beloved Papa Ramdas said at the start, "You are going to be meeting every attachment and aversion that you ever had, because attachment holds you into the senses and into the physical, and aversions are that which you don't want, so you hold it in the mind and therefore create it." Attachments and aversions keep us stuck in wrong identification, rather than knowing we are infinite spirit beings. Everything we're trying to find in the outer is within: total love, bliss, joy, peace, and contentment. When we relinquish the lesser for the better, the lesser just isn't as exciting anymore. We can still enjoy the experience, but it isn't the same. Karunamayi once said when you do years of *sadhana* you look at the same people and things differently, because the veil of egoism is gone. Even the "good" things don't seem that good anymore, which is why people pursue spiritual lives.

When I met Brian, I was no good for sex, and that was fine with him. We'd lie together and go out of our bodies into high states of bliss. No sooner would we embrace than we'd be out, sometimes half a day at a time. We'd see the Masters, and they would say, "We are so glad you two are together again." There was no thought of coming down to the body for sex. Who would want to? Brian's the only man I have known with whom who I could have this type of relationship. In truth we are complete in ourselves and never have to complete ourselves in another. Brian and I were in our own bliss, and when we came together we would transcend into Oneness.

When I was young I also experienced Oneness in meditation with Muktananda and Ramana Maharishi (through Hugo.) They were already established in that spiritual identity, and the experiences solidified my decision to not get entangled in sexual relationships. The pure and beautiful state I experienced was all I wanted and I didn't need an object for it. I was my own complete being.

As I look back on my life, I did everything backwards from everyone else. Even in high school I was interested in boys only as friends. The yearning of my soul for pure love is what took me to India and to the Masters when I was very young. I saw the highest, lived in the highest from the beginning, and, for the most part, didn't get into maya. It didn't prevent me from going through the difficult process of releasing karma and attachments. I had learned in solitude to ask, "Why am I hanging onto this? Why can't I let go of it?" And then an entire story line would come up from the unconscious. The source was usually from a trauma, and before I could release the attachment, I would have to release that trauma. As the karma unraveled, I could relax, and become completely detached from that person, as if I had never known him before! The intense longing to be with someone, in what we call love, is not love; it is attachment. It's hell! For every bit of love we receive, if we lose the object of our love we often feel rejected and go through hell.

I didn't want duality the way most people do, and I stayed beyond it to a degree. Even when I was going through the karmas, I tried to stay above duality. I refused go to bed with someone simply because he wanted me to. I would explain that I would enjoy his friendship, but was not interested in a sexual encounter. Friendship is divine. I didn't want the play of sexual magnetism and all the games that go with it. The men would either become my best friends, like brothers, or they would quickly retreat, and have nothing to do with me again. And that was okay with me!

My whole life was different from most people, because I wasn't going for a perfect this or perfect that. My karmas were being played out in 3-D because my primary goal was to grow and to become realized in this lifetime. I had no clue what I would have to go through when I started on this path, and I'm so grateful it is behind me. I remember Swami Vivekananda's words when he finally entered the total *samadhi* beyond duality, "I am grateful I was born. I am glad I did suffer. And I am glad to enter peace." Even Vivekananda, who was an ever perfect being, had to go through karma. I wonder what karma he experienced? He had to go through something; perhaps he was taking on Earth's karma.

It was after this last year the Yeshua lifetime was mirrored in me. Other stories came out as well, such as a life-

—

time in Greece where I was an oracle and high priestess and a great instrument of God. I fell in love with my advisor, Brian again, who was about seventeen years younger than me. I left all my duties at the temple and we got married. He later betrayed me when he left me for a younger woman, and I was left with nothing. I didn't have my job in the temple, and didn't have a husband.

The same story repeated itself throughout many lives. Brian was my lover. We'd marry, and I was in heaven each time. Then I would lose him. It's the cycle of maya, of highs and lows, and opposites. We're as high as a kite because we just bought the most expensive car on the market, but how long does that joy last? Then we want something else. I was seeing the endless cycle of birth and death, and how desire keeps taking us on and on. We are reborn over and over again, exposed to the same mirrors, repeating the same lessons, although the lessons get harder and harder when we miss the point. Karma returns in another, more difficult form until we finally get it and say, "I don't want this anymore. I want to go beyond delusion." It's then that we meet the great teachers, find inspiring books that reawaken us, and meet the right people to begin our spiritual journey.

I had worked through so many past lifetimes with Brian. Just when I thought I was free of him, another bubble would surface. I'd miss him or I'd feel more pain. So I would pray and ask for all the karma to be completed.

When Brian and I were living in Santa Fe, he became depressed at one point, so we did a healing session. A

Chinese lifetime opened up where he had fallen in love with an empress who wanted to marry him and leave all her duties. Then with no warning, he was told by her people that not only could he never see her again, but he must leave the kingdom. He was devastated, and felt completely betrayed. How could the love of his life do this to him? She didn't even have the decency to tell him to his face. As I was working with him, I became angry at this empress for treating my Brian like that!

After our work together, I wasn't feeling well, so I went into meditation. I saw that I was a young beautiful Chinese girl, about nineteen. I had long flowing black hair and dark dancing eyes, and was full of mischief. My father in this life was my father in that life as well. He was a Chinese sage and great leader, and as I meditated I felt incredible grief and saw that he was dying. I was the heir to the throne, and was overwhelmed at the thought of being empress. After he passed, I began to see my coronation ceremony. I was dressed in a beautiful white gown and saw myself walking up a long aisle with people on either side. I felt great strength and power as I walked, as if God had taken me over and had empowered me to be empress. There was no ego and I felt the glory and power of the Holy Spirit, and any doubts that I previously had about handling this lofty post were gone. I knew that honor and duty would be my life's purpose, and were more important than anything else at that time.

The period after the coronation wasn't so much fun. I had people looking to me for direction at every moment.

I missed my father, was forced to grow up fast, and was expected to be wise. I appointed a monk to be my spiritual advisor, and he assisted me with my meditation, prayers and decision-making. He became my best friend, and I ended up falling madly in love with him. He was none other than Brian. We kept our love affair discreet, except for a few close attendants. If the affair had become public it would have caused a huge scandal. I don't know how long it lasted, maybe a year, but it became clear to me that I couldn't continue that way. The worry of being discovered and the guilt of committing such a dishonorable act were taking me away from my duties. I had to choose: to leave with him, or have him leave so I could assume my own power. I knew I couldn't let my father or God down, and decided I must choose duty over love. It tore my heart apart to tell him personally, so I had my friends handle it. We were both heartbroken. Later it was arranged for me to marry another man, who was a creep. It was all for show.

In this lifetime, I have always wanted to be with Brian for the rest of our lives, and for us to become enlightened together. I was trying to fix maya, trying to make maya beautiful, which is not possible, because it is all illusion! We have to go beyond the story. In one of my letters from Hugo he said, "You've seen one side of the coin, but now you have to go beyond the coin." For every high we experience and every desire that is fulfilled, we will always lose, through death or circumstance. Human existence is fickle. The only pure love I have experienced is the love of the

Masters, and the state of Oneness. Over and over, we give and receive love. These experiences are what make life beautiful. Human sexual love is the highest experience that most people know, but it is all temporary. We can merge with another high being, but it is a merging of spirit with no desire. Only through the soul will we know Love.

TRANSFORMING KARMA IN JADE

If someone comes into your life who continues to hate or resist you in spite of your good will efforts, that person may have committed a destructive act against you in a past life. I have personally experienced it a number of times, although never before as close to home as with Jade.

Annie and I have been friends since childhood. I am also very close to her family. One of the things I love about them is how attuned they are to each other. That changed when Annie's granddaughter, Jade was born. From the first time I met Jade, I didn't feel close to her. During her first four years, my attempts at connecting with her were met with resistance, and she wouldn't let me into her heart. Not only that, but she wanted to control everyone and everything, and even her parents were becoming alienated from one other. I had always felt a deep connection with this family, so it was painful to watch.

During a visit to Annie and her family, I watched Jade in action. A group of us had come back from a shopping trip, and Jade was still strapped in her car seat. Her mother and Annie were busy unloading packages, so I went to get Jade. She began to scream, because she wanted her mother or grandmother to come get her. Working at my father's camp taught me from an early age not to give in to tantrums. I decided to confront Jade on her outburst. Children are aware beings and I knew never to "talk down" to them, so I said to her, "You have an investment in staying in control, and I'm not going to let you do that. It's not good for you." She cried for two days because she knew she could not control me. The need to control is a valence for hiding fear and to avoid being hurt.

I visit Annie several times throughout the year, typically during the holidays, so I don't see Jade often. However, the anger she exhibited toward me at that last visit lingered in my mind. About a year had passed before I saw Annie again. It was Thanksgiving and I hoped that Jade had matured and would let me into her heart. This was not the case; in fact, our relationship worsened. The dynamic between us was so disruptive I considered not going back at Christmas.

When I returned home, I knew I had to find the cause of this rift, so I sat down in meditation and asked what the karma was between us. I saw she was an angel from an original soul group but had been coerced over to the dark side; apparently her soul wanted to find out what power was about. At some point, each of us has a time when we choose to misuse power and control, so that we can understand the difference between power and surrender.

—

To seek power is to desire manipulation and control. Surrender to God and to the higher forces is release of control, and a return to the love of spirit.

Jade was my enemy in several lifetimes, and she had me killed more than once. We lived during a time before Earth, when the light and dark were involved in intergalactic warfare. In one lifetime, both she and I were captains of our own starships. I was the commander of a group of light workers who were trying to save a planet from being destroyed. I was unable to complete the mission because I was killed, and the planet was destroyed. The dark forces continued creating havoc in the universe through misuse of power and refused to surrender to the Light. Eventually God banished the dark souls to a planet of their choosing, which was Earth. Our karma continued on Earth as I recalled two more lifetimes where Jade had me killed.

When I was going through these karmas with Jade, I knew I had to deal with the control issues now, or we'd have a Hitler on our hands as she became a teenager. Jade was dividing Annie's whole family against each other. She wasn't completely successful, but she was definitely on her way. I knew that if a child is into power, and is not confronted early on, he or she will continue. Jade is an Indigo child, and some are hell for their parents because they have similar control issues to work out.

I prayed to Jesus and Babaji for help. They came in laughing, and said, "She is your charge. We will help you, but she chose to come into this family so you could straighten her out."

I went into meditation and asked for Jade's permission on a soul level to help her, which she granted. I then prayed to the angels, guides and Masters to bring up all Jade's karma concerning power. I asked that a diamond pyramid be placed over her with mirrors facing inward, to reflect back her own power and manipulation, and then have it transmuted with the violet flame. I stayed with her on an inner level for three weeks while she went through this. Every time I stopped, thinking the work was finished, I could feel her psychically attack me, because there was more work to be done and she didn't want to be left in limbo.

I was focusing not only on our personal karma, but on her misuse of power. In one life she was a king, and had many people killed because they wouldn't listen to her. As her ego was being dissembled, and karma was transmuted, on an inner level, I could feel her journey through hell. I can't imagine what it must have been like to deal with her personally during that time!

After three weeks, I felt the karma had been lifted and the misuse of power was totally dissipated. Later, during a meditation session with a group of friends, I sensed Jade's soul there with me in love, friendship and gratitude.

That Christmas when I went to visit Annie and her family, Jade was a completely different child. Her whole personality had changed into one of sweetness and surrender. She was thoughtful, loving and kind.

—

ST. GERMAIN AND RETURNING
TO THE CONSTITUTION

St. Germain has been many characters on this Earth. During the French Revolution he was Count Comte, a member of royalty. He knew his total Ascended Mastership at that time, and Napoleon and Marie Antoinette were his disciples. St. Germain was very adept at earning tremendous amounts of money. There is a big joke among the Masters, "Give all the money matters to St. Germain and don't let Yeshua near it because he doesn't have a clue!" St. Germain was also the master responsible for the establishment of democracy. During the French Revolution, he attempted but failed to unite all the European countries and bring them into a democracy. St. Germain was also Christopher Columbus— it is his karmic destiny to be a part of America, and as such, he was instrumental in the formation of the United States of America. Democracy is the reason our country has been so great. But just when the

Republic seemed to be progressing, the Illuminati reared its ugly head again in 1913, and implemented the Federal Reserve Act. Eventually our treasury banks were no longer backed by gold, as mandated in the original Constitution. Unbeknownst to the people, much of our democracy was destroyed at that time. The Federal Reserve introduced credit so that banks could accrue huge profits from the interest, and they instigated taxes to pay for government jobs that served the people. In the original Constitution, certain taxes were allowed, but service jobs were exempt.

The conflict between the light and dark has repeated itself since Lemuria. The Illuminati have inserted themselves into every great culture, to manipulate, control and make the people a slave race. The fallen angels are very jealous of the step of Ascension, because they cannot achieve that status, unless they surrender to the light and go through all their karma. They have done everything in their power to hold humanity down and slow the progress of evolution. We would never have stayed here on Earth unless we had agreed to be programmed and implanted. The evolutionary plan was for the angelic beings to descend and to hold energy.

When I was a little girl Yeshua came to me and said, "In your lifetime you will see tremendous change. You will see the government and monetary system change." I've waited for a long time to see this happen.

Nine years ago I had the opportunity to become part of a project, under the umbrella of a very wealthy man.

He had a good heart and was devoted to Jesus. One day Jesus appeared to him and said, "Help my little ones." The wealthy man was part of a lucrative business venture where a huge sum of money could be loaned to small European banks. The interest earned from those loans is beyond imagination. After his vision of Jesus, he decided to open his investment to "the little people," in whatever amount they could afford, to be included in his investment. People put in various amounts, but when the money is paid out, it will be equally distributed among all the recipients of this project. For many years the money has been rolled over, and there are trillions of dollars available. The United States government has held back the project's distribution, knowing that if this money is paid out, those in power will be exposed for their illegal actions. Everything will be made public, including the fact that because the sixteenth amendment was never ratified, it is not part of the Constitution, and as a result, the Federal Reserve is not legal. Those who were born in America know the potential of this country, and many are waiting for its return to greatness.

As is becoming painfully clear, the war in Iraq appears to have been initiated under false pretext. It seems that it was based principally on the United States' intention to control the Iraqi oil, and the anticipated wealth that could be gained. The United States government is responsible for the deaths of many innocent beings for the sake of selfish gain. The karma of the Illuminati is so horrific that when they die this time, they will get the choice of going through all of their karma or a "second death," whereby their individuality is relinquished and they merge into matter. Some will choose to go through their karma, and others will choose the second death.

This is the final showdown, and in order for humanity to finally wake up, certain things still need to be mirrored back to us by the dark forces. When over half of the people can see truth clearly, we will not need these mirrors anymore; it is happening rapidly. Numerous books and movies are exposing the deception. Many Masters are here to awaken us and, as was signified by the Harmonic Convergence, Christed ships are amping up the crystalline energies on the Earth. With every outpouring of light from the higher realms, people start to awaken. It's like popping a bubble where everything has to surface, evil included.

The Illuminati have a belief that they can defy the Law of Karma and continue to act with impunity, until now. At this time, a shift in the collective consciousness is apparent, and change is imminent.

Our project was originally started by St. Germain in France during the French Revolution. Many of us were there as adepts of St. Germain to hold the energy. Napoleon was one of his greatest disciples and could have united all of Europe, which was St. Germain's plan. However, Napoleon chose the path of power. St. Germain is in charge of this project coming through, and the Masters have been working nonstop to make it happen. My feeling is they underestimated the dark. It's similar to what Krishna went through when he battled the demons in the Battle of Kuruksetra; He said it was beyond anything he'd ever imagined, and consequently had to devise more complex strategies. The demons also know the principals of light; they just reverse them.

When the project is released, there will be a stock market crash. If all transpires as intended, everyone who has a mortgage on a house will own it free and clear; all credit card debt will be excused. The money from these projects will be equally distributed to everyone in the world, and as the Bible says, "the meek shall inherit the Earth." There will be no starvation, there will be housing for all people, and educational programs for the poor will be implemented to enable them to care for themselves. The Illuminati will no longer control the money or hold people hostage in a semi-survival state. Everyone will be able to do their spiritual practices and seek the truth. Among the Illuminati's protocols are the elimination of the pledge of allegiance and prayer in schools, control of money/communications/media/politics, and weakening the people with allopathic and "illegal" drugs, and the chem trails project (poisonous jet streams).

When I realized how much I've been clobbered by the Illuminati lifetime after lifetime, I despised them. The same thing happened on Maui. If we could have stayed together as a group, we could have opened up the karma in the world much faster, but the group wasn't ready to confront the Egyptian karma; timing was off. I was on my own to experience that karma, forgive my enemies and go beyond the delusion. Forgiveness has been an integral part of my spiritual path, because if I don't forgive, I suffer. The minute I release it, the karma goes back to the perpetrator.

The Illuminati have been trying to tear down the fabric of democracy, and create a one-world government with themselves in power. They mock the efforts of the Light Beings by control and manipulation, lacking humility and surrender to God. The conflict of the Dark and Light forces is one of perpetual control and manipulation versus surrender, while Light Beings are firm in the understanding that God alone is the Doer. One cannot reach the higher states without humility and understanding, and without accepting the consequences of karma. Papa Ramdas had a story about reaching realization, "We offer God one rupee for realization, and God says, 'No' and then we offer two rupees! 10 rupees! 100 rupees! And God says, 'No, no, full price has to be paid.'"

All imperfection has to be released in order for us to come into the original blueprint of who we are. For every karmic action we release, and every level we ascend, everyone, including our ancestors, benefits. We are working out so much ancestral karma from all lifetimes and for all beings. As we release all karma, it goes forward and back seven generations. Most of the beings coming in now are here to help their ancestors. We are just beginning to see changes. Politicians' illegal actions will be exposed through the judicial system, with rock solid cases and indisputable proof of their guilt, painstakingly prepared by the White Knights over many years.

Everyone, the Light and the Dark Forces, is on the planet right now. Everyone is signing up for a ticket to Earth, knowing it's the fastest time in Earth's history to evolve, and a key moment for which we've all waited a long, long time. In surrender, we cannot know the outcome. We have to remain in the moment and take the next step, which is what we have been taught. We must learn equanimity in all things— happiness, pain, success and failure— because it is all part of duality. The only way we can succeed is to overcome ego and release karma. It's not what happens to us, but it's how we handle it. Those who evolve the most use suffering as a stepping stone; my dad taught us that when we were young. Suffering is a great privilege— we can either go down with it or use it as a step to go to another level. God looks with favor upon those who have the greatest trials and suffering in order to become free.

Suffering can take many forms, either self-inflicted or through apparent innocence or victimization. Good karma-bad karma- labels don't apply. A humble little person in India who is fortunate enough to go to Karunamayi's school may learn all the mantras, but goes home hungry because of extreme poverty. That one may suffer throughout the whole life, but will learn to embrace suffering, rise to perfection and become a saint.

I believe one reason why so many Great Ones have become realized in India is because most people have so little, attachment is not an issue. It's much easier to get attached when one has access to money and material things.

Yet many throughout the world are becoming more conscious. Mary, one of my clients, has been a cowgirl all her life, and said, "I have everything that should make people happy. I have thousands of acres of land, I'm outside every day in the fresh air, I'm my own boss, I have plenty of money, but I'm miserable. I want the *Big One* now. I want to get through the suffering to go beyond suffering. I'm removing the boulders, not only from the cattle trails, but from my own eyes now. I'm on the big trail for keeps. I want something that is permanent, not something that can give me joy one minute and sorrow the next."

We're all here— little people, Great Beings, avatars and their disciples— for the *Big One*. Auditoriums full of people will go into the Holy Spirit and experience the *Shakti*.

THE FINAL SHOWDOWN

Many tools are now available to help us evolve, including natural substances containing antioxidants that can release cellular memory. My friend Charles was talking about recent scientific research of the effects of sound on water. Actual tests have proven water can be purified through prayer. It's a coming together of science and religion, so to speak, in that science is providing quantifiable data on the effects of prayer and energy. I believe there is a machine in existence now that can undo the engram command phrases, or implants, that were programmed into us many lives ago by the dark forces. It scans the brain and determines exactly what is missing according to the person's original blueprint. I remove implants through prayer to the angels and Masters, by asking them to bring up the phrases and to quickly and painlessly release them.

The Illuminati will be exposed, and those men and women of power will no longer be heroes, nor will they control. It may seem odd, but we want them to have money because we want everyone to have money. I personally don't want them on the planet if they are going to play the game of manipulation, harm others, and create wars. War is big business for the Illuminati, as in Iraq, when they first deceived us with regard to their motives, then diverted our attention in order to gain control over Iraqi oil. Now they want to invade Iran for selfish purposes. Those involved will live their karma. For everyone they have hurt through their greed and misuse of power, they will face the karmic consequences. This is the Day of Judgment the Bible talks about. The deeds of men will be speeded up for everyone to see, and it's happening on the other side too. A time will come when everyone will meet in a common frequency. The veils will be gone and we will see the Oneness of worlds, and be able to go wherever we want just by thought. We will be inter-dimensional.

Just as Princess Diana went into her high causal angelic form, so will all of us go into those forms. That is who we really are. Princess Diana, John F. Kennedy and John Kennedy, Jr. are all great souls that came back to uplift and bring truth to this world. JFK said all of his family members are members of the White Brotherhood. Before he died he knew about the Federal Reserve and that our money was worth absolutely nothing. We were in total debt. He tried to restore the gold standard according to the original Constitution, and he was killed for it. It wasn't time. Everyone knew he was a great hero, but many didn't know why. When I had the experience on Forbes Island when he downloaded me with all the information, he said, "We are all working for our beloved America. It is such a blessed country. We *must* succeed in our original plan. All the great ones who love America are working tirelessly for her on the other side."

All the Great Beings— Lord Shiva, Parvati, Lakshmi, Vishnu and all the Hindu Gods, the Egyptians and Native Americans— all beings and religions are working together. I see Mother Mary and Quan Yin working together to look after the children of the Earth because they both love us dearly. Quan Yin is on a board of great healers and brings in teams of healers. She is a *bodhisattva* of the Buddhist tradition, but She is not a buddist as such. All are Great Beings of Oneness who have gone beyond all dogma and concepts, and are not of any one religion. Babaji is not a Hindu, nor is Jesus a Christian- They are beyond all religions. They are placed in a hierarchy and are put into service according to their levels. They all have responsibilities and are continually working on our behalf. The angelic beings we call on to help us are humble and need no praise, but they appreciate us when we honor them. We don't know their names— there are legions of these expertise teams. They need no personal gratification, and are simply working for God, out of profound Love, and beyond ego.

In this lifetime I have been called to hold huge segments of energies for Earth. When I went to Germany I worked on the prison camps of the Holocaust and saw many discarnate beings hovering over the Earth, still in shock over being killed. It was the same at Pearl Harbor. All those beings had to be cleared. Frequencies from Indian battles, wars, and brutal deaths are held within the Earth until they are cleared. We can clear whole areas of the Earth, and she carries a lot.

I received a call from a man who said he was getting visitations at night from spirits. I saw right away they were from a Native American battle. I cleared all of them by asking Archangel Michael and legions of angels to bind and take any Earthbound entities off the planet, to a place where they could evolve. Whole areas can be liberated this way. I then asked for the trauma of the Earth to be released through the violet flame. I do this often- it's like a computer game, getting the negative energy of the affected area decreased from a level five to zero!

Anyone can do this through prayer. All we have to do is ask. Angels and beautiful beings will come in and lovingly take the Earthbound beings off this planet into realms where they can evolve. They are Earthbound because of trauma or attachment to this Earth. They may have had money but couldn't spend it because they died or were addicted to alcohol or drugs. Earthbound spirits will attach to other alcoholics or drug addicts to get the high. Regardless of the reason, they just get stuck here and need to transition to the higher realms.

When I came to Sedona seven years ago I was told by my guides to work on karmic time periods in history, and to send healing to every soul who lived during that time, and who was willing to receive the healing. I called it "sending it out to the field." We've been doing that since Maui, but this was a mission to clear in a more concentrated way. When we got into the Atlantean time slot in Maui and sent the healing out to the field, we received calls from people wondering why they were going through hell; a result of the "field" healing working on them. I've been doing field healing for over 25 years, and when I came to Sedona, the work became more concentrated. I met a beautician, did some healing work on her, and she soon began psychically attacking me. I tracked it back and learned she had been a sorceress in Egypt who posed as my friend and later had me killed. She was jealous and wanted me out of the way in order to take my position.

Time and time again everyone is getting busted. There are no secrets anymore because we can track karmic action back to its source. (*Who did this? Okay, I forgive him or her.*) Then, we let it go.

It's been amazing to see the web of karma unravel on Earth as a whole, watching the Illuminati try to take over again, and succeed for a time. In order to see delusion, the collective must evolve consciously. No victim, and no perpetrator. Everyone has a role to play. The suffering shows where we need to grow and what we are unconsciously holding onto, such as a trauma or desire.

Lester taught us that every ego reaction can be used for growth, by taking responsibility and asking, *is it control or approval?* I want to control. I want approval and I'm not getting it, and so on. The ego is so very simple. It is offended when it doesn't get approval. But approval isn't love. Love is giving, sharing and all the divine qualities of trust and understanding. Approval is wanting appreciation for being beautiful, funny, smart, and is impermanent. Love is helping people to see the truth and giving with no strings attached. That is what we are seeking in all relationships. That is also why most of the relationships between male and female have failed. My friends Ehrton and Naomi are divine beings who love each other in a spiritual and unconditional way. It's not based on *What can you do for me?* They love helping each other and other people and it is a love that is not based on exclusivity.

Human love has caused nothing but pain and separation, an endless search for happiness outside of ourselves. We fell from the divinity of spirit into the senses and sought gratification from them in order to be happy. It became a vicious cycle. We couldn't get beyond the senses and that became our only satisfaction. We forgot how to find ourselves in spirit.

Many souls will achieve the final realization after countless lifetimes of going toward spirit and conquering karma. Papa Ramdas used to say that if enough of the rope is burned, the whole rope will drop away. Going beyond duality through deep *samadhic* states also burns the karmic rope.

The light workers today do not have the luxury of retreating into the forest to find realization, as the *rishis* taught us ages ago. Still, we must put God first if we want to be enlightened. At the same time, we may need to earn a living and raise a family too, among other things. The result of this struggle has been incredible growth. Most devotees have tried to evolve right in the middle of daily life, juggling the material and spiritual. They are the heroes.

MEETING MIRABAI AND VISHWANANDA

B efore my trip to India last year I met Mirabai, a beautiful English woman from South Africa. My friends encouraged me to meet her because she gives *Shaktipat darshan.* The first time she gave me *darshan* we held each other close and I felt that she was an old, familiar friend. I knew her soul, and she knew mine. She said, "Thea Ishwari, go into the void." I totally let go and fell back onto the floor and into a trance. Attendants had to move me over to the other side of the hall because many people had come to receive *darshan.* I was in that absorbed state for two hours.

I went to the Yoga Center where she was giving *darshan.* She wanted me to sit next to her because she knew I was a healer and could transmute energies and karmas. As she hugged people she would take on their karmas and transmute them, and I would help her to release it in half the time by bringing in the angels of the violet flame. Usually it took her 48 hours after giving *darshan* to release everyone's karma, but through prayer the angels would lift it off much faster.

Mirabai became very instrumental in helping me mirror the Essene lifetime, and I loved her very much. She's a Westerner and it was easy to talk to her about my deep experiences. I shared one about a supposed saint that psychically attacked me, and she said that the same "saint" psychically attacked her also. I could share things with her that I couldn't tell anybody else because they would think I was blooming mad. It was wonderful. She wanted to connect with me when I went to India, but it wasn't possible because I had already been in India for four months, and my body was falling apart. I would have loved to have traveled with her, but it was time for me to get back to the states.

Mirabai had told me before I went to India that I would leave certain karmas behind, and in order to get to the deep states I would have to go through tremendous periods of darkness. I was relieved that it didn't happen in India, because I was vulnerable there, with too many people around, and no safe place to go through such things. Her book *Samadhi* helped me to understand the soul must go through the darkest of dark periods because we are reliving the beginning of creation, which began out of light and darkness. She was a great teacher to me for a short time, and my soul told me I could be her friend.

Mirabai and my friend David told me about a great master, Swami Vishwananda, who lives in Europe and is from a Hindu community in the Mauritius Islands. Mirabai talked a great deal about this incredible being. As *prasad* for Mirabai He regurgitated a *Shivalingam*, an oblong object that symbolizes the omnipresence and primeval energy of Lord Shiva.When he materializes an object through regurgitation, Vishwananda's followers call this "giving birth." He can also materialize objects from his hands. Mirabai and a few of us that were at David's house used this marvelous *Shivalingam* for a Shivaratri celebration. That night I slept in David's shrine room with the *Shivalingam* and it put me very much in touch with Vishwananda. I was fascinated with him, but at the time I didn't know if he would become my teacher. I just knew there was something I needed from him.

Meanwhile, David had made several trips to Europe to see Vishwananda and had seen him in trance-like states where rose oil would stream from his head. David told me that since he was very young, Vishwananda had *Stigmata*[39] and absolute miracles would happen around him. David and several other Americans arranged for Vishwananda to come to California, so David asked if I would help because I'm accustomed to serving Masters.

Several months before, a Sedona newspaper asked me to write an article about Vishwananda and I enthusiastically agreed. I started writing questions for the interview and prayed to him that I would ask the right ones in order to reveal who he is. At that point the questions started flowing so fast I couldn't keep up. After I had written a num-

39 A mystical and unexplained phenomenon where an individual experiences the suffering and/or bears the wounds of the crucifixion of Christ.

309

Sri Swami Vishwananda

ber of questions I suddenly became absorbed, and I saw
my beloved and ancient guru, Babaji, and Vishwananda
together in their light body forms with both of their hands
up in blessing for me. It was as if they were a team, work-

ing together. When I came out of meditation I said, "Holy mackerel! How can this be that he is in his physical body, but I can see him in his light body the same as Babaji? Who is this guy?" The only other Masters who had come to me in their light body were Babaji, and Dhyanyogi, but this wasn't the same. I was very excited to meet Vishwananda, and knew he would have key information about Babaji. When I was in my first month of solitude at Lester's ranch in Sedona, Babaji had shown me that I had been with him many times in the Himalayas, and between worlds. I had a memory of Babaji sending me to Mataji, his spiritual Ascended sister, to look after me. I also recalled journeying with both of them. I knew Vishwananda was a devotee of Mahavatar Babaji, but didn't know the details. Then Babaji showed me that not only was Vishwananda a devotee, but that they are a "package deal."

Some weeks later I started working on my questions again and asked for Vishwananda's help, and a similar thing happened— I was taken into an absorbed state and saw Babaji and Vishwananda in their subtle light bodies blessing me. I couldn't get to California fast enough! I left a few days early so I could help David prepare. Because a great deal of preparation was needed, and David was frazzled, (like I usually am when Karunamayi comes to Sedona,) I was happy to take the pressure off him. David put me in charge of the reception committee for Vishwananda's arrival. Mirabai was to garland him, and the remaining devotees would form two lines and chant to Vishwananda as he entered the retreat center. We bought lovely flowers, and beautifully decorated the altar and retreat center. Many of his German staff had arrived early to serve him and set the energy for Vishwananda. A group went to the airport to meet Vishwananda; I stayed behind to get the reception committee ready. When he arrived, he was wearing western-style clothes with his long hair pulled back in a pony tail. The reception committee performed according to plan, but when I saw him it was as if I were in a state of shock. It was like seeing Yeshua for the first time in 2000 years. I thought, "This guy is so familiar, and is someone I know really well." As he walked past, he only briefly acknowledged me.

I went up to my room and got ready for dinner, and when I came down I somehow managed to be seated at the same table right across from Vishwananda! Mirabai and other beautiful people were at that table, and I felt so honored to be there. Vishwananda is more of a Westerner. Not only can he speak perfect English, but he uses slang as well! He joked around and seemed very approachable. Sitting across from him, seeing an incredible blue ray around him, I finally said, "I don't know who you are, but I'm seeing the blue ray of Krishna around you. You've come to me in your light ascended body with Babaji, and I don't know how Masters in their physical bodies can do that?"

He just grinned, and looked into my eyes with beautiful, loving, and dancing brown-black eyes. Everyone watched to see where he was looking because every look would shoot so much *Shakti* into our being, we'd be higher than a kite. In a very short time, he lifted me to a very high state of bliss. While in that state, I became very bold, because I felt one with him. I learned years ago from Hugo to go within and not follow the master around, so I wasn't accustomed to a master walking in our midst and sitting at the same table! I was used to a master coming out, giving *darshan*, then leaving. I surrendered the desire to be around him, although it was easy to become addicted to his eyes and the bliss. Everyone was hanging around and following him, and I did as well, to a point, but I also spent a lot of time in my room going within. My friend Jen, who had overcome bipolar disorder, and Joe, a student from Albuquerque, had come with me. Joe was trying to follow Vishwananda around, so I told him, "I'm going to give you good advice— get him within. Go into your room and do meditation, meditation, meditation, and he's going to give you tremendous grace as you go within." Joe did as I suggested and not long after, Vishwananda walked into Joe's room, sat on his bed and started talking with him! I had had a similar experience with Ananda Moyi Ma, which is why I knew this was the right thing to do.

That first night after dinner, a number of people came over to meet him. He sat on the couch and one of the ladies asked, "Why are you here? What is your mission?" He said, "My mission is to bring Love." Another woman told Vishwananda that she heard he might be a very great saint from the past who had been her teacher. He smiled at her with recognition, put his hand over her head and said, "You are my disciple." Suddenly, ash poured out from his hand onto her head.

My room was upstairs near his, and David and Vishwananda were sitting on the stairs talking. I wanted to be invisible, and sneak past them so I could go to my room, but Vishwananda took my hand, and said, "Sit down!" So I sat down with him, the same boldness I had felt at the dinner returned, and I blurted out, "We need an ashram here, where people can be safe." He responded, "Yes we do, and I'm working on that."

Mahavatar Babaji

I told him that I had been on the path since I was young, and wondered if it were harder at the end than at the beginning. He gave me a beautiful analogy, "It's like the ocean, with the waves hitting the sand. At the end of the ocean, the waves crash down upon the sand. It's likened to karma. As the waves hit the shore, it's harsh; and so it is at the end of the path, you bring up the bigger karmas you couldn't handle before, and it's very rough at times. Yes, it gets harder, but it also gets easier, because you become more of a witness, and it goes faster."

Every moment with him was like gold. I cherished being with him, receiving such clear answers. I wondered, why I was so fortunate to get in on this?

The next morning I left my room thinking of Karunamayi, and realized that I felt detached from her. I still loved her deeply and felt her within, but I knew somehow there was another step for me to follow. Weeks before, when Babaji and Vishwananda came to me in meditation, I sensed that Vishwananda might be my next step. For years I had been so one-pointed on the Divine Mother, that I had forgotten my connection to Babaji, and Ram, and the Great Ones whose praises I used to sing. I felt that Vishwananda was opening up another door for me. Then, as I walked out into the hallway, I saw him. Each time I saw him I went into shock, and this was no exception. I was about to say something when he took my hands, looked into my eyes and said, "Amma is compassion, I am love. You have completed that course with Amma. You are now in my course." I knew it was so. My tears were streaming down, and I asked him to initiate me into a mantra, and He said, "Yes, but you have to be patient, and wait." That seemed to be his lesson to me- waiting and giving up, and when I least expected it he'd surprise me!

There were about 500 people that met Vishwananda the first time in the United States, and he said, "I have come for my old friends. I've come for a certain group of people."

Later, when I had interviewed him for the Sedona article, he said to me, "You must advance. You have come to advance. Babaji has been watching you since you came in. Babaji is your ancient guru." And when I asked who he is to Babaji he said, "Babaji is my mother, my father, my everything." At those words I became overwhelmed with emotion and started to cry. He just looked at me with his loving eyes, but didn't say anything. When I was able to continue with my questions, I asked if he was an ever perfect being, a soul coming in without karma, and he said, " Yes." When I asked why he had the stigmata and what relationship he had with Jesus, Vishwananda said, "Jesus is my big brother. I wanted to experience what my big brother went through. I don't do it anymore."

"What did you experience?" I asked.

"I experienced tremendous bliss, and suffering at the same time."

I told him how I had always longed to be with Babaji in the Himalayas, and how Babaji had told me I couldn't be with him physically this lifetime. Vishwananda said, "You have had many lives with Babaji and I will open them up for you." Boy, has he ever! He continued, "Are you ready to take the big leap with Me?"

I responded, "Yes, but I don't know how to do the big leap. I can only do little leaps. I surrender in the moment."

Vishwananda said, "That's how you take the big leap. You surrender and live in the moment, and then the big leap comes."

I knew he was the guru to take me to the next step. I had

thought Karunamayi was that person, but I needed another piece. I needed to get back to my ancient gurus, to the very beginning, Babaji, and to Krishna.

I had a whole notebook filled with questions for Vishwananda, but he grabbed the notebook from me, read the questions himself and responded only to the ones he wanted to answer! He said, "We can have a big interview later of all of these questions, but now is not the time."

Then he told me that I have come to advance, and that Babaji sent Vishwananda to me. That really did it. I was determined to spend as much time as possible with him. I went to all his public programs where the finest *kirtan* musicians in all of California played, and I received his *darshan*. I became very close to Vishwananda's German entourage. Through them I learned more about who Vishwananda is, and they saw how attuned I was to him. I sat in front with his entourage, and we set the pace for the *kirtan*. I went wild over the Krishna bhajans. The *Shaktipat* was being totally awakened again and I wanted to dance and sing, but I was so blissed out I couldn't even get up! I was in heaven again through Grace. When it was my turn to see him for *darshan*, he put ash on my forehead. It was such a powerful transmission of *Shaktipat,* that I had to practically crawl back to my seat.

On July 4 we did a fire ceremony, or *homa*, where we chanted the *Gayatri* mantra, and offered up all our sins into the fire. At that time, he asked us to make a wish and a prayer, for America. I asked him for a new administration in our government, with God-loving and conscious people as our leaders. He laughed and nodded. I could tell he is very involved with America. His mission in Germany has been to help heal and lift the horrible wound from the Nazi regime, as has Mother Meera, and the Germans are now experencing tremendous growth of consciousness. Vishwananda's schedule is solidly booked as he travels throughout Europe and to America.

There was a young man traveling with Vishwananda who was in constant *Shakti*. Vishwananda kept hitting him on the head or looking him in the eye and the kid was in bliss all the time. Those who get close to Vishwananda feel great liberty; at the same time, they feel as if they could even sit on his lap in total surrender.

The German people that traveled with him were beautiful, yet I could tell they were a little threatened by the growing numbers of people surrounding Vishwananda. They knew that his mission was starting and that they couldn't be as intimate and close to him as before. We all knew that. We also knew that he will have a huge following. One Frenchman, named Pierre, was rubbing Vishwananda's feet, and asked, "Master, will we ever again be able to be as close to You, like this?" Vishwananda lowered his eyes, and sadly shook his head. My feeling is that he has come to bring millions of souls across. He is dynamic, and beautiful.

The time I spent in between programs with him I saw such playfulness. I've never seen anything like it. Papa Ramdas was playful too, but not quite as playful as

Vishwananda! I went to Ojai Valley with them and stayed at the retreat center there. I went into the living room, and Vishwananda jokingly placed his foot on the chest of a young man who was in a deep state. Then he took Pierre's wife, in her wheelchair, on a spectacular joy ride through every room in the house. He went so fast, he nearly collided with everyone, and just laughed the whole time! Pierre's wife was delighted.

When I was attuned to him, I was very bold, but when I was going through my stuff, I totally stayed away from him. I knew he was bringing up old tendencies; it was intense. One day some old pain about Brian came up, and I tried to stay away. I also needed to visit my sister who lives in the area, and I decided to tell Vishwananda that I was leaving for a few days, and that I would rejoin him later. He stood overlooking a panoramic view of the valley, wearing a white robe and I could see the Ascended Master in him. He was in a state of *bhava,* completely absorbed in bliss. The Germans who travel with him knew to hold and balance Him while He is in this state. It touched my heart to see a gentleman lovingly put his arm around Vishwananda, and support his beloved master. I was standing fairly close, watching this, when suddenly Vishwananda turned around, put his hands on my head, and whispered the mantra in my ear. I was so shocked and overwhelmed, I didn't even hear the mantra! He knowingly smiled, and told me to go to my room, get paper, and he'd write it down for me. Later that day, when I was able to approach him again, he wrote it down, and when I bowed to him, He sweetly said, "See you real soon."

As I drove back to my sister's house, all I could do was cry. When I got there, I cried more. My older sister has been like a mother to me at times, and she held me in her arms as I sobbed. There was no judgment from her, as she knew how emotions can be unleashed when one is in the presence of a realized being. I was so grateful for her understanding and comfort.

A few days later I was on my way to Rancho Mirage and Palm Springs, where Vishwananda was having more programs. My friend Gwen came from Sedona, and we stayed at a hotel together. Gwen had missed out on a private interview with Vishwananda in Ojai Valley, because we had to sign up beforehand, and he was already booked. I would have loved to get in on another interview, but those slots were filled up too. We had to be quick to sign Gwen up for an appointment, because they filled up very fast. Gwen and I drove to the house where he was giving interviews, and waited in the living room. There were many people sitting and meditating in silence, waiting for their turn. I was happy to be close to him again, even if it meant just sitting in the living room. I was excited for Gwen that she was able to get an interview. After her interview, Gwen walked out of the room, and I heard Vishwananda shout, "Thea!! Thea's here!" (He pronounced it *Tayah*!) The attendant came and led me into his room. Once again, I was in shock- I had not been prepared for this, so I got down on my knees and totally surrendered to him. His eyes sparkled. I said, "Swamiji, nobody ever told me what this path would be like. Nobody tells us what we have to go through. It's been so hard, and yet so beautiful too. I've gone through such suffering." He replied, "Yes, you go through the suffering to go beyond the suffering." He then lifted me out of everything behind the tears at my sister's, and brought me into bliss again. Then I said, "I don't know how I deserve to be here with you and what my connection is to you, but it is so ancient. I look at you and I go into shock." He just said, "Yes, it will unfold."

I walked out of there feeling like I could levitate! When we got back to the hotel I was still in bliss and wanted to maintain that experience, so I stayed in my room and meditated, and chanted the mantra. That night, I went to *darshan* and I sat next to a lovely American woman in a Punjabi outfit, who was beaming like the sun. I put my hand on her knee and I said, "I don't know who you are, but you are so beautiful, and I love you." She took her hand and put it on my knee and we went into meditation together. It was so sweet. When the Krishna bhajans began we both went wild. I could see the *Shakti* was completely awakened in her. She told me that she had been with Muktananda. She also said, " We were *gopis* during the lifetime of Krishna, and that is why we can't stop crying, dancing and loving each other." I thought, "It must be, it must be, because I love him so much, and go into these beautiful states." Carol Parvati, who is a very high soul later became my friend. She lives near Palm Springs, and we talk regularly by phone. I met my friend Regina, another high soul, in a similar way. These women are really working at it, and going through karma fast. Both have become very dear to me.

I felt like Vishwananda was working out more karma, and accelerating my sadhana with every *darshan*. I was either in total bliss or in hell— nothing in between. After three weeks wih him, I needed to get back to Sedona, where I had clients waiting for me. His people pleaded with me to come back for Guru Purnima, and I said if some miracle happened, (because I was running out of money) I would.

One of my friends in Sedona recommended a woman named Mary, for a healing session. I was so charged up after being with Vishwananda, that her session was really charged too. She said, "I don't know what you're doing, but I want to do it too! Who is this Vishwananda, and where is he?" I explained who he is, and told her my plan to return for the next public program, Guru Purnima, if enough people went with to share the cost. To be honest, I had given up on the idea, and had resolved to stay at home, and recalibrate with everything he had already given me. To my surprise, Mary said, "I'll go! My husband and daughters need to go too!"

Two more friends, Linda and Keith, also wanted to go. It appeared the money problem was solved with enough people to share the cost of the trip, but the air-conditioner in my car wasn't working. Driving across the desert in July with no air conditioning would not be pleasant.

I had told Frances, my friend from Lester's ranch, about Vishwananda, and how much I wanted to go back for Guru Purnima. I explained the situation with my car, and to my surprise, (and I think to hers), she said, "I can take you to California!" Suddenly the trip was on!

Her offer in itself was a miracle. Having been emotional hurt from her relationship with Lester, Frances had been totally turned off to Masters for many years. After that relationship ended, she had focused instead on turning to the Guru within.

Swami Vishwananda and Thea at Cathedral Rock in Sedona, AZ

Later, Frances told me she had had no desire to go to California, or to meet Vishwananda. She couldn't understand why she had offered to drive. But after attending Guru Purnima and receiving Vishwananda's blessings, she began to understand that he knew more about her spiritual needs than she.

Vishwananda's Guru Purnima celebration was not far from where Karunamayi was giving hers, and Mirabai wanted me to go to hers as well. Many incredible celebrations being held simultaneouly, and I wanted to be at all of them! We checked into the hotel where Vishwananda was, and headed down to the dining hall. David was there, and said, "You have five minutes to get to Vishwananda's room. I'll take you there." Because she was with me, Frances came as well. About 15 of us were there. Vishwananda sat in *bhava* state with a huge picture of Babaji behind him. When he saw me, his eyes lit up. I knew he was happy to see me. I could feel his love for me- for everyone. My feelings of devotion grew stronger because of my love for him. My heart longed to surrender at the Master's feet, so I silently prayed, "Please give me a chance to be at his feet and offer the water and flowers." At that moment, a woman announced that all of us would be able to do *pada puja* to Swamiji's feet! Everyone was permitted to offer water and flowers, and to bow down and touch his feet. I was in heaven.

I glanced at Frances, who said to him, "I need your help." He replied, "Okay, we'll arrange a time." I could see that He was opening her heart, and that an internal shift was happening to her.

By then, the crew had the hall set up, and we all moved into that beautiful space. Mary arrived with Tom and her kids. Suddenly all my friends were there! I saw many of the same faces that had been at Pacific Palisades, who came for *darshan,* and those who had met him in Encinitas and at Rancho Mirage. Those he drew to himself, couldn't stay away. I felt close to every one of those devotees.

My great friend, Art Tarby, follower of Karunamayi, was in charge of all the sound equipment for Vishwananda. I felt privileged to see him there too. He showed me what Vishwananda had materialized for him, and I showed Art what Vishwananda had materialized for me. I could see that Art was drawn to Him as well.

Humble and childlike, Vishwananda walked in, wearing a beautiful white robe. His eyes revealed how happy he was, how much he loved everyone, and how grateful he was that the devotees he had come for, were with him now. He sat down and began to speak. "My beloved Babaji is my beloved guru, and I pay tribute to him. He came to me when I was five years old and showed me my connection to him, and showed me my translucent body." Vishwananda continued with his tender feelings toward Babaji. As he spoke, I recalled the moment when Vishwananda and Bababji had appeared to me in their translucent bodies. The ancient tie to them was really opening in me, along with incredible love and bliss.

Swamiji started the *kirtan* by singing to Krishna. The devotion, love and *Shakti* that came through his voice set the vibration. We had the best *kirtan* bands there and all the vocalists were great, but I wanted only to hear Vishwananda sing! As I looked around the room I knew that everyone there had also been with Krishna, and was feeling that same connection with Vishwananda. We were ancient souls from all traditions, from Yogananda and TM (Transcendental Meditation) to Karunamayi and more. Some people had felt conflict about whether to go to Vishwananda's or Karunamayi's Guru Purnima, and I had said, "Go to both! That's what I'm going to do." But I got so high from the *kirtan* and the *darshans* that not only could I not attend Karunamayi's Guru Purnima, I couldn't even get up to go to the bathroom! I was totally absorbed. I told Art, "I can't go, I can't even move. I will be there in spirit thinking of her feet and all the flowers they will be placing on her. I'll be bowing at her feet, but my physical body just can't go." He reassured me it was okay, and said he would bring something back for me.

Vishwananda imparted a Guru mantra to me. The Guru mantra is an aspect of the Divine Mother which I hadn't concentrated on before, but an aspect to which I felt a strong connection. In the past 20 years I have had remarkable encounters with the Divine Mother in all forms. She had come to me as Radha in the temple in Barsana, and at the ranch in Sedona. When I went to Rama's birthplace, I felt very connected to Sita, who is the same being as Lakshmi. She reincarnated as these beautiful aspects of the mother, when the avatars of Vishnu came here. Vishwananda told me, with a dance in his eye, to do the Guru mantra constantly. I thought, "oh my God, this is so exciting."

I have had many experiences since then, about my lifetimes with Babaji and Vishwananda, and that ancient tie. I've been with Babaji very recently, and in between lifetimes I get to be with him. When I started getting *Shaktipat* from Muktananda and going to those *lokas*, or heavenly realms,

I would go to three places. One was in Babaji's cave in the Himalayas, the Divine Mother's *loka*, and wherever Jesus was, I would try to catch up with him. These are the three I've always seen around me, and when I'm quiet, I see They are with me. Others too, appear: Shiva, Vishwananda and Karunamayi. Many more are with me, but Babaji, Jesus and Divine Mother are the three that seem to be constant.

Vishwananda said he would open up my connection to him and to Babaji. He certainly did. One day I was meditating doing the Guru mantra and an incredible grief about Babaji began to rise in my heart. It was a Sunday, and I spent the entire day meditating in front of his picture, getting into the grief and seeing its cause. As the story began to unfold, I saw myself as a young girl living in the Himalayas. My mother was dying. Because my father didn't want us to be without a mother, he brought my older sister (my friend Jeannie Harper in this life) and me to the monastery where his guru, Babaji, resided. Babaji has spent time in the physical plane throughout the ages, but because his work is so intricate and concentrated, he can't be here for long. He must return to the subtle ashram, where he can focus on world events, and constantly monitor the Earth. He has vowed to be on this Earth until every last soul has ascended. Talk about a powerful *bodhisattva* vow!

During that lifetime, I was a beautiful little Indian girl. I would cry constantly for my mother. Babaji would hold me and say, "I am your mother, I am your father, I am your everything." That is exactly what brought me to tears when

I asked Vishwananda who he was to Babaji. Babaji was so tender and loving as he raised my sister and me. I learned all the mantras and how to do all the *pujas*, such as washing and worshipping his feet. Later I took the vow of renunciation, became a *sanyasini* and wore the orange cloth that Babaji gave me. I gave up all my desires, to be only for God. I experienced incredible, blissful states with him and was so happy to be at the feet of a Great One.

The villagers took care of us by bringing food, because they loved Babaji too. One day an influential man in the village brought his critically ill baby to Babaji to bless. The baby died the next day. The father did not understand that Babaji's blessing had freed the soul of his sick baby. The man sought vengeance by starting rumors that we were having sex with Babaji, and that he was a black magician. About that time Babaji was preparing to return to his subtle ashram in the high Himalayas, to perform more intricate work for the world. We stayed behind to run the ashram, but shortly after he left, life became unbearable. The villagers believed the rantings of this man, so they cut back on our food supply. Our once blissful lives were being replaced with hunger, fear and ridicule. The villagers continued to accuse me of sleeping with Babaji, even though I had taken the vow of renunciation. It became a hell realm; it was horrible. I decided to leave and become a wandering *sadhu*, but that was a very difficult existence too. For years I traveled to different holy places and eventually a profound grief began to rise, not only because of losing my mother, but of losing my guru as well. I knew he was within, but I missed him and wanted him back in the physical. I thought of Babaji day and night as I traveled, and finally I resolved to go to the Himalayas to find him.

I took the same trail from Mana Village that Brian and I climbed last year, with Hanuman's help. It was very cold. I was hungry and getting weak and a snow storm began. Villagers never go up there alone because it's too dangerous. At that point I didn't care if I died. I climbed higher and higher, thinking of Babaji constantly, and from a high peak an avalanche came crashing down and buried me. Death wasn't a tragedy, because Babaji was with me instantly.

I knew I had been at Babaji's subtle ashram many times before, but only in between lives, since it is impossible to reach in the physical body. After my death from the avalanche, I was able to be with my beloved Babaji, and Mataji, who is also Lakshmi, and whom I love as much as I do Babaji.

When I was in solitude at the ranch in Sedona and read about Babaji in *Autobiography of a Yogi* by Yogananda, I knew I had to backpack to the Himalayas, and most likely hike up that same valley where I had been killed! It was at that same time, however, Babaji came to me in a vision and told me I would not be with him in this life, because my *dharma* is in the west.

Vishwananda also mirrored my past lives with Krishna and Rama during the Golden Age when we were all

—

taken into tremendous love states, and tremendous ecstasy with the Blue One. Krishna comes from a supramental world, and Krishna and Vishwananda represent the love ray.

The great Masters know that by a certain time, I think 2009, specific frequencies must be in place within the collective. This is the reason so many Great Ones are here now to uplift humanity as fast as possible. Vishwananda said it is up to many beings to advance and evolve in this lifetime, and that we all have our missions.

My friends, and all the people I'm commissioned to work with are evolving quickly, and yet some people are stuck and unaware. I've seen devotees who have been on the path for many years, following gurus and doing mantra by rote, but they seem to be stagnating, or, at the very most, growing slowly. Others, growing at the speed of light, have come in as a group this time, to reach a certain level of consciousness. Always there are seekers who are more or less advanced than ourselves. Yet the goal is the same for everyone: to reach self-realization and to help one another evolve as quickly as possible.

When the collective consciousness reaches a certain frequency, the love of all the Masters will return. Yeshua, Babaji-Krishna, the Divine Mothers and ancients will literally walk the Earth with us. It will be the return of the Christ within us. It will be a tremendous celebration for the first, second, third, and probably many other waves of beings, who reincarnate again and again, to participate in this incredible *Play of Consciousness*.

The guru's job is to point you back to yourself. Gurus may fall temporarily, and if that happens it is a great opportunity to look at your reactions and codependencies and move on. You also may pass a teacher in consciousness. Keep walking ahead, and follow the guru *within*! There is only the guru within anyway. Even if you have a living guru, you still have to find him or her within. In the end there is nothing outside except yourSELF! The *only* relationship there is is with your Self, everything else is a mirror.

MY FINISHING SCHOOL:
MASTER MOHANJI

"If you love one master, all the masters will get that love,
because all masters are one!" – Master Mohanji

In March 2017, a friend of mine brought a master named Mohanji to Sedona for a yoga conference. I am an old-timer on this path, so when I met Mohanji, I immediately knew he was my "finishing school for enlightenment" in this lifetime.

As I stood outside the event that March where Mohanji was to lead a meditation and give *shaktipat*, an Indian man approached me. Since he was the only Indian man there, I asked him if he was Mohanji, and he said, "Yes." He took a moment to talk to me, and as I looked into his big black eyes, I felt recognition and familiarity. We all entered the room for the event and received his *shaktipat*. After the program ended, I immediately went home to integrate the experience. I felt many different masters come through him and had the urge to go to his retreat that was being offered in Sedona.

The retreat was very powerful. We were all granted a one-on-one interview with this great master. I was the first! As I sat before Mohanji, I received a transfer of energy from his eyes. I felt so close to him and asked him many questions. He said he had come for me, which seemed so natural, for he felt like an old friend that I knew so well.

Mohanji told me in my interview that I had very little karma left, but what seems little to the Masters seems like a lot to us (as I'll describe later)! I gave him total "power of attorney" to complete any karmic residue in my subconscious. To this day, Mohanji has been consistently doing his part, as I have tried to do mine.

We were taken to a place known as Buddha Beach, which is located along the beautiful Oak Creek and has a magnificent view of Cathedral Rock, one of our most powerful vortexes in Sedona. We were meditating with Beloved Mohanji on the beach with the stream flowing in front of us.

As I got ready to meditate, I was leaning against a tree and looking at the beautiful reeds in the stream when all of sudden I heard a flute playing so rhythmically that I thought someone nearby was playing it. I asked a lady sitting next to me if she heard a flute playing and she said no. I continued to go inward and felt the ecstasy of Krishna! The reeds swaying in the stream triggered the past life memory of me being with Krishna in some ancient time when I was in a state of pure joy and extreme ecstasy.

When we left the beach area, Mohanji and I were walking arm-in-arm and I told him about the experience. I knew he gave that experience to me, but he is always so humble that he doesn't take credit for it. He said, "You raised your vibrations to a level where that could happen!"

During the retreat, he gave shaktipat again, and when it was my turn, I fell back onto the hard floor—my head missed a chair by several inches! I felt that unseen hands cushioned my fall. This *shaktipat* revealed to me the many masters that come through him, such as the Self-Realization Fellowship's (SRF) Swami Paramahansa Yogananda, and gurus of the great Kriya lineage of Mahavatar Babaji.

I knew once again that he was my next step to my Path to God Realization! I took his Kriya initiation. Mohanji said that he would always be with me.

The night after the Kriya initiation, I was up all night with the Kriya breath going up and down my spine. We were only supposed to do the Kriya for ten minutes, but I felt Mohanji with me all night directing the Kriya breath. From then on, I felt Mohanji's presence in all the healings I performed on people throughout the day. Before, I would always see Babaji when I closed my eyes. Now, I see Mohanji!

During Mohanji's birthday celebration, I started feeling depressed. I went into it and experienced the life of Rama. I saw that Mohanji was Rama and I was closely connected to him in that lifetime. I experienced a brutal death at a young age. There were many people jealous of me as I was of the bloodline of Rama. People seemed to be jealous of bloodlines!

As the months passed, I relived many past lives with Mohanji. In Krishna's lifetime, I was his daughter, and again, being his bloodline, also experienced a brutal death. The battles were violent in that lifetime, and included a lot of black magic, hatred, jealously, etc.

I wondered why an avatar like Krishna allowed him and his bloodline to be cursed by Gandhari with, "May you, Krishna, witness the death of your children and your children's children and may you die in the forest hunted down like a beast."

Krishna hugged Gandhari and accepted the curse as a solution to end the age-old vendetta. It had to end sometime, and if this demanded the sacrifice of his clan, then let it be so. I was one of his children, which is why this was in my memory bank and I got the information. Now I understood the plan. We asked Mohanji if the curse finally ended for all his generations of children.

When asked about Krishna's decision to sacrifice his clan to violent deaths, Mohanji responded:

> "Dearest Thea,
>
> "I understand this point very well. Krishna knew that his presence was not only strengthening the Yadava clan but making them tamasic, noxious, and arrogant. He, like all avatars before and after him, came to reestablish the eternal 'sanatana dharma.' Sanatana dharma is 'the eternal way' on earth. And, the state of the Yadava clan was not acceptable. He couldn't have left his body and leave his clan in the adharmic [not in accord with dharma] state.
>
> "Krishna lived only about 125 years in an era when the average life span was 1000 years. He couldn't have left the Yadava clan to accept the advent of the era of Kali by their bad deeds. Gandhari's curse could not have happened without the active consent of Krishna. It was not Gandhari's curse that created the destruction of the Yadava clan. This was already scheduled. Gandhari just reaffirmed what was already scheduled to happen. This is why Krishna smiled. That saga is over. The Gandhari curse ended in that yuga itself.
>
> "Kali Yuga has brought back all kinds of adharmics to earth. It has also brought Krishnas. But the mass only can see the obvious glitter and not the subtle glow of eternal sun within.

336

"You are continuously praying and cleansing. I want to assure you that your prayers are being answered. Much love and affection." —Mohanji

Meanwhile, a group around Mohanji became jealous of my close relationship with him. I could see that the Krishna lifetime was being played out again in this lifetime. I had been a Pandava, the side of Krishna, and these people had been from another group who were enemies of the Pandavas. Mohanji was being true to his promise of clearing past karmas. So, not only were the masters of the Kriya lineage coming through him, but he was also Rama and Krishna! Little did I know there was more to come.

When Mohanji took a group to Mount Kailash in 2018, I was unable to physically handle the trip, so I went astrally! I ended up inside the mountain in my light body where I saw Shiva sitting on a throne with sages sitting around him. Next, I saw Mohanji merge with Shiva! Okay, Mohanji, now you are Rama, Krishna, and Shiva – I bet you are Dattatreya!

It so happened that around that time a client took me to small claims court accusing me of giving him the wrong information in a session. I had been working with this man for about a year and he was a challenge. I do healings, not psychic readings, and this man wanted me to tell him about his 3D moves. I felt that he was getting co-dependent and wasn't happy about healing, as he wanted psychic advice.

I was summoned to small claims court and I was experiencing a psychic attack by this client. I got in touch

—

with Mohanji and he advised some mantras and practices that I could do. I knew that Mohanji was helping me, as I felt his strong presence.

Two days before I was to appear in court, I had a dream that the man was not going to show up.

The day I was to appear in court, Mohanji lifted me to such an amazing state of grace and bliss that I was worried that the judge would think I was drunk or on drugs, as I could hardly function! As we entered the courtroom, the plaintiff didn't appear. The judge walked in and his secretary followed giving the judge information. Later, the judge informed us that my client was not coming and that the case was dismissed! Mohanji's grace!

The third time that I went to see Mohanji was at a retreat in Virginia. I was privileged to meet him at the airport. We walked arm-in-arm, and as usual, I was able to talk with him as a very deep friend. I told him that he was always with me and I saw him in my Third Eye. When I did my healing work, he was always there working miracles on all dimensions. I always used to see Babaji in my Third Eye, but now I saw Mohanji. I knew that Babaji had brought Mohanji to me as my final guru. I told him of my experience of him being Rama, Krishna, and how he had merged with Shiva at Mt. Kailash!

I said, "I think you are Dattatreya because if you are Vishnu, Brahma, and Shiva, then you must be Dattatreya!"

He was silent, and then he said that this was revealed to me and that other people were beginning to see it. Other people and masters had seen Dattatreya in him, but for Mohanji, he only ever sees himself as Mohanji. This is his incarnation in the world, and this is his relevance to the world.

At the retreat, he conducted a fire ceremony to burn up individual and generational karma. I was in such bliss and loved Mohanji so much. We had beautiful moments together where he told me he was here to bring in the Golden Age and that he would not be here long! He also told me he was speeding up time.

After the retreat, I relived two other lifetimes. One in which he was a king, not Rama or Krishna, maybe an incarnation of Dattatreya, when I was his daughter again. I was brutally killed in that one too! It's no joke being bloodline to a great being.

My Trip to Peru with Mohanji

My second trip to Peru was inspired by Mohanji. When I heard that he was going, I got an inner pull to be with him there. When I arrived in Cusco, I collected my luggage and waited for someone representing Mohanji to meet me. I waited an hour, but no one showed up. I prayed to him, and shortly thereafter, a man with a sign representing Mohanji stood before me. I was so relieved to get in the van and met two other beautiful ladies who were also going on the tour. We arrived at a lovely hotel, La Casona De Yucay Hotel, in Valle Sagrado where we met up with the rest of the tour, had dinner and then went to a meeting where Mohanji greeted us. I was so delighted to be with this great master again. I held onto his every word and was ready for the adventure that lay ahead. I surrendered to my next step with him and cherished each moment under his direction.

On the first evening at the hotel, we had our formal *darshan* (meeting) with Mohanji. Many questions were asked, and he drew each of us into his being. The next morning at breakfast, we had the great privilege of having Mohanji sit at our table. As usual, I could ask him anything I wished with such freedom. It seemed that all of us had a hard time getting to Peru. On pilgrimages, we get tested! And, I noticed that Mohanji's solar plexus was blocked. I wondered why, so I asked him. He said that the body is attacked by the dark ones and that it is easier for him to be out of his body as consciousness, so he would not be attacked. I thanked him for getting me through the dark force attack the past winter with the court case. I knew it was because of his grace!

We then boarded a bus to our next excursion. Mohanji took turns sitting with each of us and answering questions. There were about 27 people on the trip, so we got to share our time with him. We had a beautiful group of people on the trip, no ego flare-ups, and everyone was using this time to truly be with our great teacher.

The special places we visited in Peru were very powerful, especially Machu Picchu and Lake Titicaca! We had a fabulous ride on a train that took us into Machu

Picchu. I was sitting in the corner of the train in a state of bliss and oneness. Mohanji was working on all of us constantly. When we reached Machu Picchu, Mohanji took us on a hike to the ruins and showed us the key energy spots. I went on all the hikes except to the Sun Temple. I chose to stay behind in the ruins with five other ladies.

As I was meditating in the ruins, my mind was on Mohanji and I saw a miracle vision where his body was elongated into a huge light form and it seemed like he was blessing the universe! That Indian man in blue jeans and a T-shirt was much more than what we saw as a human body! He was huge, blessing universes!

At one point, as we were hiking in the Andes, and I asked Mohanji why we were going through ancient lifetimes as Rama and Krishna. He said to Jyothsna, who was standing close to me, "Thea always asks these questions that only we understand." However, he didn't answer my question!

Later, when we were in the Maras salt mines, Mohanji told us how he met a great saint in India, near Mumbai, who was famous for being angry. People still would go and take his blessing even though he scolded them or used abusive language, as the saint's blessings helped them through layers of karma and brought abundance. However, when Mohanji went to meet the saint, his face lit up and he was smiling. The saint came down from his seat and fell on Mohanji's feet. Mohanji was surprised.

Then, the saint took him to his sanctum sanctorum and showed him the idol of the Nath Guru Kanifnathji – an ancient Hindu saint and avatar, and one of the nine maha yogis of Navnath Sampradaya, who looked exactly like Mohanji! Mohanji told us that Kanifnathji was the only Nath Guru who was a Raja Yogi.

I later got the answers about why I was reliving Rama and Krishna's lifetime because humanity was not ready to relive these times before now, it was all a matter of timing! All the players of these lifetimes are back releasing the past feelings of fighting and separation. After millennia, here we are again, Pandavas and Gandavas, releasing division and coming into unity and forgiveness.

During our trip, I started to get a terrible head cold and sinus infection. I felt miserable for a while, and then I called on Mohanji and the whole thing disappeared as fast as it had come!

My most favorite place that we visited was the Doorway of the Gods. It was a doorway in the rocks that was a portal into other worlds, other dimensions. I received a lot of shakti there and had to lie down to absorb the experience.

Our next stop was Lake Titicaca. We boarded a boat and I sat next to Mohanji on our way to the Floating Islands. I asked him why he never talked about Ascension. He answered, "Ascension means somewhere to go. When you are everywhere, there is nowhere to go!"

On the last leg of the trip, I was boarding the bus and Mohanji was sitting in the front seat. He said to me, "You have gone full circle now; you are complete!" I didn't know what that meant but I knew it was good!

The night before we left, we were privileged to receive

shaktipat from Mohanji. The next day, I felt the results of that transference of energy. On my way to the airport, I was in such bliss and oneness that I could hardly function. By God's grace, I had friends to help with my luggage and to board the plane. God always looks after every detail so beautifully!

What gratitude I felt as I flew back to America to have been on this great adventure with one of the greatest beings on the planet!

I Am The Altar

The greatest adventure of my life resulted from the prayer that I made to Jesus when I was just 21 years old. I prayed to Jesus to take me to a man who knew God! That prayer was immediately answered by my journey to the very old land of India, the land of Saints and Sages. Papa Ramdas was the first great master that I met there (see Chapter 2 for that story).

What followed was the lifelong journey to all the great Masters in my book. I know that I couldn't have started on this path without learning about the Path of God Realization from the "realized souls" themselves. By their example and grace, they gave me the strength and courage to go inward and discover the numerous experiences and karmas which I needed to go through in this lifetime. The Masters gave me such high experiences from the beginning of my path and encouraged me to go where I needed to be—permanently.

My beautiful parents brought me up in a "universal way," which helped me to understand that all religions led to the One Heart within and that all prophets were great messengers of the One God. All the saints from all religions have always inspired me!

This path has been lonely for me at times as I have been a pioneer. Dogmatic people, even in my own family, told me that I would go to hell if I didn't accept only Jesus as my personal savior. And yet, it was the Beloved Jesus who took me to India to meet these great Masters! It was Jesus who I even understood better after meeting the masters. If you understand one master, you understand all masters.

It was Jesus who took me into an experience of knowing that everyone was myself. I remember when this insight happened: I was with my sister in a shopping mall in Newport Beach, California! You never know when grace will hit.

In retrospect, I see that every step of my life has been orchestrated, and every event, and every mirror was what I needed for growth. And, if I didn't go beyond that experience, the same experience would come up again for me to conquer! By conquering, I mean that I had to forgive everyone who hurt me, or betrayed me, until the experiences no longer stuck to me and faded away as if in a dream. All attachments and aversions were presented, and these were very painful until I let go.

Every master who came into my life was orchestrated by God. They always kept me moving to the next level and they gave me the strength and courage to go on to the next step.

I am at the end of this incarnation now. I have walked a long way on this path to perfection. My part is to never give up until I have stabilized the experience to every moment.

Yoganandaji said, "A saint is a sinner who never gave up." Each experience in my life was and is a perfect play of events with friends, enemies, ups and downs, until all the karmas are completed and then I sink into the altar of my own Sacred Heart and the Bliss of my own Being. When I am settled into the altar of my Being I know that I am the altar and there is nothing but me in endless blissful contentment. My Masters are consciousness and I am one with that consciousness. There is always another step to take until we know we are One with every atom.

Mohanji said, "There is no me or you. There is only consciousness. This constant awareness is called perpetual meditation. Whenever we see and feel you and me, there is work to be done."

Endless Blessings to all Beings, Thea Ishwari

About Mohanji

Credit: Mohanji.org

Mohanji was born in 1965 and made a successful career in the shipping industry in the Middle East. He married in 1992 and welcomed a daughter, Ammu, in 1995. In 2000, Ammu was killed in a tragic car accident. This left a huge void in his life and precipitated a series of hardships, including separating from his wife, and years later, the loss of his job, and ill-health.

He traveled to the Himalayas to search for inner solace and silence. When he returned to the world of "noises," he began connecting to the silence between two breaths, two heartbeats, and two thoughts. It took him ten years to stabilize and establish himself in the world of silence. In

2003, he started ACT (Ammucare Charitable Trust™) as a platform for selfless service beyond all man-made barriers and to support the helpless and needy.

In 2010, Mohanji married Devi Mohan in a simple ceremony. It was not a typical marriage. Mohanji explained to Devi that he belonged to everyone and must serve the Nath gurus by his service to the whole of humanity. Through his marriage to Devi, his beautiful daughter, Ammu, was reborn as Mila to the couple. Shridi Sai Baba had told Mohanji that Devi was a very high aspect of Mother Mary. Devi serves Mohanji tirelessly and is a perfect mother to their dear daughter, Mila.

Mohanji's introduction to Mahavatar Babaji began in the mid-1990s when he read the book, *Autobiography of a Yogi* by Paramahamsa Yogananda. After he lost his job in 2004, he met a man who was in constant communion with Babaji, and who gifted him with a picture of the saint.

Throughout the years, Mohanji had "communions" or telepathic conversations Babaji, and his style was always abrupt. The first time was when he mentally heard the message, "Come to the puja room." He did, and as he sat for meditation he heard: "Do not meditate. I am working on you." Immediately, strange bubbles started to rise from every cell of his body. He felt the bubbles rising, clustering, conglomerating, moving, and bursting.

It felt as if someone was massaging his insides. Meanwhile, the voice explained Mohanji's tradition and the importance of the Golden Path, i.e., the Path of Shiva – a path of perfect beingness, total nullification, annihilation, and dissolution. Those on the Golden Path need nothing from the outside. They remain in complete fullness and need no recognition, fame, etc. Golden energy is the highest energy, and once gold becomes purified in light, it is forever pure.

In Mohanji's subsequent communions, Babaji told him many things, including the higher unity between all Masters and all the knowledge that he would need to continue with his life's mission. Mohanji also knew that Babaji is not just a man or a guru, he represents the God Almighty in all His subtlety. Words cannot explain Him.

Babaji also told him to teach. Being an introvert, Mohanji objected, plus, he felt he was just an ordinary man and not qualified to teach. Immediately the answer came: "That is not your problem. We will send people to you. Understand that those who come to you are sent by us. Others will not reach you. Nor will they understand you. Your strength is your subtlety. You are empowered. You will represent our tradition."

In 2014 Mohanji met Thyagananda, from the lineage of Bhagwan Nityananda, Rakhadi Baba, Poornananda, and Sadananda. Thyagananda was given a mala in 2000 by Poornananda just before he left his body. Poornananda had worn the mala for a long time. It was like an atomic bomb it was so powerful. Poornananda told Thyagananda, "One day Mohanji will come. Give it to him and transfer all your powers to him." When Thyagananda asked him how he would recognize Mohanji, he said, "Look into his Third Eye. You can see a blazing sun."

So, in December of 2014, just as Poornananda had predicted, Thyagananda saw Mohanji and, overcome with emotion, asked Mohanji if he could transfer his powers. Mohanji said, "Yes," and received his powers and the powerful mala.

Later, Mohanji was conferred with the title of "Brahmarishi" by Guru Avadootha Nadanandaji, along with the transference of spiritual powers on the direct guidance from the Guru Mandala (the Masters of the Tradition).

Devi Amma, a great saint and follower of Augustiar, a guru to Babaji, adopted Mohanji as her spiritual son. She describes Mohanji:

> *"Mohanji is a very great Siddha who has been sent to this world by the Divine Masters, The Guru Mandala. He is an extremely compassionate being. His role in this avatar is to spread unconditional love on this earth and beyond. He is not only a Jagatmitra but Mohanji is a Vishnumitra. I will clarify, he is not Vishwamitra, the sage, but Vishwa-mitra (friend of the universe). Being an incarnation of compassion, Mohanji can only offer unconditional love under all circumstances. That is why despite many negatives and obstacles coming his way, he still offers love."*
> *– Devi Amma*

That is his pure nature. This is an important message to mankind, giving the inter-galactic dimension of Mohanji, coming directly from the masters conveyed through one of their purest and true representatives.

A famous saint wrote this about Mohanji:

> *"Mohanji was not compelled to take this incarnation but decided to do so out of love and compassion for those who called him here. He will fulfill all kinds of desires of his people as he is not going to take another physical incarnation. He was an accomplished Jhana Rishi in his last incarnation and dissolved into infinity at his Samadhi. Yet, he came back as a Raja Rishi in this life just to fulfill the desires of all those who have been connected to him, even though there was no karma for him, for Mohanji is equal to unconditional love. At the same time, Mohanji will be present on earth in the subtle form until the last soul that is connected to him is liberated. Mohanji will be on earth for 1008 years and his place of Samadhi (tomb) will become a great shrine of worship for thousands of people."*
>
> *– Swami from the lineage of Bhagavan Nityananda*

Mohanji Experiences Shiva

Credit: Mohanji.org

In 2007, Mohanji had an experience that permanently shifted his consciousness and enabled him to move effortlessly between different levels of awareness. It was his birthday and he and his parents decided to celebrate at a nearby ashram and feed the poor children. However, that day, he was feeling dizzy and nauseous and by evening, his eyesight was blurred. He told the Swami at the ashram, who led Mohanji to another house in the complex and sat him on a chair. Moments later Sacred Ash started coming out through the top of his head and cascaded down his body. According to the Dattatreya Tradition, sacred ash sprouting out of *Sahasrara* is a sign of burnt karmas. When the last remnants of karmas are getting exhausted, like a volcano with high intensity, they are burnt and expelled through the Sahasrara.

His body became transparent and his eyelids golden as a huge bright light from within radiated outward. The Swami shouted to the nearby ashramites, "Shiva is here! Come fast... Bring the camera!" At first, the light was so bright and the level of energy so high that no one could enter. But as Mohanji slowly started regaining his body awareness, photos were taken of his body covered in ash.

Mohanji said, "When we touch the realms of Shiva, the Supreme, everything dissolves. Everything merges into one. It is only a vast, expanded brightness, peaceful, and all-knowing.

"All the planets, various suns, stars, and various spheres of existence simply become parts of the vast existence of Shiva, the Supreme. It is all contained within the infinite brightness which has supreme awareness. When the limited entity called Mohan became Shiva, at first, there was only the bliss, indescribable bliss that encompassed me. The bliss of infiniteness. The bliss of liberation. The bliss of 'bodylessness.' Existing in that expanded state, I became one with all the beings of the Universe. Limited awareness of Mohan merged with the entire cosmos and became one with both, the limited and unlimited existence. In that expanded state, one can only express Love, our very nature. I became every being, and every being became me."

Private Conversations with Mohanji

Credit: Mohanji.org

In candid conversations with Master Mohanji the summer/fall of 2020, I asked for more detailed information on the spiritual questions that kept coming up with me as an East/West-educated woman, living in Sedona, AZ. Though many years had been spent in the East to deepen my wisdom around masters of the East, I always sought the truth contained in all religions and spiritual systems by probing more deeply beneath the superficial differences and finding the core of authenticity, which unifies the human spiritual experience. Sitting in my aerie retreat, looking over the towering red rock beauty of Sedona, I connected with Master Mohanji in Bangalore, India. He graciously consented to grant this interview. It is with profound gratitude that I present his answers here for all those who are students of world religions and the shared experience of seeking God-realization as individuals and collectively for our planet.

Thea: *Are you here to bring in the Golden Age? When does it start?*

Mohanji: I think all of us are here to bring in the Golden Age if we become conscious about it. The Golden Age is a state where we are one with the whole consciousness. That means we experience consciousness in each state, each day—waking state, dream state, deep sleep state. When we are in tune with this consciousness, it is spread over the whole world, and then we are in the Golden Age. That is the age when we have no divisions, separations, confusions, comparisons, competitions, nothing. We are all One. We will not be worried about people, characters, constitutions, and stuff, because that's just individualistic. We will only look at the energy which is spreading through all these people, animals, and beings—through that, we see the thread and not the beads.

If you reach a level where nothing outside affects you, then you're in the Golden Age. That is a stage of stability and stillness, and that tells us where we are. So, just look at how many people have reached that state of stability. If a million, billion, or five billion people have reached the state of stability, earth has come into the Golden Age. If five percent have attained stability, that many people are in the Golden Age. If ninety percent of the people have reached stillness and stability, then ninety percent are in the Golden Age. We have to look at it in that way and not just a blanket Golden Age.

We can see a huge variety of frequencies operating in today's world. There is the very low frequency of greed, hatred, and jealously, and comparisons, and criticisms, which must come up to a frequency where we see everybody as one. It may take time, and everybody may not even understand. Many of us are working in that mode to bring forth the Golden Age as much as we can, to create uniformity and harmony in this whole world.

Earth is not the only plane of existence. There are many planes of existence, and various planes of existence are already in the Golden Age. It is not something intangible, it is tangible and can be in our own lives. When we have no enemies, its tangible. When we do not look at people but instead look at purpose, then it's tangible. In various levels we can see the Golden Age at work even now. In some degrees, it is a state of wellbeing. We are in supreme power. When you are one with the whole consciousness of the world, you command life. Life or karma does not command you.

My job is also part of it. I think many people who have understood their purpose are all doing the same job. I am not unique in this. Probably, I am being used by the larger tradition. I normally practice insignificance so that I can relate to people better. If you become abnormal or supernatural then you're already separated. So, I prefer to be one of the normal people with all my weaknesses and all my strengths, not at all special, so that I am able to relate to and communicate with people.

Thea: *Did you choose to come to Earth to set an example? Did you have full awareness since your birth?*

Mohanji: I would like to believe that I am sent for a purpose. That's what people have said. I didn't have the inclination to come to earth and do the same pattern over and over again. I do not feel much attached to any of the aspects of earth, such as materials, people, places, time, etc. I respond to it as a normal human being, but I do not have much connection with any of this. Even as a child, I never felt that something is so precious that I should preserve it. So, I don't know whether it was a very conscious, fully conscious awareness, or it was just my nature. Now, I feel that I have a job to do.

I try to bring light into people's lives, but you have to be light to give light. The nature of light is to give light. My benchmark to myself has been for my presence to be the reason for transformation, not my teachings. I give guidance but I don't sit down and teach a lot. I don't go into the category of teachers, but instead, I would like to say that I have been sent here for some reason, like all of us.

Everybody has a reason for coming here, and most are karmic reasons for experiencing life in various flavors.

Karmic processes are the ego and will take care of "me and mine" ownerships. The mind will take care of emotions and relations, and the intellect looks for answers, information and knowledge. My operating platform is usually not like that. I am not craving for knowledge and if knowledge is needed, it comes automatically. Whatever I am speaking, I have never learnt. It just happens. So naturally I think there is a bit of awareness right from childhood. I never felt too inclined for possessions and positions.

I never shied from working hard and I still believe that there is no substitute for hard work. When we are lazy, we lose. I believe that we should always try to excel in whatever we do. If there is a reason to do the work, you do the work, and if the platform demands an action, do the action. Don't expect results or any reward, so that you're free from that desire.

I believe in freedom in activity and compassion, which means you should not look at yourself above anybody. I always make sure I deliver more to others than I ask for myself. I do not think that I am bigger or better than anybody else. That is the aspect of compassion. I am giving you all broad yard sticks and you can figure out who I have been and who I am, but it doesn't really matter.

People can have opinions and I have seen people changing opinions. The world has been talking, speculating, gossiping, and pouring forth their opinions. All opinions are not based on truth, most of them are based on assumptions, people's understanding, people's positions, and people's level of evolution. All opinions are not really truthful. But people believe that they are because when four people say the same thing, people believe it. This is how the world works.

So, we have to stay away from all these things and do the job. Whether people like you, dislike you, understand you, misunderstand you, it doesn't matter. You keep doing your job and you try to excel in whatever you do. I always ask myself, is that the only thing I can do, or can I do more than that? I refused to be satisfied with my action because the moment you're satisfied with your action you stop growing. I normally push myself a little bit more and the result is the Mohanji platform today.

When I started Ammucare in 2003, everybody said that without money, without a "Godfather" you can't run it. Now seventeen years later, we are still running it. What degree of growth we don't know, and it doesn't matter. It's serving somebody, helping somebody. Some people are getting the food in the name of Ammucare, ACT Foundation.

If what we do is effective for the world and whatever we do is good for the world, nature will keep it. Our job is to act, to move forward. Nature, God, guru will give the power, the wind beneath the wings. All of us are here to assure a state of Golden Age in the lives of people and it is everybody's responsibility.

Thea: *Is this your last incarnation on Earth?*

Mohanji: This is my last incarnation on earth, which I

have already clarified many times. I knew this and various masters have said the same thing. I don't intend to come back in another body, but I will probably work without the body for a much longer period.

Thea: *What is your connection to Mahavatar Babaji?*

Mohanji: I have written my experience on blogs because these are my experiences. Whether people appreciate them or think it is real or unreal doesn't matter. It's my experience. Talking about past lives does not really have value in this life because it could be imagination; it could be hallucination; it could be sheer bluffing.

I will say that Babaji had a great influence on me. He took me from a level of non-understanding and going in circles in my life, to a level where He guided me to some usefulness. That is a big work that He has done for me. But I normally do not use His name. I generally see a lot people use His name for their purposes, which I disagree with. We should not do that. We should never use the name of any great masters for our personal benefit.

I had two major interactions with Him and both those times Babaji transformed me. I believe that He runs the show a little bit, as with Nadananda, also. Babaji guided me to him and eventually under the instruction of Brighuram Paramahamsa, He transferred his spiritual powers to me. That was orchestrated by Babaji. Babaji's hands have been visible in my life many times.

Once I had a serious attack from someone due to jealousy. Jealousy and comparing yourself to others are emotional, mental things and the reason some people decide to defeat others. If you're stable in your spiritual practice, you will never try to defeat anybody or try to create enemies. So, when I had this attack, Babaji helped me. A few times he has come and helped me to survive. Same with Shridi Sai Baba. He has been a pillar of strength.

Thea: *Who are the Bodhisattvas? Who was Buddha?*

Mohanji: I shall give you my opinion. I do not know if this will be acceptable to various minds. The Bodhisattvas are enlightened beings, or beings who are connected to their soul essence, more than the identities of each of their incarnations. They are those who live internally, or I would say, "settled within themselves."

Buddha is the "Enlightened One." When bodh or awareness of who you truly are eventually stabilizes, one becomes a Buddha.

Thea: *We know that Rama and Krishna are Avatars of Vishnu; are Jesus and Buddha also Avatars of Vishnu?*

Mohanji: I do not think Jesus and Buddha were avatars of Vishnu, such as Krishna and Rama. Krishna said, "Whenever there is a decay in righteousness, I happen." So, all the avatars are happenings when a situation demands their birth; it is not karma that provokes a birth, like most people. Avatars only come and live for a purpose and then they leave for a purpose, leaving behind the residue that the next generations can continue.

In the case of Jesus and Buddha, they were more like teachers. They were re-aligning stuff, not fully preserving dharma, as such. What they did was mostly correcting the faulty machines. They tried to realign what was going wrong, but in the bargain, they lost their lives. Buddha didn't die like that, but Jesus did.

Buddha had a purpose. He was deeply touched by the sadness of the world and the bad things happening in people's lives even though it was karmic. People, because of their unconscious living, kept on repeating the patterns of sorrows. That disturbed Buddha and provoked him to go and make a difference in the world through his philosophy. He became enlightened and conveyed his enlightenment in such a way that the world could go beyond sorrows by just living consciously.

He talked about breath and spoke to people about awareness and consciousness and all those things. So, that is the nature is of a teacher. There is a distinction and difference in their life.

If you look at Krishna's life, Krishna had every aspect complete from childhood. He is worshipped as a child and had perfection as a youth, husband, cow herd, king, warrior, charioteer, or whatever he did. You can see that perfection in him completely.

In the case of Rama, he lived like an ordinary prince and he went through all the ups and downs of life just like an ordinary person, and he did the impossible. At the same time, he did not use all his powers to do the impossible.

He used everybody. He empowered everybody. He had a very clear distinction as a being and his job was to preserve dharma, and that's exactly what he did his whole life.

All the masters are the same, they attain their perfection like a graduate. Once you cross over as a graduate, you will be graduating in various things and subjects, but you all are graduates. So, in this coming back as avatars each time, there is a pattern, a distinction. In this age when people talk about Kalki, the tenth avatar, it is said that it will be a situation and not a person, so the virus situation could be a Kalki avatar. We don't know. We can presume all this.

When a person is operating on a particular level, he will be considered an avatar, especially when his operating level is only for purpose and not selfish reasons. He is doing everything for a larger good for the world and for the resurrection of mankind to transform to people from utter unconsciousness to full consciousness. There are masters and teachers who guide people to that state, but avatars literally transform people with their presence. That's the difference.

Thea: *Was Christ a cosmic being who descended to Earth and incorporated into the body of Jesus at the Baptism in the Jordan by John, the Baptist, as put forth by modern Christian Gnosticism?*

Mohanji: Christ consciousness means a state of consciousness, a state of full awareness where there is a oneness with the entire universe. Jesus became the Christ when he became aware of His purpose on Earth, and realized who He was, rather than what he seemed to be-the son of Joseph and Mary.

Thus, he became Jesus, the Christ. St. John was an Avadhoota—someone who was occupied only with his inner world; and hence, for the outer world, he looked like a mad man. Avadhootas are the ones who have dissolved their minds (capacity to handle emotions), intellects (capacity for analysis), and egos (seats of personality connected to positions, possessions, names, and fame in the society). When John baptized Jesus, the veil of ignorance, the identification based on his incarnation as Jesus, was removed and the pure consciousness descended into him. Thus, when the illusion of his identifications with his incarnation was removed, Jesus became Christ, the Enlightened. The man transformed into purpose and gave him focus and freedom. He became fearless. "Life" (purposeful life) began at that point for him, and John was well aware of this. Looking at the grandeur of his purpose, John said that Jesus was far ahead of him and that he was not worthy to even untie his shoelaces.

My understanding is that Jesus' baptism was a wakeup call for him to start his work of bringing light into the ritualistic, dogmatic, priest-controlled society of Israel and to bring the truth of human refinement and possibility of God-realization to man. Finally, it took crucifixion to shake up and wake up the conscience of his society. These are my observations. And, perhaps there could be disagreements amongst scholars on this topic, which is natural as everything is rooted in individual perceptions.

Thea: *Yogananda spoke about John, the Baptist, and Jesus as having been Elisha and the Prophet Elijah, prominent Biblical figures in the Old Testament of the Bible. Elijah was taken up in a fiery golden chariot at the end of his earthly life. They both reincarnated near each other in Palestine at the beginning of our era and Prophet Elijah was reputed to be Elisha's teacher. Could Mohanji add anything to this great story?*

Mohanji: Paramahansa Yogananda did explore many unknown and unseen aspects of various incarnations, especially Jesus. He had the challenge of talking to a society (in the West) that did not believe in reincarnation. Now, with the acceptance of reincarnation due to exposure of the wisdom of the East through various teachers, regression therapy, and numerous testimonials, the mind of the society is more adapted to the truth that people could possibly come back in another body to complete what they have left unfinished or incomplete.

We are programmed to think in a linear manner because we are deeply oriented to our existence in the flow of time. Just consider taking time off from this business called life. The vertical time or timeless state is where the past, the present, and the future exist together. There is no yesterday, today, or tomorrow. There is only the NOW. This is what Lord Krishna demonstrated in the 11th chapter of Bhagavad Gita. The stories and theories that we usually entertain, lose their validity except for their academic or their entertainment value. True spirituality is recognizing, connecting, and transforming into the essence that is behind all creation; yet is unbound by any creation.

Elijah and Elisha could have been John the Baptist and Jesus of Nazareth. Each individual has his or her own frequency. When we witness similar frequencies, we assume those individuals could have been this or that person. Enlightened beings have existed in each generation to uplift their society. Elijah and Elisha might have come back, but it was the years when they delivered to the world that matters. Nothing else is important. The same goes for all of us. Our relevance is only what we give to the earth and not what we take from the earth for our gratification. Our mind craves associations, especially with past incarnations. But I always believe that it dilutes the present incarnation.

That is why when many people wrote and told who I was in my past lives, I not only refrained from endorsing it, but I also even played it down. This incarnation is the only relevant incarnation because we live in the present. What I give to the world has relevance, and what I could have been, has no relevance today. When we are totally occupied with the essence within, the supreme, we are all beings, and all incarnations, across time and space.

Finally, I have seen many purposeful reincarnations in this time, and they hate to be revealed because it affects their work. So, some secrets are always good because the message has more relevance than the individual.

Thea: *Amma Sri Karunamayi told me that Ishwari, the highest form of the Divine Mother, took on the job of planet Earth. Could Mohanji add anything to that?*

Mohanji: Shakti (female divine energy) is the source of all creation on all worlds, including the Earth. In beings, it operates as Iccha Shakti (Will Power), Kriya Shakti (Power Behind Actions), and Jnaana Shakti (Power of Knowledge). The Divine Mother is the source of all three. Since she operates as consciousness, which includes waking, dreaming, and deep sleep, she is also considered the source of the three siddhis (mystic powers achieved through meditation and yoga) or the three tangible states. We are a combination of all three even though inherent Gunas—Sattva (purity), Rajas (activity/passion), and Tamas (darkness/inertia)—determine us.

Mother is spread within and throughout the universe. The Gayathri Mantra invokes the 24 centers of our structure where the Mother predominantly resides. Kundalini Shakti is called Maha Shakti (Great Power) because that shakti detaches us from all bindings, identifications, and establishes us in a state of consciousness known as Shiva. Each state or frequency is named as per its nature.

Transcending states and merging with the supreme consciousness is the journey of the soul, which always remains detached from the body and life, even though it seems as if it is attached.

Shiva is the source, pure consciousness, spread over the manifested and uncreated universe as infinity. The Mother stays as the manifestation and the possibility for creation. So, all creation in all the worlds has the Mother's hand in it.

Thea: *What does Mohanji think about the Second Coming? This idea should be compatible with the Avadoot concept.*

Mohanji: The Second Coming according to me is the changeover of a phase or a new era. No real incarnations have gone from here to come back. Everybody exists here in essence form. The consciousness of Jesus, Buddha, Krishna, Datta, or Babaji are still available and active. Shirdi Sai left his physical body in 1918 but is still tangibly active. So, only those who have gone need to come back. I believe that if another purposeful incarnation has to happen from the same essence that we call as Jesus, it will happen as per the need of the hour. The idea is to detach the current generation from ignorance based on identifications, to the possibility of what I call the highest awareness of the God principle on the experiential level. The new incarnation will take such a form, perhaps as an engineer, doctor, or an IT professional to be able to communicate what he came for, with this world, easily and effortlessly.

The essence of Jesus, Krishna and Buddha are already working through many incarnations. But the question is, who listens and who understands? People try to put a master into a frame that they have kept for him in their minds. Masters fit into no frames. They usually reject the master but keep the frame. Then it will take posterity to understand and appreciate a true master, in his originality. There are numerous examples of this with us. Jesus, Socrates, Buddha, Adi Shankara, Hazrat Babajan, Jnaneshwar, Yogi Ramsurat Kumar, Ramana Maharshi, Sai Baba of Shirdi, and many of the true masters living or not living today. They were not accepted, appreciated or respected in their time, and it took posterity to honor them.

Even if Jesus were to come again today, how would we have him? If he dresses up like Jesus of Nazareth, how he was, won't we put him in a lunatic asylum? There are numerous enlightened masters in asylums and prisons in countries like Iran. Their crime is "they polluted the minds of the youth, the thinking generation, with 'their truth.'" Some are scandalized, accusing them of paltry matters such as money and sex. We cannot handle absolute truth. We prefer relative truth that is changeable which the mind can understand. There are numerous masters in India because we have always allowed the unconditional individuality of everyone.

As the world is conditioned and oriented in the gross aspects of life, it is not easy to see nor appreciate a true master deeply rooted in supreme consciousness. Their rules are different. They are unbound. They are free. They are rooted in righteousness, compassion, kindness, and selflessness. The self-centered, selfish world fails to see them. Yet, they leave their mark and the future generations eventually see them.

Jesus would have lived longer if his society had accepted his originality. Even if Jesus comes now, the established religious institutions may crucify him a second time through social media, at least, because they might not be able to accept truth and originality even now. Time has changed, minds have not, and society has not. Society is still ridden with theories, concepts, prejudices, opinions and comparisons. This takes their ability away from recognizing, understanding, and appreciating anything original, unless skeptically.

Thea: *Can you describe more about Bhriguram Paramahamsa, who guided Avadoot Nadananda to Gyan Ganj, which is spoken about in* The Autobiography of Avadoota?[40]

Mohanji: Bhriguram Paramahamsa is the "General Manager" of Gyan Ganj. I do not intend to bind him with a title because he cannot be bound at all. He is the central administrator. It is a metaphysical plane. This is a place where the gross and subtle coexist supporting each other. Gross can enter and exit this plane only if it attains sufficient subtlety to accept, receive, and appreciate this plane as it is. It was Bhriguram Paramahamsa who took Avadhoota Nadananda to Gyan Ganj. It is to Bhriguram Paramahamsa who I met in Shirdi along with Nadananda, that I gave Dakshina to (offering myself as in a symbolical surrender through some money).

[40] https://www.amazon.in/Autobiography-Avadhoota-Part-I-Nadananda-ebook/dp/B01LYXGMSI

After this incident, Nadananda said, "My job is over. You are now directly connected to Gyanganj."

This is mentioned in the second volume of *The Autobiography of Avadhoota*. Bhriguram Paramahamsa is considered to be the Guru's Guru of Bhagawan Nithyananda of Ganeshpuri.

By the way, Avadhootas are those who are only occupied with their essence within (themselves). They may not care about the external world at all because, for them, nothing exists outside their inner universe. They witness the macrocosm in their microcosm. They may look like mad men or eccentric people. They are drunk with God.

Thea: *Tell us about how you meditate.*

Mohanji: Every day from 3 a.m. to 8 a.m., I used to sit and connect to myself. I would connect to my spine and assimilate myself. Eventually, I could go deeper and deeper into the world of noises, the core of noises, which is silence. We are in a world of noises, and we are contributing to the world of noises every moment. But there is a source for all these noises. Where have these noises come from? Absolute silence. So, you need to get back to the original source, the core, and that's silence.

When you go deeper and deeper into the core of noises, you will finally reach the world of silence, where there is no noise. All the noises like waves come out of it, and they go back to it; you are stillness. It took time for me to settle down, and so many things broke down at that time: physically, emotionally, intellectually. At that time, it was not very comfortable because we are a bundle of sounds, you are settled in silence and you are fully in that mode, you feel oneness with every master.

Thea: *Is Planet Earth going to ascend?*

Mohanji: Our mother earth is a beautiful place for experiencing the various flavors of life. From gross sensory pleasures to total dissolution or merger with the supreme consciousness, when a drop becomes the ocean and loses itself in it. Hence mother earth is indeed a sacred space. No doubt.

Thea: *I understand that the position of Dattatreya is an office or position which is appointed; what has Mohanji to say about this?*

Mohanji: Unmanifested consciousness is only pure energy. There is no creation, space, or time. There is no beginning or end. Neither death nor decay. Creation began with the conglomeration of energy into a particular frequency that we call matter. Matter gave the opportunity for time and space. In this vast creation, Earth is a relatively new planet. Existence has manifested before in multiple planes and multiple frequencies. Earth is a vast canvas with a massive potential for the formation of various species and several layers of frequencies also through a play of the elements (earth, wind, fire, water, and ether). Despite this huge canvas and potential, it is minuscule when viewed against the vast cosmos (manifested creation), which also is minuscule compared to the unmanifested consciousness.

We should think about a master of the stature of Lord Dattatreya in the context of the cosmos and not just Earth. In his original form, which is described in the scriptures as an energy brighter than a million suns, no one will be able to see him, much less recognize him. He has to condense himself to a level where he can communicate. He manifested Himself as a representation of the three aspects of the created universe (creation, sustenance, and dissolution), yet remaining all the while as the unmanifested consciousness. This is very complicated for a human mind to comprehend.

Lord Dattatreya's energy or that aspect of universal consciousness can manifest through various bodies simultaneously. When one raises one's frequency and shifts from the mind to consciousness and gains the awareness of being a unit, the energy of that aspect of consciousness that we can call Dattatreya merges with you and eventually connects you to the awareness of the Universal Consciousness. As Krishna says, "We merge with what we are connected to."

If we are consistently connected to Lord Datta, we merge into that consciousness. Thus, you become That. But then it is difficult to say that this aspect of you is Lord Dattatreya because it is all One. That consciousness is as vast as the entire infinite universe. Being finite can only represent it but cannot be it in its entirety.

"One who can contain the oceans in his jug, can be called a master." – Adi Shankaracharya

Here, the ocean is the grand consciousness and the jug is the unit, the visible being. Various avatars such as Dattatreya, Krishna, Jesus, Buddha, and so on, happened at the right time for the distinct purpose to redeem the decay or decline of dharma (righteousness) and restore the order of the world. I am operating as Mohanji in this life – a projection of the Tradition to facilitate a frequency that allows communication with some people. Not everyone may understand me. Not everyone may accept me. Not everyone may reject me. If you ask me, "Am I Lord Dattatreya?" The direct answer is, "No. I am not Lord Dattatreya, because I know I am not Lord Dattatreya." If you ask me again, "Am I Lord Dattatreya?" The answer is, "Yes. I am Lord Dattatreya," because I consider him as my great Guru, hence, I am a part of Him. Whoever you are deeply connected to, you become a part of that. You are where your mind is parked. Dattatreya resides in everyone. He becomes evident and predominates when one's frequency is raised beyond mind.

The key question should be: Am I delivering what I am unconditionally to the world? In the Tradition of Liberation, a master delivers transformation. When a person consistently connects to a master, transformation must happen. Hence, my relevance is my performance. Does it really matter if I was another in the past? Is it important if I was Jesus, Krishna, Buddha, Dattatreya, or anyone else? I don't live in the past nor do I like anything superimposed on me because it dilutes my present existence, my being Mohanji. If I'm considered someone else (a manifestation from the past), how will I perform? People will expect me to behave like someone else. If I have to comply, I have to pretend, which I refuse to do, since it will dilute my work. That's why I keep insisting that I'm Mohanji in this life. I will live as Mohanji and will die as Mohanji. Tomorrow, or after my death, another may resemble me, and people may think that he is the incarnation of Mohanji.

Thea: *Please explain how the Nath tradition and the Datta tradition are merged, and how are they connected to Krishna and his teachings?*

Mohanji: When Lord Krishna realized that the time to leave his body was near, he wanted to ensure that the purpose of his avatar and the resulting teachings wouldn't get diluted after his death. Mostly after death, we forget the gurus and their teachings, or we interpret their teachings as we like. This naturally happens with every guru. What was Krishna's teachings? In a phrase, life in all its practical aspects. Be practical. Be flexible. Live your purpose. Always remember that you are the universe, and you are universal. That is how he lived. Lord Krishna discussed with Lord Dattatreya who was the yugacharya (the teacher of the era) during his time, to create a system that would allow his teachings to continue. Accordingly, Lord Dattatreya codified the Nath tradition based on the state of Shiva. What is Shiva? Totally expanded, completely detached, and fully consumed in ecstatic bliss.

Lord Krishna called all higher beings before he left his physical frame and told them that the purpose and message of his avatar must continue. He chose nine people as its messengers. They are the nine Narayanas. "Narayana" means "destination of man." Lord Krishna, himself Narayana, summoned the nine Narayanas, who were projections of himself, and ordered the formation of Nath Tradition. Thus, Krishna expanded himself from one to many. They became the Nava (nine) Nath saints. Lord Dattatreya is the primordial master, who delivered the Tradition. The Tradition is created to spread the message of true love, beyond all boundaries, and preserve the ultimate dharma of existence. The Nath masters also are beacons or representations of the human potential for higher awareness to the level of the consistent ecstatic state of existence without dependencies on any aspects of Earth. Nath Tradition represents the aspiration of a true seeker to find Shiva within himself, with a promise that it is achievable and practical. Kriya is one of their methods.

In contrast, the Masters of the Dattatreya Tradition are perfect beings, born accomplished Avadhootas who happened as per the need of the times. The Masters of the Dattatreya Tradition like Shripada Shrivallabha, Narsimha Saraswati, Swami Samarth, Sai Baba, Bhagavan Nityananda, and so on, were considered incarnations of Lord Dattatreya. They came to effect certain transformations in people and the world, and their service continues as long as it is required. Completely detached, they were consumed in inner stillness and had nothing to do with the outside world. Their presence was transformative. They allowed people to be themselves while taking them to the highest on the path of liberation. With a mere touch or glance, they made stones into pure gold. They never created disciples. They never taught anything. Their life itself was their teachings. They have been living Gods. Their goals were similar to the Nath Tradition, but they differed in delivery. To progress, one has to be consistently in tune with the master's consciousness, which was not easy. Transformation took place in their presence without any initiation. It was just their presence on Earth. They were brought by collective consciousness of people who craved for redemption. There have been no demands from them. They asked nothing from anybody, even to follow them. They never revealed themselves. They did not cater to the general people's routine expectations. But when people connected to them consistently, without doubts, prejudices, and other mental barriers, they delivered them FREEDOM. Avadhootas are not teachers. They are living Gods on earth. Dattatreya not only delivered Nath tradition, he also delivered the Dasa Maha Vidyas (10 Great Techniques) of the Shakti (feminine energy) worship. Dattatreya cannot be defined in words at all.

Mind needs frames. It cannot have a frameless state. Mind needs demonstration, methods, and activities. The Nath tradition is more suitable for the masses since it is vast and systematic with detailed methods and practices that one chooses based on one's orientation to achieve the highest. To suit all orientations, it supports all yogas: bhakti yoga (devotion), jnana yoga (knowledge), karma yoga (service), raja yoga (meditation), and so on.

Earth is a relatively new planet. So, when a planet happens, there are high frequency points and low frequency points and there are in-betweens and various frequencies in every land. Not all things are high or low. One of the high frequency points is Mount Kailash, and some points are very, very, powerful. People are attracted to certain points and have the potential to reach that frequency. It is like a flower that attracts butterflies, honeybees, and insects. Everybody gets attracted to that frequency, but not everybody is getting the same thing from it.

A person of elevated frequency will find culmination there, but a person of a different frequency may find gratification. It's all different. You cannot say this is it—ever—in any one aspect. There's nothing final. There are always options. There is always a change. There's always a transformation. It's mostly connected to how we are and what our state is.

So why do we connect to a master? When you consistently connect to a master, your frequency starts to shift. When you connect to a master as an object to get something, then you will get something, maybe some knowledge, some guidance, that's all, but you will not connect to the master's frequency until you're consistent. You're serving the master and serving the master doesn't mean that you have to physically serve. Serving the master means in tune with the master's consciousness. That is why all the masters have always said to take your time to understand the master, and then you connect, otherwise doubts will come. When doubts come, it's opposite.

Shiva may not have been from here. He could have come from elsewhere and not be part of the evolutionary teaching of the Kailash frequency. Representing infinity means that he could be timeless. Lots of beings living at Kailash may not be from the earth plane. On the earth plane, you take a birth, you go through frequency shifts, and evolve, and evolve, and evolve through lifetimes, then you reach a particular state of awareness. Each state takes you to different levels, or each state stabilizes you somewhere. So, this is the evolutionary way. The beings there may not be part of the evolutionary way. They might have been existing elsewhere and have found that this place is good and stable for their existence. They need nothing. Once you have crossed over to the unlimited space, you need nothing because everything is yours. If you don't have something that you need you are everything. What would you need? This is the clarity you should have.

The Nath Tradition is a tradition of a certain Order to stabilize a certain frequency in people. Datta apparently made that happen. If you take Dattatreya separately, he is an Avadhoota. He said, "I'm the nature. I'm everything in nature. I am the Shakti as well as the Source." That is how he delivered the Dasa Maha Vidyas (the Ten Maha-vidyas) to Parashurama. He delivered it as a guru. This is exactly how Datta operates. He is an Avadhoota. He has no interest in following the people following him. He is here like God, representing supreme consciousness, which has three aspects: the creation, the maintenance, and the dissolution. Datta was a "yugacharya." He was the acharya of the yuga and he delivered what he had to deliver.

Shiva is dissolution. When people connect to Shiva, they're ready to dissolve into him. But when they connect to Mahavishnu, it's more about sustenance, of daily stability. If you connect to Brahma, it's about creation. So, this is how the whole structure works.

For me, Shiva is the ultimate. That's where I want to reach and why I am here. If I deliver a certain message and do good things for the world, it can inspire people.

If you talk about the path of liberation, but then do whatever you want, it will not be acceptable to the mind. The mind will say that this is bullshit; it's not working. The path must be highly practical to get there. Just keep moving, moving and you will get there.

Krishna told Arjuna to pick up the arms and fight. Arjuna said, "I cannot do this!" Krishna replied, "Isn't that why you were born a warrior? If you are born a warrior, you're supposed to fight to win. Do it purposefully." Certain frequencies demand or facilitate a certain presence. This is the fundamental problem. If you look at it from the earth point of view, it is how he's projected and how he has to be.

Look at it this way, there are a few dams and they block the flow of different rivers. At some point in time, someone opens the tap, and then water emerges. The water existed before, and the water was complete even before it emerged. Once three rivers merge, who can say which river is which? It's like that, so very difficult. This is Datta.

– With love, Mohanji

Credit: Mohanji.org

HEALING TECHNIQUES

As you read this book you may feel sad or heavy, and if so, you have probably lived with me during these times. I would like to share with you techniques that I have used to transcend illusion, faster than chanting the mantras or other healing techniques I've learned. When I was sitting during the years in solitude, I had to learn how to move karma fast. The techniques, along with my intention, could expose the next step of growth. However, I could still remain stuck in whatever surfaced, for an awfully long time. For this reason, I learned to call directly on God, and ask for a specialty team of Angelic Master Beings to help me quickly transmute karma that was already up. God is the Supreme Being, the Mother/ Father God. All Masters, avatars, saints, devas, and departments of angels report to God, who has the final say. When we say a prayer to the Supreme Being, a specialty team will be sent to help. God knows exactly what we need, and who to send; however, the clearer our intentions, the more quickly we will receive. The following is a prayer that will cover any situation:

Heavenly Father and Mother God, I/We ask that You bring in your specialty team for (say person's name.) I/We ask that You bring in the light, color, and sound frequencies and magnify and intensify the God light frequency through a diamond pyramid at the highest frequency that person can take. I/We ask the Angels of the Violet flame to instantly transmute by grace and bring up from the unconscious to the conscious, any blockage that is causing this problem. I/We ask that this healing go through all the bodies, the RNA and the DNA (physical cells).

OM, PEACE, AMEN.

There are many departments of God's angels. The archangels and their divine feminine counterparts, archeiai, rule the angelic kingdom and protect mankind. There are seven archangels assigned to carry out God's work through a designated color ray and its corresponding quality. For example, the sapphire blue ray embodies the power and will of God, and is lead by Archangel Michael and Archeia Faith. Michael brings forth the will of God and Faith materializes it. The book, *Angels of Love and Light* by Lynn Fischer beautifully describes the hierarchy of the angelic kingdom as well as the rays and qualities. The second ray, the golden yellow ray, is associated with illumination and wisdom and is led by Archangel Jophiel and Archeia Christine. Pink is the ray of love and adoration and is gov-erned by Archangel Chamuel and Archeia Charity. The white ray represents Purity, Ascension and Resurrection, and is ruled by Archangel Gabriel and Archeia Hope. Emerald green is the healing and truth ray that Archangel Raphael and Archeia Mary (Mother Mary) oversee. Archangel Uriel and Archeia Aurora rule the sixth ray, which is a combination of gold and purple, representing grace, compassion and selfless service. The final transmuting violet ray gives us the power of transformation into God Consciousness, and is governed by Archangel Zackiel and Archeia Amethyst.

As I mentioned before, there can be no doership when we ask for God's help. We act as an anchor for God's energy, which can pass through us, but God's team, not us, does the work. If the ego becomes involved and we think we are any part of the doership, the higher ones will leave.

The most important part of a healing is *intention*—the knowledge that it will be done. Each of us is part of a team, a co-creator with God. Know *WITHOUT A DOUBT* that your prayers will be answered, and *IT WILL BE SO* if that prayer is for the highest good.

For protection from negative energy, call on God to bring in Archangel Michael's angels and to place a diamond pyramid over yourself, with a mirror-like substance facing outward, to reflect any negative energy back to its sender with love. Ask Archangel Michael's angels to stay with you, to protect you while you are under the pyramid. Another way is to enfold yourself in an egg or cocoon of Christ-white light, which no negativity can penetrate, and to which only good can come.

If negative energy or psychic attack is caused by jealousy, its source can be used as a negative switchboard for dark energy. There are many categories of dark energy including dark spirits, earth-bound spirits and demons. Earth-bound spirits are people who are still attached to something on Earth, such as money or addiction, and do not want to leave. They are not very evolved beings; otherwise they would release the attachment, and go on to higher spheres of light. If you feel there are negative spirits or energies around you, or in a particular area, or if you feel an evil spirit is coming through someone, you can offer the following prayer:

Heavenly Father/Mother God, please instruct Your angels under Archangel Michael to bind any dark spirits in my auric force field and bodies (or name of person.) Take them off this planet and bring them to You for trans-mutation in Your Divine Love and Light.

You can also reinforce the prayer by bringing in any of your personal Masters, such as Buddha, or Jesus, etc. Repeat the following prayer with fiery conviction as an instrument of God. After the initial prayer, the underlined command should then be repeated three or more times with great conviction until the clearing is complete:

In the name of Almighty God, creator of all, I COMMAND ALL DARK SPIRITS TO LEAVE ME NOW! Please hold Your hands over me and under me and place Your angels of light all around me. Seal off my auric force field and safeguard me against all dark spirits, psychic attacks and evil influences. OM, PEACE, AMEN.

Always clear yourself if you feel off balance. Negative energy or entities can be picked up from other people and places (such as bars), and it is very important for your own protection to clear areas and people in order to bring yourself into balance. To clear another person or area, use the same three-step clearing process above by stating the person's name or place. More than one person can be cleared simultaneously.

The angels have been asked to go with this book, so that if you have lived during the same karmic time slot and become deeply affected after reading it, the angels will lift the karma instantly.

LETTERS TO THEA

From Brian, Mid-1970s

Namaste Sister!

Some ripples of thought to share in the wake of your call yesterday.

First, I feel your sense of loss and confusion in regards to Swamiji [Prem]. I am amazed as well at your incredible balance and honesty in dealing with this heavy development. Jai! That time we sat in silence together was a movement of three souls towards the One. Perhaps he needs us badly, too, for I felt he had so much to teach me. But what a blessing it was revealed, now, that he is not yet free. Like you I desire the highest. "My Lord, all I want is thee!" I can only follow with all my heart, soul, mind and strength, one who is truly a realized master, Paramhansa Yogananda. He has even given me teachings in a lucid dream! I feel at present so very strong and sure, out of that center came the inner vows of brahman-chari for this incarnation. We shall seek God together and find him too!

Your soul is on fire and my own eyes have seen its bright light around the very embodiment of Divine Mother. I am your son and most humble spiritual brother. Our souls seem so open to each other's spirit, our energies so compatible and complementary, our karmas so intertwined. What grace that Mother has brought us together for the holy work of getting free! Nature, seclusion, India and Samadhi, we share the same dream, but all is up to Ma in the end. "Thy will be done!" She is also going to have to arrange for finances, mine are almost non-existent. All we can do is yearn for spirit with all our being and everything else shall follow. "Seek ye first the Kingdom of God and his righteousness and all these things shall be added unto you." "Take no thought for the morrow for the morrow shall take thought for the things of itself."

As you foresaw, Mother is helping me work through a lot in a very short time my last weeks here. I wrote this chant to her:

> *My Divine Mother, My Divine Mother,*
> *Bless me with Thy wisdom and Thy sacred Om.*
> *My Divine Mother, My Divine Mother,*
> *Bless me with Thy beauty and Thy wondrous light.*
> *My Divine Mother, My Divine Mother,*
> *Bless me with Thy pure love and Thy boundless heart.*
> *Jai Ma*!

Yours in God, Christ & Gurus,
Sadhu Ram

From Ananda Moyi Ma, 1970
Written to Thea from Mrs. Vasudeva

First of all Ma smiled and was very glad Indu had written– "read, read, read!" she said. She lit up at your name and said, "This work is complete."

When you mentioned you were discouraged because your work was so hard and didn't feel like you were encouraged, etc., and felt lost without grace – she said, "That's because your japa is incomplete! You must do it constantly – 24 hours! Continue on it until the light manifests from within. *Swayam* (light) *Prakash* (within)."

You asked her to teach you to love her– she said, "Love comes about by its own accord from within– you can't teach it– practice japa!!!"

I told her how you were getting keen to come to Mother. She at once replied, "Tell her Ma is there with her."

Excerpts From Papa Ramdas

September 14, 1962

Beloved Mother,

Ramdas is very happy to read your loving letter of the 6th instant. It is excellent that you are now serving your mother. The service of the elders is greatly helpful to one's spiritual progress. Since you have Ramnam on your lips, no external hostile forces will attack you. Ramnam is so powerful. May it be always on your tongue and in your heart. When you feel like coming here again, you may do so; but try your best to attune yourself to the environment in which you are at present. The way is to behold the Divine in all beings and creatures, to have the universal vision. Then you will not feel the need of changing places and surroundings. May God grant you perfect peace and bliss in His remembrance...

Ever your Self,
Ramdas

October 6, 1962

Beloved Mother,

...It is true that in all matters we are guided and inspired by God who dwells within us and everywhere outside us. In fact, He dwells in all beings, creatures and things. He is omnipresent and omnipotent. May you be ever conscious of His presence. May His name dwell ever on your tongue. You are spiritually growing into a beautiful flower and the fragrance of it is very far and wide. All victory to you or, in other words, victory to Ram within you.

Do feel purity and joy as your true and real qualities. You are always in tune with Reality. All joy and peace to you. Please do write us from time to time...

May divine grace ever pour upon you all.

Mataji and Ramdas send their hearty love and blessings.

Ever your Self,
Ramdas

March 20, 1963

Beloved Mother,

...Your previous letter intimating about
your mother's regress in her health has
not reached Ramdas. If you feel you
should remain to serve and nurse her
you must of course do it and postpone
your coming here. There is a line in the
Upanishads in which it is given: "Matru
Devo Bhava". This is in Sanskrit which
means "Mother is God". So to serve the
mother is to serve god.

What you say about complete dedication
of life to God giving up all attachments
to father, mother and the family is also
true. But, in your present circumstances
your place is with your mother. After she
gets well you may think of coming here...

You have poured your heart in this letter. Your faith in Ramnam and your Papa
is simply wonderful. It is seen clearly
that you are swimming in an ocean of joy...

May you ever be immersed in divine
bliss and peace.

Love and blessings to you, your mother,
father and all others there.

Ever your Self,
Ramdas

From Hugo
November 8, 1965

Beloved Theo,

Dry periods are a sure sign of progress and one has not at all to be disturbed by them – all that is Ram also. After all, the mind gets tired sometimes from that much walking so it seeks rest in drying up. You know love is He. Thus love can-not be gained or produced since it is the uncreated Eternal. As soon as we try to catch hold of it to possess it, it has gone – since love cannot be subjected to anything but love alone. The moment we try to possess it we try to subject it to our (the ego's) will and wish. How could that be?! It must be the master and we the slave wholly possessed by it entirely an instrument of it. We have to give ourselves up to it – dissolve into it then Ram is the master and the mind the servant. Not Ram should be ours but ours ought to be Ram's. Give up all that you possess and are and when all has gone then Ram is You. Your path surely leads to this end.

All the love of the Almighty is very with you in the form of Ananda Moyi Ma, Bhagavan and Papa. You have abso-lutely nothing to worry but just to know – the path is like that. See all problems are within thus also the solution must take place from within.

How? When by chanting His Name the mind gets still and aware of that resting place within the mind from where shines forth deep undisturbed eternal peace. Holding onto this focus it holds on to the hand of the Guru within. Holding it strongly and looking back at Theo – then you know what is to be learned and what matters – since from there you see Theo not as yourself but something else. From these Theo never matters but that what holds you hold on – try to sink-sink – that's all! No teachings nothing required – just forget, forget and Be!

–Hugo

REFERENCES:

Eddy, Mary Baker (2000), *Science and Health with Key to the Scriptures*, Boston: Christian Scientist Publishing Company.

Kahlil, Gibran (1923), *The Prophet*, New York: Alfred A. Knopf, Inc.

Nikhilananda, Swami (1942), *The Gospel of Sri Ramakrishna*, Volume1, Visit to Vidyasagar. Retrieved May 29, 2006 from www.rama-krishnavivekananda.info/index.htm

Nikhilananda, Swami (1953), *Vivekananda A Biography*, The Parliament of Religions. Retrieved May 29, 2006 from www.rama-krishnavivekananda.info/index.htm

Yogananda, Paramahansa (1993), *Autobiography of a Yogi*, Los Angeles: Self-Realization Fellowship.

Montgomery, Ruth (1984), *Strangers Among Us*, New York: Fawcett Books.

RECOMMENDED READING

Paramahansa Yogananda (1946), *Autobiography of a Yogi*, Self-Realization Fellowship.

Eide, Rita (2001), *Celestial Voice of Diana*, Findhorn Press.

Maxwell, Glenn (1999), *Glances at Eternity: A Memoir to Remember*, Angelic Encounters.

Papa Ramdas, *In Quest of God, In the Vision of God*, and *God Experience*. For more information contact:
Anandashram, Anandashram P.O., Kanhangad 671531,
Dist. Kasaragod,
Kerala, India.
Tel: (0467) 2203036/ 2209477
Email: cnn_ramnagar@sancharnet.in or
papa@anandashram.org

GLOSSARY

Akashic records – Refers to a subtle substance called akasha where every thought, action and word of every human being in existence is recorded and kept for all time.

Amma – An affectionate name for the Divine Mother.

Ananda Moyi Ma – (1896-1982) Known as the "Bliss Permeated Mother," one of the greatest aspects of the Divine Mother, as mentioned in *Autobiography of a Yogi* by Yogananada.

Arati – Holy light in Hindi and is a Hindu ritual where lighted wicks soaked in ghee (clarified butter) and camphor are offered to a deity.

Archaiea – The feminine aspect of the archangels.

Ascension – Perfecting the physical body into the Light Body. The act of ascending.

Ashtar – An Ascended Master who belongs to the Galactic Federation and is the Commander of many fleets of starships.

Augustiar – (Also "Agastyar") one of the teachers of Mahavatar Babaji.

Avatar – Avatar means "the descent of God" in Sanskrit and refers to the incarnation of the Supreme Being who is free from the laws of matter, time and space. Avatars come to this world to spiritually uplift humanity and to remind them of their true eternal and divine self. Famous avatars are Krishna, Rama, Sita Devi, Gautama Buddha and Jesus Christ.

Babaji (Mahavatar Babji) – Mahavatar Babaji is an Ascended Master still living in the Himalayas. He is said to be thousands of years old, although no one knows when he was born or where. He is one of the great Masters who watches over humanity and appears to people periodically to impart his message of love and peace. Babaji has yogic, or super human powers, such as great strength and the ability to appear in different forms.

Bhakti – Deep spiritual devotion.

Bhagavad Gita – A sacred Hindu scripture based on the Indian epic *Mahabaratha* where Krishna and Arjuna have a philosophical dialogue about the nature of God.

Bhajan – Devotional songs to God written in Sanskrit.

Bhajan Hall – Temple where holy songs and worship is performed.

Brahmachari – A spiritual student dedicated solely to God who has renounced the physical pleasures such as sex, alcohol, gambling, eating meat, etc.

Brahman – The Supreme God in Hinduism.

Brujas – Black magicians who perform rituals to harm others.

Chai – Indian spiced tea.

Chakras – From the Sanskrit word cakra meaning "wheel," they are energy centers along the spine that give life force to the body.

Dark spirits – Earthbound souls and other souls who work for the dark forces.

Darshan – Blessings from an enlightened master.

Demons – A devil or evil spirit.

Dharma – A term in Hinduism to represent living one's

life in a righteous manner and according one's own divine plan.

Dhoti – Traditional Indian garment worn by men that consists of a long piece of cloth wrapped around the waist and legs.

Divine Mother – The Divine Mother is the dynamic and creative force of the Godhead and lives in all things. She is known by many names, such as the Goddesses Devi, Shakti, Durga, Kali, Isis, and Mother Mary.

Durga – The Hindu Goddess and all-pervading force of the Divine Mother representing fearlessness and patience.

Durga Puja – Worship to the Divine Mother, Durga.

Entity Release – Release of the dark spirits from people or places.

Essenes – The community of people who prepared, taught, nurtured, and celebrated with Jesus 2,000 years ago.

Ganesha – The Hindu Elephant-God who is the Lord of success, wisdom and the remover of obstacles on the spiritual path.

Garawa Cloth – An orange robe that symbolizes a renunciate.

Gopis – The famous group of cow herding girls who were completely devoted to Lord Krishna.

Guru Kripa – The Master's grace.

Hanuman (Hanumanji) – Hanumanji is the Monkey God, the greatest devotee of Lord Rama.

Harmonium – A free-standing keyboard instrument similar to a reed organ or pipe organ.

Himalayan scriptures – A manuscript of the Akashic

Records that were dictated by a master telling of the future of Planet Earth. They warn humankind that if we do not change we will be taken over by the dark forces.

Implant – A device superimposed in people's energy fields to alter the DNA and hold one back. A form of black magic.

Jai – Also "jaya" or "jay", Sanskrit word for victory.

Jin Shin Jyutsu – A Japanese healing art which works with balancing pulses.

Judith – Essene teacher of Yeshua (Jesus).

Kali – The Hindu Goddess Kali is the warrior aspect of the Divine Mother who cuts through illusion with fierce aplomb. According to ancient text she was born from the brow of the goddess Durga, a slayer of demons, during a battle between the good and evil.

Karma – The Sanskrit word for "action," in the sense that for every action there is a reaction. It's meaning is rooted in the law of cause and effect, or "As ye sow, so shall ye reap."

Kirtan – Indian devotional chants typically accompanied by muscial instruments sung in a call and response fashion.

Krishna – The eighth incarnation of Vishnu.

Kum kum – A powder made from turmeric and lime juice and in Hinduism is applied to the forehead during pujas, or sacred ceremonies. It represents a pure soul who sees the divine in all beings.

Kundalini – Sanskrit for "coiled up" or "serpent power" representing the female cosmic energy existing in every atom of the universe. In humans it originates in the first chakra, or energy center, at the base of the spine and remains in a dormant state until awakened through disciplined yogic practices or by a realized master. The unmanifested kundalini is symbolized by a coiled serpent with its tail in its mouth. When this energy is awakened it travels up the spine to the top of the head where the person experiences a Oneness state with God.

Ladus – Offerings to a deity in the form of flowers, food, etc.

Lakshmi – The Hindu Goddess of beauty, abundance and fortune.

Lokas – Heavenly realms.

Mahasamadhi – When a realized master leaves the physical body through death and goes into a God-illumined state of Being that is forever beyond karma.

Mahavatar – "Maha" in Sanskrit means "mighty" and "avatar" represents the incarnation of the Supreme Being who is free from the laws of matter, time and space.

Mala – "Garland" in Sanskrit, a necklace with 108 beads.

Milarepa – Milarepa was a great Tibetan master whose guru was Marpa. When Milarepa was a young man he used black magic against his family who unjustly stole his fortune. He repented and his guru Marpa was working out Milarepa's misuse of energy by having him build houses and then dissemble them. Milarepa spent years meditating in a cave where demons would come at him, and he learned to tame the demons and bring them to the light.

Mother Meera – Born in 1960, she is believed to be an embodiment of the Divine Mother, residing in Germany.

Murti – An image of a deity used as a focus of worship.

Nadis – Subtle energy channels in the body that are connected to the physical nerves, with the main nadi running up the spine from the base to the crown chakras. Depending on the source, there is said to be anywhere from 1,000 to 72,000 nadis.

Nadi Leaves – Ancient written records from the Akashic Records, which describe in minute detail the lives of individuals who are living in this day and age.

Narvana – Another name for Vishnu, the Preserver aspect of the Hindu triple Godhead which also includes Brahma and Shiva.

Nirvana – Supreme Enlightenment. Liberation through Self Realization.

Om – (Also Aum) in Sanskrit the primeval sound and symbol representing the non-dualistic universe as a whole.

Pantheist – Pantheist literally means "God is All," and refers to one who sees God in all of nature and the universe.

Parvati – Consort of Lord Shiva.

Powah – A Tibetan practice to help a soul exit through the top of the head in a very high state.

Pradakshina – Circumambulation or walking around in a circle as a form of worship in India.

Pranam – A form of greeting in India by holding the palms together and bowing.

Prasad – Food that has been imbued with the blessings through puja or sacred ceremony or from the touch of an enlightened master.

Puja – Hindu ritual worship.

Radha Krishna – Radha was a gopi who became Krishna's supreme beloved and represents the Supreme Goddess.

Rama – The legendary king of Ayodhya in ancient India and considered to be an incarnation of Vishnu.

Ramakrishna – Ramakrishna was a great, realized soul who lived in the mid-nineteenth century. He mastered all the types of religions and proved through the elevated state of meditation or samadhi that every path or religion could reach the final state of Oneness or God.

Ramana Maharishi – (1879–1950) A famous Indian sage who attained liberation at the age of 16.

Renunciate – One who renounces the world and lives a monastic lifestyle.

Rishis – A "seer" or "shaman" to whom the Vedas (ancient scriptures from India) were originally revealed through states of higher consciousness.

Sadhana – A spiritual discipline, such as meditation, prayer and healing that leads you to God and release illusion.

Sadhu – A wandering monk who begs for his food.

Sahaj Samadhi – The Universal Vision, where one beholds one's self in every atom.

Samadhi – The Sansrkit word Samadhi refers to a completely absorbed state of God consciousness experienced during concentrated meditation.

Sananda – The Oversoul of Yeshua (Jesus). Yeshua was only one of the lifetimes of Sananda, who has had 33 other lifetimes on the Earth plane.

Sannayasin (sanayasini) – A renunciate.

Sanskrit – The classical language of Indian and the liturgical language of Hinduism, Buddhism, and Jainism. It is also one of the 22 official languages of India. The name Sanskrit means "refined", "consecrated" and "sanctified". It has always been regarded as the high language and used mainly for religious and scientific discourse.

Saraswati – An aspect of the Divine Mother, representing wisdom and the arts.

Satchitananda – A compound of three Sanskrit words, "sat," "cit," and "ananda" meaning existence, consciousness, and bliss, respectively.

Shiva (Lord Shiva) – Shiva is regarded by some as the supreme being and by others as forming a triad with Brahma and Vishnu. He is worshiped in many aspects: as destroyer, ascetic, lord of the cosmic dance, and lord of beasts, and through the symbolic lingam. His wife is Parvati. ORIGIN from Sanskrit Śiva, literally 'the auspicious one.

Shakti – The female principle of divine energy, especially when personified as the supreme deity.

Shaktipat – An ancient Sanskrit word that refers to the transmission of divine energy by a realized being, or guru, to activate the kundulini energy that lays dormant in all humans in the first chakra (one of seven energy centers) at the base of the spine. Shakti is the creative energy that animates all life, and pat means to descend. When a guru gives Shaktipat, it awakens an individual's own inner divine energy and leads to spiritual awakening.

Shankaracharya – An aspect of Lord Shiva, incarnated in the 8th century A.D. in India. He brought forth the Vedanta teachings which include the doctrine of non-duality. Vedanta is the pure essence of Hinduism.

Shivalingam – An oblong object that symbolizes the omnipresence and primeval energy of Lord Shiva.

Siddhas (siddha powers) – One who has achieved spiritual realization and supernatural power.

Spiritual Self Inquiry – A method of going directly to the higher self within. Whatever question you pose, the answer comes from within in the form of a realization.

Sri Ram – The name of God and is considered to be the impersonal Godhead, or it can be the personal prophet who was the great avatar Rama.

Stigmata – Marks on one's body corresponding to those left on Jesus' body by the Crucifixion said to have been impressed by divine favor on the bodies of St. Francis of Assisi and others.

St. Germaine – An Ascended Master who gave humanity the gift of the Violet Flame of Transmutation in the 1930s, and who has been overseeing and assisting America to fulfill her soul destiny for several hundred years.

Subtle Body – The subtle body is a non-physical energy that all beings possess. Just as the physical body is made up of matter, each non-physical body has its own attributes and exists around the physical body. The physical body is the densest, and each subsequent body is progressively more refined and resonates at a higher frequency.

Swami – A Hindu honorary title, typically received by one's guru or spiritual master, that signifies one's mastery of Yoga.

Swami Vivakananda – (1863–1902) The primary disciple of Ramakrishna and considered a key figure in the introduction of Vedanta and Yoga in Europe.

Tamasic – A Sanskrit word that describes one of man's three attributes, or gunas, which are: tamasic (darkness, inertia); rajasic (activity, passion, the process of change); and satvic (purity in mind, body and soul). Tamasic represents laziness, clouded power of reasoning, dark emotions, anger and greed.

Tantra – A Hindu or Buddhist doctrine dating from the 6th to the 13th centuries involving mantras, meditation, yoga, and ritual.

Tamil – A Dravidian language spoken predominantly by Tamil people in India.

Teleport – To be transported across space and distance instantly through thought.

Tulsi Beads – A necklace (mala) made from the wood of the holy tulsi plant, which is sacred to Lord Vishnu and all of his incarnations, like Sri Rama and Sri Krishna.

Tulsi Twig – From the holy basil plant that is highly revered in India for its healing qualities and is used for worship in Hindu religion.

Universal Vision – A state where an individual perceives himself/herself to be One with everyone and everything.

Upanishads – Ancient Hindu scriptures that constitute the core teachings of Vedanta.

Vedanta – A spiritual philosophy explained in the Upanishads that says the ultimate goal is to go beyond self-identity and realize one's unity with Brahman.

Violet Flame – A spiritual tool of the violet ray of transmutation which is invoked to purify and transmute old, stagnant, unqualified energies from the physical, etheric, mental, emotional and spiritual bodies, or from the earth.

Yogananda – Paramahansa Yogananda (1893–1952) was an Indian yogi and guru who introduced many westerners to the teachings of meditation and Kriya Yoga through his book, *Autobiography of a Yogi*.